MY PENITENTE LAND

Reflections on Spanish New Mexico

Fray Angélico Chávez

With a New Foreword by
Thomas J. Steele, S.J.

MUSEUM OF NEW MEXICO PRESS   Santa Fe

To All the Diverse Peoples of Our Other Forty-nine States

Manufactured in the United States.
10 9 8 7 6 5 4 3 2 1
Library of Congress Catalog Card No. 74-83380.
ISBN: 0–89013–255–0.

Cover design by Linda Seals.
Decorated versal letter by Mary Lou Cook.

Museum of New Mexico Press
P.O. Box 2087
Santa Fe, New Mexico 87504

Contents

Foreword

My Penitente Land is my favorite New Mexico book, very simply the most beautiful book about New Mexico. But like the best (and best-loved) work of fiction about New Mexico, Willa Cather's *Death Comes for the Archbishop*, this present book has its irritating and even outrageous dimensions.

In this way, *My Penitente Land* resembles its author: cantankerous, waspish, opinionated, outrageous, entertaining, charming, delightful, knowledgeable, intuitive, intelligent—everything that is the opposite of boring. *My Penitente Land* is a book full of the author's personal favorites, and it is so irritating precisely because it constantly punctures the reader's personal favorites—*my* personal favorites—scolding them for being unauthentic, untrue, unenlightening. If I want to describe the characteristic *Nuevomejicano* of two hundred years ago as a peasant farmer, Fray Angélico calls him a stockman. I thought I had gotten it right; Chávez tells me to think again.

Chávez, probably the leading authority on the detribalized and Hispano-acculturated Native Americans known as *genízaros*, dismisses them as not indicative of what is truly New Mexican. All along, I thought they might be the key to comprehending the medieval character of the place. Similarly, I have tried to make something central of the penitential Brotherhood of Our Father Jesus the Nazarene and of their allegorical image of death, Doña Sebastiana, and Angélico brushes confraternity and image aside as unauthentic and unenlightening. Outrageous! I am partial to the depictions of San Francisco de Asís as a penitent, meditating upon the skull and the crucifix that he holds in hands marked by the stigmata of Jesus' passion—and this Franciscan friar brushes him aside in favor of the happy Francis. *Whisk*—and there goes the Shroud of Turin. *Whisk*—and there goes the

Santuario of Chimayó! *Whisk*—and there goes Our Lady of Guadalupe!! Doubly outrageous!! Triply outrageous!!! Who is this devil's advocate with the name of an angel?

But though at first I may not like some of the Chávez hypotheses, I have to admit that the man knows what he's talking about. I may know one item here and another item there better than he does, but he knows the whole subject-area, the whole Spanish culture, better than I ever will if I live to be a hundred and fifty. Francis Parkman (or perhaps it was Dave Barry) said of my religious order, "Not a river was crossed, not a cape was turned, but a Jesuit led the way," but if he had known Fray Angélico Chávez and New Mexico he would have added something like "Not a library aisle was crossed, not a filing cabinet was opened, but a Franciscan led the way." I don't know how many times I've thought I've discovered something only to find that Chávez (or occasionally E. Boyd) had beaten me to it by twenty or forty years. And let me take the occasion to say with gratitude how kind and helpful both E. and Angélico were to me when I was just a beginner, overflowing with enthusiasm and dumb questions.

Devil's advocate he may be at times, but Angélico writes like an angel. This book is more of a prose poem than it is anything else, a poem composed by a poet who knows history. The meditative reader will notice bits and pieces and whole chunks of poetry on nearly every page. Chávez skips things, for every historian and every poet must learn how and what to omit. But he tells all of it that's worth the telling, thereby providing the reader with more New Mexico than any other author can tell even by telling everything. Chávez's book embodies *Chávez's* New Mexico, *"my* penitente land": his personally appropriated New Mexico, the New Mexico that formed him into the man he is, the New Mexico that is profoundly and vastly more *his* than it is anybody else's.

And *My Penitente Land* is doubly angelic because it is a book about spirituality, about persons as persons, or, in other words, about persons as interpersonal. (The dogma of the Trinity insists that "person" is a not an absolute concept but a relative one.) It is a book about persons in love: in love with their dreams, in love with their land, in love with each other. This book has given me a very great gift by making the Hebrew word *hesed* as real to me as my own hope for happiness, as real as Lucero Mesa and the Big Lewis pasture and the Rio de las Vacas, as real as Roan Carrillo and Thelma Romero and Sotero Sena and Agnes Amadór and Eddie Sánchez. And as real as Angélico Chávez. *Hesed* is God in love with us, and *hesed* is our response, made with the help of a finite share of God's own infinite love. With this *hesed*, we can love God as He deserves and love one another as Christ commands us. *Hesed* is a Jewish, Christian, and Muslim experience; it is a Pales-

tinian, Spanish, and New Mexican experience; it is Francis of Assisi's experience
that attracted followers who loved God as Francis did. As just a musical motif
lights up one of Wagner's operas, so this word lights up many of the pages of this
fine book. It is a great contribution to New Mexico's religious understanding
of itself.

You can look up in the index all the forty-eight pages where Fray Angélico
uses the word *hesed*—and I hope the Museum of New Mexico Press and I haven't
ruined the wily author's plan by adding the index and thereby making *My Penitente
Land* into a book for quick and easy reference. As some people say when I mention
the index, one of the book's many annoying charms is that whenever you look
for something you're sure is there *some*place, you end up rereading fifty or sixty
pages, totally blowing your time-schedule, and loving every minute of it. It's like
getting lost in Santa Fe: when you do, you almost always discover something you
never could have found even if you'd been looking for it, something that was
worth every minute it cost you.

Who knows what you'll find as you saunter through *My Penitente Land*? There
are numerous other Wagnerian motifs there, like Nuestra Señora de Guadalupe
in contrast both to the Señora de Remedios (Cortés's Lady of the Conquest) and
to Santa Fe's own Conquistadora, a Lady of the Assumption statue that came to
New Mexico in 1620, fled with the survivors of the Pueblo Rebellion sixty years
later, returned a bit over three hundred years ago, was remodeled into a Lady of
the Rosary, was kidnapped ten or fifteen years ago, and still reigns over the hearts
of Catholic New Mexicans from her altar in the north transept of the Santa Fe
Cathedral; Chávez has written many works of all sorts about her. There are Fray
Angélico's ruminations about the economic foundation of Hispanic New Mexico
before the land-losses of the nineteenth and twentieth centuries pulled the
Hispanics out of their homes in the mountain valleys, away from the extended-
family values that can survive in a village setting but not in the urban world of
wage-work, consumerism, democratization, and individualism. There is Angélico's
delightful lesson about four traditional status levels: *labrador*, *obrero*, *ganadero*, and
conquistador—farmworker, craftsman, rancher, and soldier–conqueror–*hidalgo*—the
last two of them wonderful examples of the nearly universal man–on–horseback
archetype so especially powerful in the Spanish world. You'll encounter Hebrew
Nazarites and Spanish *Nazareños*, and you'll examine "Sangre de Cristo" as the
name of a range of mountains.

As you wander through Fray Angélico's land, you'll notice his frequent
assertion of a moderate environmental determinism, somewhat along the lines
of Ross Calvin's in his 1934 classic *Sky Determines*. Fray Angélico's even–more–classic

volume takes the reader first to the ancient Biblical world of Palestine–Israel–Arabia, crucible of the three great "peoples of the book" who share the love of a God eternally in love with them. Then it moves to the look-alike herding world of Extramadura and Castile, where Jew and Moor and Christian lived together and fought among themselves for centuries. And finally it brings the reader home to a third holy place, a new-world facsimile of the other two. This holy land of the new world developed *un misticismo tosco*, a roughhewn spirituality of ceremony and prayer that brought men and women wonderfully close to God, an incarnate God who shared with them the pain and wonder of being human, vulnerable, and mortal. In accomplishing this loving reminiscence of New Mexican history, Spanish history, and salvation history, *My Penitente Land* goes back to Oñate and Villagrá, further back to the Cid and his anonymous poet, and all the way back to Abraham and the writers of the Torah: to the culture heroes and the talented chroniclers of the three arid lands that formed the *anima hispanica*, the *casticismo*, of Spanish New Mexico.

This tendency to "go back to Adam and the egg" is a point that invites comment: the tendency of nineteenth- and earlier-twentieth-century historians of New Mexico (like their contemporaries elsewhere) to search for the earliest paradigms, the epic founders of nations and colonies, as if whatever was older and more Spanish was somehow more authentic and important than anything later and more Mexican (or more Anglo). Chávez's frequent use of the term "Spanish Colonial," a 1920s creation of Mary Austin and Frank Applegate, suggests such an aging historiography. Is this book the creation of a Victorian gentleman-historian, a quaint being far different from the contemporary scholar-historian, that academically trained virtuoso who takes pride in history as one of the social *sciences* and even lusts (in a purely academic manner, of course) after the condition of a real science like physics? Maybe so; maybe so indeed.

But most of the better Victorian historians did not so much lack scientific methodology as distrust it, relying instead upon their own intelligence, experience, and insight. Following in their footsteps, I believe, Fray Angélico Chávez reached the right conclusions about New Mexico more often than all the would-be scientific historians, "politically correct" revisionists, and "patriotically correct" *vendidos* put together. Given some fine tuning (such as William Wroth's findings about the New Spain sources and analogues for the penitential Brotherhood of Our Father Jesus the Nazarene), Chávez's pronouncements about the religious history and culture of Hispanic New Mexico are probably going to endure like the dialogues of Plato, to which all later western philosophy has been mere footnote. Chávez's thesis about the origins of the Penitentes as an organization was first floated in the early 1950s and substantially repeated in this book in 1974, and it is reprinted today because it is still better than any alternative offered.

For Fray Angélico Chávez has that fine insider's sense of what's really Franciscan, what's really New Mexican, what's really Christian, and what's really culture. Furthermore, he can state exactly why it is what it is, and to what extent and to what degree it actually is what it pretends to be. So while I might feel personally that Doña Sebastiana is more New Mexican than all the *gachupín* great-grandmothers that ever existed (or, more numerous by far, that never existed), I will be forever plagued by that self-doubt that is the outsider's most needed social grace. And I will hold my tongue.

For whenever I have read this book I have felt myself in the presence of a powerful practical wisdom, the wisdom that educates and forms the young by means of the *plática de los viejitos*, the discourse of the village elders, of which Charles Briggs has written so well. This is a *viejito*'s book above all, written for the benefit of all novice New Mexicans whether born here or adopted. This crotchety, cantankerous, waspish, opinionated, irritating, outrageous, thoroughly delightful book is designed to share with us a life lived in New Mexico. Chávez learned to live New Mexican in his memory when in an Ohio seminary or at an army base in the Pacific during World War II or in Germany during the early 1950s: "I began reliving the experiences of my people in the past," he tells us early in the book; and this Wordsworthian reliving of experiences—this "emotion recollected in tranquillity"—made Chávez the quintessential *castizo Nuevomejicano* as surely as Wordsworth's calm recollection of his experiences of nature made him the premier romantic nature-poet. And as we begin to read this book and begin to relive the pattern-setting experiences of the Hispanic people of the past, we become like Wordsworth's sister Dorothy or like any later reader, who needs only read the "Tintern Abbey" ode with full openness to share the nature-mysticism Wordsworth the poet exemplifies. *My Penitente Land* is the formative text for anybody—born here or born elsewhere—who wants to become a complete New Mexican, who wants to appropriate, to make his or her own, the four centuries of Judaeo-Christian Spanish Franciscan life on the land of New Mexico.

So, read this book. Get into it, get it into yourself, and let it challenge and expel any received ideas that don't measure up. Read it over and over. Rip out the index, if that'll help. And when you've finally arrived in Fray Angélico's pentiente land, apply to the New Mexican Bureau of Spiritual Immigration and Naturalization to take the oath of citizenship. You've come home.

Thomas J. Steele, S.J.

Prologue

A boy's will is the wind's will, said a popular poet of yesteryear, and it was just such a gust of boyish impulse that made me do something rash and thoughtless long ago, with consequences I never forgot. Indeed, it all turned out to be the seed from which this book grew, slowly and imperceptibly through a lifetime, as trees do, depending for shape and size on circumstances of nourishment and weather.

I must have been some ten years old at the time, that spring day when a playmate and I found ourselves peering into the open rear window of the village cobbler's, who also doubled as the town barber. He was our friend, letting us play in his cozy shop during those long and bitter winters for which our high New Mexico mountain valley was noted. He and my father had a mutual respect for each other; and my mother, as parish organist, valued his faithful and creditable bass in those operatic Latin masses still being butchered in the years following the First World War.

But he also belonged to that brotherhood which performed bloody flagellations during Holy Week at a stark and windowless *morada*, or adobe lodge, on a mountain flank well away from the village. It was not long since he had returned to resume his rumbling *kyrie eleison*s in the church's choir loft at Eastertide.

This man was working intently at his low shoemaker's bench, in a far corner beyond the empty barber's chair, when my mate and I stuck our heads through the open window and burst out singing an insulting parody we had learned from the older youths in town. Even the melody mocked the "flamenco" nasal wail of the brotherhood's own *alabados:*

Penitente pecador,
porqué te-ándas azotando?
Me comi-úna vaca gorda
y-óra l-ándo desquitando!

O Penitente sinner,
why go flogging yourself?
I ate a fat (stolen) cow
and I'm paying for her now!

Only because the surprised and angered man had to round the strung-out adobe structure (of shop and contiguous dwellings) in order to get at us, and for what we immediately realized was a well-deserved trouncing, did we have time to scurry to our respective homes. I sped past my mother in the kitchen into a bedroom and was not surprised to hear soon afterward a hard steady pounding at the kitchen door. Then I overheard the cobbler's low rumble relating my crime, as well as my mother's loud and clear apology, which carried a promise of prompt retribution. The man went away and she came straight to me, unable to move as I was, and cuffed my skull; then she led me by the ear to where my father's razor-strap hung from a nail.

But her emotion had weakened her also, fortunately, and I was spared a bit of flagellation which in this case would have been poetic justice to the full. Instead, she sat me on a bed beside her, and gravely she began explaining to me the mean thing I had done.

The Penitentes, she said, were not to be made fun of. They were sincere Christian men, most of them poor and unlettered, who loved the Suffering Christ so much that they felt themselves compelled to flog their backs and carry heavy crosses during Holy Week. They were also imitating many of the saints who had scourged themselves for the sins of mankind. In doing so the brothers bothered no one else, she went on; only mean and uncouth people tried to spy on their penitential processions, or mocked them as I had just done.

She was careful to point out that one or the other of the *hermanos* (brethren) might not be such a good fellow outside of Lent—I thought of the verse about a stolen cow—but most of them were like the cobbler, good and honest folk. Besides, she added with something like a tone of relief, only a very small portion of the men of New Mexico had ever been Penitentes.

Later on, I asked her when and how the Penitentes had come to be, but she said she did not know for sure. Nobody seemed to know. People took it for granted that the flagellant society was something very, very old, like Lent and Holy Week.

*   *   *

This matter of antiquity, the very vagueness of it, played havoc with my young mind. I also remember asking my mother more than once why we were not exactly the same in speech and demeanor as the priest from Spain who was our assistant pastor at the time, and why we differed in the same way from a family from Mexico living up the street from us. She would flush with impatience—at her own inability to explain, I am sure—merely saying that our forebears had come from Spain a very long time ago. But she didn't know when or how. All this made the double puzzle of Penitentes and ancestral origins merge most confusedly inside my inquisitive young head.

It was in this same boyhood period that I asked my mother if any of the menfolk of her own immediate family had ever been Penitentes. She bridled visibly, declaring proudly that her side of the family had always been such good Catholics that they had no cause for joining the Penitentes. Secretly amused by her answer, I asked about my father's side. She replied curtly: "Your father's people were not even good enough Christians to be Penitentes." My father grinned in good humor when I mentioned this to him afterward.

Decades later, during my many years of documentary research on the Spanish colonial history of New Mexico, I had the rare good fortune of being able to trace both my parents' branching-out families back to the sixteenth century—well over two hundred pairs of grandparents in all. Imagine my amused surprise upon discovering that my mother had been instinctively right: While her own direct ancestors were for the most part ardently devoted to affairs of the Church, a goodly portion of the twelve generations on my father's side had not been quite so devout.

For in their detailed meaty information, the documents were teaching me more about my people than mere chains or lines of descent. Although we were truly Hispanic in blood, language, religion, and customs, we were no longer Spaniards like the clergyman from Spain just mentioned. Nor were we really Mexicans, as our North European–derived neighbors chose to call us. The differences, I was beginning to suspect, were all a matter of cultural and linguistic development from a parting of the ways with both Hispanic Europe and Hispanic Middle America down three centuries and a half.

As to the origin of the local Penitentes, I had kept on wondering about it ever since that early day when I barely escaped a whipping on their account. The question kept coming up during my youthful years away from home, while studying for the priesthood in the Franciscan Order. Perhaps it was a buried feeling of guilt, deeply impressed upon my soul as well as on my skull by that timely maternal cuff and admonition, which stirred in my subconscious whenever I came upon corporal penance in Scripture and church history, along with the general religious story of mankind down the ages. But even in subsequent adult years, after I had plowed through about every known document of New Mexico's Spanish colonial period, nothing in the seventeenth and eighteenth centuries came up to satisfy my curiosity.

*   *   *

What had been written so far was in the past century, and in English, by American newcomers who knew little of local Spanish history, and nothing of ancient Spanish religious belief and custom. Ever since the United States had annexed New Mexico in 1846, some persons with a bent for writing journals had begun publishing the most unflattering reports about our people from their distinctively different point of view. Shocked by what they considered our benighted religious customs, they focused upon a strange society of flagellants which they had discovered in certain mountain villages.

What was commonplace in this regard to the local folk seemed most bizarre to these newcomers, to say the least. Their accounts, understandably sensational, did not differ much from what I had known since childhood. These were Lenten and other processions in which some of the penitential brethren scourged their naked backs to blood, while others carried heavy timber crosses upon their bruised shoulders; and on rare occasions, it was told, one of them had himself tied to a cross, as if crucified, until he fainted away.

But then these writers went on to connect this society and its practices with scattered odd references to certain Spanish religious customs among the early colonists of New Mexico. A pioneer in this regard was Charles Fletcher Lummis, a well-meaning but impetuous author of his day, who resolved that the Penitentes had come with the very first Spanish settlers and through the agency of the Franciscan missionaries who accompanied them. Subsequent writers kept on parroting his mistaken assumptions.

That there was something wrong at bottom with all these theories came to me gradually as I began reliving the experiences of my people in the past through an ever-growing intimacy with the primary documentation of my homeland's history, and against the background I had already acquired of my remote Hispanic and Christian heritage. Meanwhile, I was also beginning to perceive how memories of race and the mood of landscape can lend shape and direction to certain impulses within the human heart. This intuition waxed stronger after the intimate story of my homeland and my people became second nature to me.

As it finally turned out, New Mexico's particular society of flagellants had not come with the original colonists more than three centuries and a half ago, but only at the beginning of the past century. While its basic ideas were very ancient, the organization as such was a new arrival. Nor was it directly Franciscan in origin; it most certainly was not a development from the lay Third Order of St. Francis, nor a degeneration of it, as will be seen.

And yet, it was not an altogether alien thing. As a relatively recent phenomenon, it simply had brought together and to the surface certain elements long festering in the otherwise healthy mystique of a people. Several years ago I published the gist of these findings in approved scholarly fashion. Since then all kinds of books and articles about my people and the Penitentes have kept tumbling out of the card files of researchers in sociology. They all bristle with rare data and photographs but miss the very essence of their subject.

All this made me more and more convinced that mere arrays of facts and dates, by their very nature, leave the inner core of human things unsaid. The intimate story of internal beliefs and yearnings, which are grooved into human beings by age-long racial development and no less colored by the seeming accidents of topography and climate, can only be told in other ways than by stringing out facts and dates. Even that Book which so many believe to be a record of God's own dealings with mankind is neither pedantic history nor spelled-out theology in its telling, but a great poem made up of many poems and poetic narratives. And the Bible's earliest protagonists are upland shepherd people on a particular landscape very much like Spain's and ours here in New Mexico.

*   *   *

This last observation is what opened rich endless vistas for me in laying out the plan of this book along with its pastoral and spiritual themes. For Palestine, Castile, and Hispanic New Mexico—grazing lands all and most alike in their physical aspects—likewise share a distinctive underlying human mystique born of that very type of arid landscape. They all differ basically from the largely agrarian and industrial Western world that we know, in both their economic and their religious outlook. Consequently, the prior Palestinian and Castilian "semitic" backgrounds of life and worship have to be outlined at some length, and in some depth, if we are to understand the intimate story of my people of New Mexico upon their very own landscape—while also keeping in mind a now-dying penitential brotherhood which continues to be a source of wonderment to many. For the latter's story cannot be adequately told without the other.

After all, we Hispanic New Mexicans are all Penitentes in some way, through blood origins and landscape and a long history of suffering. Hence this is far less a treatise on the Penitentes, who are a late feature in New Mexico's long story, than a sort of "scripture" about a penitential New Mexico wrestling with her God upon a Bethel landscape made to order.

To return to my original metaphor, the hidden mustard seed of long ago developed into a full-grown tree at last, ready for me to paint in broad strokes as best I can. Let it also be a much-belated apology to a long-dead cobbler. For, while a boy's will is the wind's will, the thoughts of youth are long, long thoughts, as the same poet went on to say.

Part One

HOLY
LAND

Yahweh alone is his guide,
with him is no alien god.
He gives him the heights of the land to ride,
he feeds him on the yield of the mountains,
he gives him honey from the rock to taste,
and oil from the flinty crag;
curds from the cattle, milk from the flock,
with rich food of the pastures. . . .

    —Deuteronomy 32:12–15.

1

Cross over Jordan

The day I was born and christened—it was a clear and flowery one in April—all kinds of colorful ceremonies marked the event alongside the big swirling river. That morning a formal proclamation was issued, and there was a solemn high mass with an appropriate sermon. In the afternoon the militia held a review. Then a stirring drama, which was composed for the occasion by one of the captains, was staged by some of the men. These things were duly recorded as a matter of course.

Later on, a long epic poem by another captain recalled the happy occurrence, also relating in vivid detail whatever took place months before the actual birthday and in those that followed. In short, everyone present knew that this was not only a happy communal celebration but a very sacred one as well.

Actually, I am describing the birth of my people and of their own way of life, the beginnings of the Hispanic inhabitants of New Mexico and their own particular culture, on that feast of the Ascension of our Lord, the thirtieth day of April in the year 1598. On that memorable morning along the banks of the southern Rio Grande, Don Juan de Oñate, *adelantado* for King Philip II of Spain, or advance leader of the first permanent colony sent to these parts—which his followers were vocally regarding as a Promised Land—took solemn possession for God and King of a brand-new infant Spain at the outermost edges of the then-known world.

"New Mexico" was the name given to this Hispanic enclave across the wilderness, fully two hundred and forty years before there ever was a republic called Mexico south of here. "Mexico" meant just a city then and for more than two centuries thereafter. The only Mexicans at that time were the Nahua or Aztec native Indians of that city and its great valley, who had been conquered by Hernando Cortés some seventy years previously.

And it was less than twenty years before, in 1581, that three little Franciscan friars had come up this very Rio Bravo del Norte, as the Rio Grande was then called, expecting to find a great harvest of souls like the one which the pioneer Franciscans with Cortés had garnered in the fabulous city and valley of Mexico. The nine soldiers escorting this zealous but naïve trio had also dreamed of finding the same golden treasures which the army of Cortés had plundered in that fateful city. Hence both the friars and the soldiers were seeking another, a *new* Mexico of that rich sort, if for totally different motives, and that is how the name took root. Those three friars—Rodríguez, López, and Santa María—were soon slain by the Tiwa Indians of the middle Rio Grande Valley, after the soldiers had set out for home empty-handed. But the name endured, to be adopted by the Crown when it sent Don Juan de Oñate to found a colony there.

His act of royal possession took place at a pleasant oasis of gnarled cottonwoods along a grassy bank of the river, some three hundred miles south of present Santa Fe. The swift murky stream was swollen by spring freshets fed by melting snows in distant high sierras. These were as yet invisible on the wide screen of the far northern horizon, but they were said to preside over a land flowing with milk and honey. For this present spot was not the Promised Land itself, only the approach to its gateway. It was, as it were, the site across the River Jordan where Joshua and his Israelites, after a forty-years' wandering in the wilderness of Sinai, were poised in eager readiness to enter Palestine.

These Spanish wanderers, too, had undergone the hardships of a great Sinaitic desert in their slow wayfaring northward from Zacatecas far south in New Spain; and, as said before, they were actually comparing their journey with the final one in Exodus. Now, in the manner of the biblical patriarchs, Oñate gave the place a meaningful memorial name. He called it La Toma, which means "the taking" of possession. By a happy coincidence, this very word is emphasized in Joshua 4, even if used in a contrary sense, as when the Lord said to him by the Jordan: " 'Today I have taken the shame of Egypt away from you.' Hence that place has been called Gilgal [*take away*] until now."

And how good the land looked to the people even then, though only an oasis by a river in that desert solitude. Their sudden relief from their Sinaitic desert sufferings made them exaggerate the reports on the land which an advance party had brought them. "Like the olive branch brought by a dove," the colony's poet-captain wrote later, painting to excess the flora and fauna much as did the reports of Joshua and his own reconnoitering party about Canaan. Even the parched and starved cattle, "like those of Nineveh," were envisioned thanking the Lord for the fresh swards of grass and other foliage.

Today the community of San Elizario below the modern city of El Paso in Texas occupies the site, but with the river running on the opposite side of the narrow and shallow desert valley.

All the birthday ceremonies having been properly taken care of, the happy and expectant colonists trekked several miles upstream along the river's left bank and, finding a good place to ford it at a bare stone-mountain pass which they named El Paso del Norte—the Northward Passage—they crossed over Jordan.

*   *   *

Several human factors in history as well as certain features of geography compel one to make these comparisons regarding the birth of a people, including the continual scriptural allusions, with the least fear of committing a conceit or striving after a tour de force. The basic material for such analogies is there in the documents. The colorful atmosphere persists even to this day throughout the same terrain and sky. The spirit of it all brims in my heart.

For a person who has closely studied his own blood lines back through the myriad-veined system of a dozen generations, and in the same setting of a particular landscape which is likewise part and parcel of his own being, knows what makes him tick. His most intimate feelings reflect this double heritage of flesh and soil, and he in turn is enabled to know what such forebears felt at that time and in succeeding instances of recorded history.

This is why I began by saying that I myself was born when those first Spanish settlers were preparing to enter New Mexico, their land and mine. A goodly number of them are my own proven direct ancestors, some by several lines. Therefore, when I intrude with personal memories or genealogy now and then, it is not to cater to a certain human weakness, but to knit the woof of narrative more tightly or highlight the colors and design. The case is very much the same with regard to biblical allusions. Scripture is brought in, not to prove sectarian doctrine one way or the other, but to follow a basic historic monotheism which, born on the dry Palestinian landscape, was grasped by its pastoral folk and later by other pastoral peoples of similar landscapes in a way decidely different from other groups of mankind elsewhere. When certain mythological factors in the same revered pages are brought out, it is only to show how so much misunderstanding came to plague the human adventure among diverse peoples in their common search for the divine. And whenever the Book's rich imagery happily coincides with the theme—as just now in this Jordan crossing—it is a literary windfall and nothing more.

"The adventure of humanity," Jules Romains wrote, "is essentially an adventure of groups." Ever since man began, groups of humankind have developed in their own beliefs and life modes according to climes and places. These have given birth to new groups who by some instinct have chosen the same kind of territory for their habitat. In this way they continued ancestral and religious patterns if in modified forms. It is this matter of habitat, or more properly of a landscape's essence simmering in living blood, which so stirs up the imagination as to lead one to speculate on matters which science might frown upon, but which art ought not gainsay.

2

Lands of Genesis

There is something about landscape which helped determine the traits and character of different peoples in ages past, when the earth seemed flat and infinite and puny man wandered about one small space of it for generations on end. What landscape brought about lies beyond those measurable factors found arranged within the cores of genes and chromosomes. It has to do, rather, with the experience gained through the outer senses, mainly the eye.

Just as mouth and nostrils took in food and air for every function and development of the body, the eye kept gathering in the familiar terrain close at hand, together with the hues and shapes of the horizon all around, and no less the various aspects of an all-encompassing sky, to store these impressions within the self. Ear and nose, too, and also the whole periphery of touch, gave their perceptions to the process. What they and the eye passed on to the brain kept draining into the living essence of the person—into his blood, as the saying goes.

There were no other distractions then, like modern print and the more pervading visual and audial electronic miracles of our day, to blur or strain away those images. They molded and tinted an individual's thoughts and feelings, betimes coming to find new being in his visions and in his dreams.

1. The People Who Found God

Take the dry interior uplands of Palestine, which people of greener countries like to call deserts. But they are not deserts to those others whom they have nourished for ages. They consist mostly of sparsely grassed, rock-strewn plains napped a tawny gold that turns to rich olive in the springtime. These plains break up into rolling hills, big ones swelling over the smaller ones, all having the same hue and cover.

Sheep and goats, especially, find it a paradise. It is a land made for erect shepherds, not for stooping peasant-tillers of the soil. True, bits of red or yellow desert also dot the terrain, but these are offset by small oases of fresh green groves and vineyards. Larger areas of true desert, like the Negeb, lie off at the edges and can be recognized as such by contrast. Part of the good land is also broken up by stony tablelands and wind-carved sandstone cliffs of varied ochre hues, and there are the blue outlines of high mountains in the distance. All over you will also find dry riverbeds that turn into swift torrents when rain happens to fall somewhere.

It is now known that in earlier biblical times Palestine was indeed "the good land" described in Deuteronomy 8, centuries before it was stripped of woods to make the land more barren. It was more like the northern New Mexico or the central Spain of former times, before climatic changes or land abuse did the same. Yet, withal, it was not the green land of the rainier areas of the world. It was more pastureland than a soil for any extensive farming.

Hence agriculture in Palestine was secondary even in ancient times, confined to parts of lowland moistened by small springs, or to the winding valley of a single Jordan drawing thirsty spirits as well as parched throats to its refreshing banks of green. The prevailing way of life was therefore *pastoral*, not agricultural, and there is a marked difference between the two which sets the shepherd or stockman distinctly apart from the farmer or peasant.

For ages families and tribes moved with their droves of domestic animals up and down their allotted grounds, ever appreciating to the fullest every tuft of grass on plain and hill, each shallow water hole or rain puddle. What few farming lands there were could not compare in extent and verdure with those in earth's regions of much more frequent rain. Yet they were a welcome auxiliary here, producing enough bread and wine to temper the heat of sun and the fat of mutton. In time, small towns grew up at crossroads, providing nests of culture as well as bastions of defense whenever the tramp of foes was heard upon the land.

But it is the gold and olive landscape as a whole, its waves lapping not only at the walls of town or garden but at the hems of the tents and very hearts of the inhabitants, which had come to make the latter love it as sailors love the sea and are salted by it. No less did the unmarred blue sky in that crystal air become a beloved and familiar acquaintance, from frequent scanning for signs of clouds that might or might not come to pour down blessings. These very clouds often took on the contours of the land below as if they were its ghostly counterpart. And at night, because of that same dry clear air, the stars in thick glittering clusters brought heaven very close, for thoughts that rose up above the daily need for food and water. Land and sky got a double hold on the tenders of sheep and goats and cattle from the time when man first started breeding these cleft-hooved ruminants in the dry uplands of the ancient Near and Middle East.

And so the children of Abraham found God in this type of landscape, so open and clear, and with a sad beauty so much like that of the human condition as to make one think that it also has a soul. Their sacred writings say that God found them instead and let them hear his voice. But they were better enabled to hear it because the dry uplands and their pastoral life had helped attune their ears and hearts to its call. This personal divine adventure found its personification in a man called Abraham, and much later in another one named Moses.

What all this has to do with the founding and the characteristics of an almost insignificant Hispanic colony of latter times, and on the earth's opposite side, may not seem apparent now, save for what has been said concerning landscape and its influence on people. What will be pursued from here on in some detail, about the relationship of an ancient pastoral people and their God upon a similar landscape, may also appear farfetched at the moment. But the strange divine yearnings which are the burden of this story go back all the way to that bittersweet romance which began with Abraham within a life mode and a landscape very much the same. Unless his own experience and that of his semipagan Canaanite kin are told, the modern mind cannot even begin to understand such a simple phenomenon as that of the Penitentes.

*   *   *

No such personal experience as Abraham's happened to the original Hebrews' mixed Semitic and Hamitic kinfolk and neighbors who chose to cultivate vast plantations and build great cities in the wide fertile alluvial valleys of the Nile on one side and the Tigris and Euphrates on the other. Now, when we speak of Semitic and Hamitic peoples we are employing a broad traditional distinction based strictly on languages which science has adopted. Physically, these ancient caucasoid peoples were a more or less look-alike mixture of still more ancient tribes who for long had inhabited that vast region. They were a fair-skinned folk deeply tanned by the sun, whether as upland shepherds or lowland agriculturists, and their prevailing black hair was either straight or frizzled.

The racial terms used are borrowed from two of the "sons of Noah," Sem (or Shem) and Ham, who represented the ancestry of these two linguistic groups to the Hebrews. The third so-called son, Japheth, represented a very distinct language grouping, among which were the Greeks' ancestors and the Philistines. To these can be added all European groups in general, and all together they can also be referred to as Aryans. This is what influenced the biblical writers themselves, who knew no other human varieties than these three, and thus the impression was created that all humankind came from three individual persons bearing these names. For this was the only world that they knew, the arc or inverted crescent curving down through their own homeland from the Asiatic steppes "east of Eden" to the Nile Valley.

The extensive agriculture of the Nile Egyptians and the eastern Mesopotamians, made possible by their great rivers' silts and the most ingenious methods of irrigation, is what gave rise to the fabulous commercial centers of Egypt and Babylon some five thousand and more years ago. Between them, later on, lay the port cities of the northern Canaanites in Asia Minor, whose builders and sailors combined and further developed what Egypt and Mesopotamia had to offer. In such agricultural and trading capitals were born the practical arts of government and commerce, along with the smelting of copper and bronze, and later iron, not to mention the more delicate crafts of goldsmithing and ceramics.

Most important of all, out of all this blossomed the much finer arts of cuneiform and hieroglyphic writing with their corresponding literature. The northern coastal Canaanites, later called Phoenicians, carried forward this primitive art of writing to produce the alphabet on which all our Western world depends. All this was long before the original pastoral Hebrews, after adopting the Canaanite alphabet and some of its literature, finally learned to lay ink onto parchment.

But in the process these lowland agricultural and commercial peoples had lost what they might have once perceived as upland herders of sheep and cattle—that primordial tradition of a single Deity who was said to have made man in his own image, and who could be addressed as person to person, as human kin to kin divine. This is not to say that monotheism came before polytheism. It could be the other way around. But, from what we know of the story of religion in ancient times, the notion of a single personal God found more favorable ground in dry upland climes than in tropical jungles or temperate forest lands, or even fertile fields and pleasant shorelines. It found a clearer response in a folk leisurely following their flocks over wide harsh horizons, and under open day and night skies, than in peoples hemmed in by their lusher types of landscape and inbound interests.

What we now like to call civilization, as based on agriculture with its consequences of commerce and industry, drew men's eyes away from landscape into themselves. True, their senses were being drawn by the elements of soil and air and water which make up landscape, but not by landscape itself. For their daily lives came to revolve with the annual cycle of planting and harvesting, instead of following the forward thrust of time that herds and flocks keep nibbling at without regard to seasons.

Whatever these farming and urban folk remembered of the Deity was also caught up in the year-round wheel of purely human interests, whereby they divinized the different aspects of Nature and submitted their lives to her cycles. In this way they produced a welter of gods who were often represented by the heavenly bodies, each one having the same human foibles as its creators. Whatever remained of the primitive Deity was applied to the chief god of the pantheon who presided over the mysteries of life and death. Thus Egypt finally ended in the gloomy cult of the divine dead which was fossilized in her pyramids and other tombs along the Nile, while Babylon's own polytheism eventually foundered when her towering temples failed to reach the heavens from their bases in the rich fields of Mesopotamia. The sacred cities of Phoenicia or Ugarit lie flattened in tiers under the soil.

But Jerusalem lives on.

This should not belittle the economic, civic, and literary heights that their hum of activity once attained. Like myriads of busy ants and bees in larger human scale, their workers developed to marvelous perfection the architecture and social system of anthill and hive around a royal culture of drones and queens. And so the later-famed Hebrew city of Jerusalem at the height of her glory could never compare with the grandeur of Babylon and Thebes and Ugarit many hundreds of years before. It is by that many centuries that the written laws of their several nations preceded any Jewish code. The Sumerian epics of Creation and the Flood, jumbled though they were by the follies of heathendom, were most poetically set down to writing centuries before the much-edited monotheistic versions of them came to be written in Hebrew Genesis. Still other ancient Ugaritic sagas of Canaan about El-Elyon and Baal left their turns of phrase within the Psalms. And there were moral sages in Egypt and Edom and other parts whose saws found their way into Job and other Hebrew books of wisdom.

Although the much more primitive pastoral people of the dry uplands, of whom the ancestors of the Hebrews were but a small fraction, were unfettered by such material trappings of civilization in those far-off times, they could not altogether avoid becoming infected by idolatry in their contacts with their neighbors of the green valleys and big cities. The southern Canaanites and other Semite groups occupying what is now Palestine, and other similar peoples roaming the deserts roundabout, still worshipped the One Lord by several names. But more often than not they had him lackeyed by lesser deities borrowed from the plantation cities.

Further north in Harran of ancient Syria, the shepherd progenitors of the Hebrews had also become tainted by their agricultural moon-worshipping neighbors in the communities along the upper branches of the Euphrates.

2. The Faith of Abraham

It was such "abominations" that Abraham had come to question in manhood, long after his shepherd father Terah had led his tribe away from the contaminating lush valleys and cities of Mesopotamia. It was the only way of keeping the memory of the One Lord pure. Like other upland pastoral tribes they met or mingled with, they had several names for the Deity in their now-forgotten dialects.

He was often called *Shaddai,* "the Almighty," or *El* and *Elyon* and *Eloah,* "the Most High"—besides other terms which scholars keep digging up from the ground or from the biblical text itself. But a most common designation was the plural *Elohim* for "God" which the agricultural and urban people had divided into many gods, although it could stand for a celestial court in unison with the single Deity.

But Abraham preferred a very special name, something like *Yah* or

Yahweh, as having come down from his forebears in times long past. In his own Amoritic speech (for the Hebrew language of his descendants was to take form long afterwards), the term meant something like "the Most High who is at hand to do"—that is, to create, to sustain, to save, to love, depending upon the circumstances of one's encounter with him. Therefore, he was not tied down to a specific time or place or figure.

Yahweh sounded more like the One Lord's very own Name—for, according to the ancients, no man could know the real Name and live. The specifically Jewish people of much later times believed it to have been revealed to Moses for the first time, and there has been none other like it in any language. Our English term *God,* our Spanish *Dios,* derived from ancient Teutonic and Mediterranean heathendom, are not so much proper names as loose terms which, like Elohim, can be applied to other gods or even human lords. To Abraham the Name meant much more.

Like certain rare persons in every age, Abraham fell in love with God. *Hesed* is the Hebrew word for it, and it shall permeate this book. It likewise means God's own love for man. And it is a word proper to Palestinian landscapes. From that moment on, all his thinking and his yearning were for Yahweh alone. Whether tending his flocks at lambing time, or at evening comforting his beautiful and faithful wife Sarah, he pondered longingly on that source of life and being that was more personal than the mysterious wind or flashing thunder. By day, as he poured endless grains of sand through his fingers in the sunny upland silences, his mind reeled with a desire to know what such a Lord might be like. Or in the still more silent night, as his eyes tried in vain to separate and count the flocks of stars, his heart listened for his voice.

And one day, what a day, Abraham heard the voice of Yahweh coming loud and clear; and he saw it, too, for that is the beauteous power of *hesed.* It told him to leave Harran, his father's family and house, and proceed without delay to a land that would be pointed out to him, adding with the solemn emphasis of Genesis 12:

> I will make you a great nation;
> I will bless you and make your name
> so famous that it will be used
> as a blessing . . . .
> All the tribes of earth
> shall bless themselves because of you.

3. The Promised Land

Abraham's God kept his word, even though it took six centuries and a half of wandering and exile before his descendants could make southern Canaan their own, as they also did its specific language and attuned it to the voice of Yahweh. This Semite dialect was already a written one before they came, and in time there arose scribes in heretofore unlettered Israel who began jotting down not only what Abraham had learned from his father Terah, but the things which Yahweh's own *hesed* had been doing for his people all this long while.

It took almost as long—Abraham himself was dead for more than a millennium—before the priestly scribes compiled in the Torah, or five scrolls of instruction, what so many generations had handed down in singsong sacred ballads and rolls of scribbled lore. In doing so they repaid Canaan's upland landscape with everlasting fame. It is in these primitive Scriptures that Palestine's landscape and the pastoral life proper to it come to the fore as in a drama. The dry golden and olive uplands are the stage for all that is faithfulness to Yahweh. Conversely, it is in the deep green lowlands that this fidelity bogs down.

At the very start, the writers begin pointing out a lush garden called Eden, situated at the fertile confluence of the Tigris and the Euphrates, as the place where man tries to rival Yahweh by coming to know the fatal stress between good and evil. Thus sin enters man's poor life to stay forever with him. Man will have to redeem himself where thorns and thistles abound, not in the fields of tender corn. The first one to sin gravely against his fellowman is Cain, a tiller of the soil, when he murders Abel, who was a keeper of flocks. As his punishment, Cain is exiled to the idolatrous cities; then, to balance Adam and Eve's double loss, Yahweh is made to give them another shepherd son, Seth, since it is from Seth that the pastoral forebears of the Hebrews have to descend, and because his son Enosh "was the first to invoke the name of Yahweh."

And so we have the upland shepherd people remembering the one Lord, howsoever dimly at times, while the lowland agricultural and urban people divide him into many gods warring or playing with each other in sinful human fashion. So depraved do these tillers and metalworkers eventually become that in their myths they have the *elohim*, or celestial courtiers of what once was the single Deity, consorting carnally with the daughters of mere men. The resulting progeny are the gigantic Nephilim of antiquity, called Titans by the later Greeks after they borrowed this ancient myth from Babylon via Ugarit.

For the Hebrew writers this is all a handy reason for the Flood and a brief preamble to their own version of it. Since the union of *elohim* and human females is not only sheer folly but rankest blasphemy, mankind has to be destroyed by the same elemental water which made the cities and plantations flourish. Only Noah and his family are found worth saving, but then this Noah, after the Deluge waters have subsided, degrades himself one day by getting shamefully drunk. Evidently he was too much attached to peasant tradition when he hastened to plant a vineyard; for Noah, the writers are careful to point out, was a tiller of the soil.

As time goes on, after humanfolk begin working new and greater plantations in Mesopotamia which give rise to ever bigger cities, they again start splitting up Elohim into many gods. They build palatial temples for them atop staired pyramids of brick and mortar rising high above their irrigated plains, for their graven images to guard and bless their crops in season. Springtime and harvesttime, the lowland peoples carry these idols in long processions, amid the din of metal horns and cymbals, returning them once more to their lofty perches where swirling smoke daily assails the sky from sacrificial victims—some of them human. They go so far as to begin a greater *ziggurat,* a tower so tall that it will reach the divine abode. And the immediate divine punishment is the breakdown of human speech, not only into the three languages of Sem and Ham and Japheth, but into the various dialects within each group.

The same drama keeps unfolding as the history of the Hebrew people with regard to Yahweh begins with the call of Abraham and his *hesed.* As time moves on in its forward pastoral course, the lives of his son Isaac and of his grandson Jacob, and of the latter's sons who founded the "Twelve Tribes," all are played before the pastoral backdrop of the same upland landscape all the way from Harran down to Gaza. Droves of sheep and cattle roam the forestage.

Then the scene changes abruptly when the slowly emerging Hebrew nation, forced by famine to go down to Egypt to purchase food, becomes enslaved for many generations thereafter, not only to the Pharaohs of those great cities and plantations, but spiritually to the urban fleshpots of the vast and verdant valley of the Nile. A return to the right landscape has to take place, through Yahweh's acting for his people and in his own good time.

4. The God of Exodus

Even after a handful of centuries in Egypt, the still landless pastoral people of the Promise remember their father Abraham and his intimate dealings with the one invisible Lord. While molding and baking bricks for their Egyptian masters, and herding flocks on the side for the royal looms and tables, they still recall the most human lives of Abraham's son Isaac and his progeny through Jacob—all a cantankerous lot who lack Abraham's full *hesed* but still are pursued by God's own *hesed* in the midst of their failings. What they remember best, for being closer in time and in connection with their misery, is the crime of Jacob's sons in selling their youngest brother into slavery, so that God's *hesed* might become manifest in Joseph's own triumph and godly humanity in Egypt.

Then it is that Yahweh picks out Moses from among them and once more reveals his Name to him. Although Moses is as primitively wayward as his forebears had been since Isaac, Yahweh now fills him with the very *hesed* of Abraham, so much so that he is enabled to impart it to his people during the time needed for the Exodus, or escape from the Nile's bondage of the spirit. But once out of the clutches of Pharaoh, they sin mortally, not so much by honoring Shaddai in the form of a golden calf, as by their clamoring for the fleshpots and lush vegetation of the Nile lowlands. As their punishment they are condemned to wander for a lifetime in the seering purgatory of Sinai before their children can enter and possess the Promised Land.

When compiling the Torah some six centuries before Christ, the priestly writers vividly describe all the events of Exodus and Joshua from the vantage point of their own times and liturgy, emphasizing the "doings" of Yahweh's *hesed* and its descent upon Moses, and going on to declare that it was to Moses that the holy Name was first revealed. And it is the power and the glory and the *hesed* of this Name which restores the shepherd children of the Promise to the proper landscape. While it is said to be "flowing with milk and honey" to describe its desirability, it consists of harsh dry uplands in contrast with the lush green lowlands of pagandom. This is the theme of Deuteronomy: that the pastoral highlands echo God's word to man better than the verdant lowlands where it can be drowned.

*   *   *

Long after Palestine is conquered, and for generations thereafter, the same pastoral theme keeps further unrolling between the spindles of the historical scrolls of Israel and Judah, and it is declaimed in the joyous or anguished cries of the Prophets and the sung raptures of the Psalms. In these prophecies and psalms, especially, is Yahweh celebrated as the Shepherd of his sheep or, in times of stress, as the upland Rock of protection and provider of living waters.

The main heroic figure of the era is David, the shepherd lad who becomes their greatest king. But from David's time on, sad to say, the scene changes rapidly. The old scenic backdrop is soon hidden in part by alien things that come to clutter the stage. For this newly experienced royalty, which depends so much on the development of agriculture and of commercial cities for tribute—as the Prophet Samuel himself had fore-warned the people—helps bring on the downfall of David's successors and the apostasy of their subjects. They forget Yahweh and turn to the shady cult of graven gods in valley groves and wooded hilltops.

And so other long purgations follow when the wayward tribes are hauled off to distant Assyria and Babylonia. Back in those lush scenes most of God's people succumb to the lowland fleshpots even after relief is offered by the captors themselves. Then most of the Israelitic tribes are "lost," drowned in the ethnic sea of paganism. Only a remnant of the tribe of Judah returns to the dry uplands of Palestine to start all over again that personal kinship which had begun with Abraham's *hesed* and headlong act of faith.

From this remnant is born the intense and sturdy Judaism that we know, as ancestral Hebraic lore becomes crystallized in the finished Torah. It is no longer that completely pastoral milieu of the original Hebrew people, but now the Jewish prophets, ever communing with Yahweh on Carmel and other heights overlooking the same hallowed landscape, add new dimensions to the sacred writings. Recalling that one promise made to Abraham in the beginning, they project Yahweh's salvation beyond Canaan's borders to all mankind. All communities of men, if in different ways and tongues, will consider themselves supremely blessed because of Abraham's faithfulness, his *hesed*.

Foremost among these will be the many varied Aryan nations of Europe—"the children of Japheth"—but none so much with his own intensity as certain ones who are more the children of Shem and of Ham than of Japheth in another Palestinian country called Spain. Also there will be his legendary sons of Arabia whose Islam, after firing up most of the non-Hebrew Semite and Hamite peoples with its stern fixation for Yahweh-Eloah as "Allah," will leave its mark on the Castilian landscape with that of Abraham's own Judaic progeny.

3

Broad is Castile

Strikingly similar to Palestine is the high central Castilian plateau of the Iberian peninsula. It is actually the western counterpart of the eastern Palestinian shore of that inland sea called Mediterranean. Semiarid rolling plains are strewn with ochre-layered table hills, and cobalt Lebanons shine in the clear distances. The bright blue arc of sky fills up at times with puffed cotton balls of cloud that, more often than not, are only promises of rain. Since the region is larger than Palestine, there are several Jordans, like the Ebro running eastward and the Tajo and Guadiana flowing down toward the western ocean.

Before modern dams were built, these rivers ran much too low in their channels to irrigate more than their immediate banks. The rest of the plateau depended on the *temporal,* or seasonal rain, which might not come at all. Hence the land was devoted mostly to the grazing of sheep and goats, cattle and horses, and the slate-gray pigs foraging for acorns under sparse scruboaks at the extreme southwestern end, called Extremadura. The landscape is more Palestinian than European. Hence, it is for more reasons than economic ones that motion picture companies have gone there to film their epics based on biblical themes, and why Sephardic Jews, summarily driven out of Spain five centuries ago, still cherish memories of a long-lost home.

1. The Land of Tarshish

Nor was Spain unknown to the Hebrews of the Bible, even if tenuously under the name of "Tarshish." In the earlier mythical part of Genesis, Tarshish is mentioned as one of the four descendants of Japheth, Noah's third son, through his son Javan; here are most likely meant the "Ionian" peoples of the isles of Greece. Others place this fabled land elsewhere. But in time Tarshish came to represent the uttermost end of the flat world to the Hebrews, as it did later to the Greeks as the Pillars of Hercules.

The Psalms extol the east wind for being so mighty as to wreck those ships built sturdy enough to venture as far as Tarshish. Isaiah berates these vessels in his oracle against Phoenician Tyre, for her men were the sailors par excellence of those times to the early landlocked Hebrew shepherds who looked upon the sea with dread. The droll fable of Jonah begins by telling how this prophet, loath to preach penance to the heathen Ninevites at God's command, tried to flee from Yahweh by braving the ocean waves against his natural fear in order to sail as far as he could—to Tarshish. But he ended in the fish's belly instead.

A passage of more universal significance appears toward the end of Isaiah, where the seer foretells how the Lord will send envoys to Tarshish and other distant lands, and

> From New Moon to New Moon,
> from Sabbath to Sabbath,
> all mankind will come to bow down
> in my presence, says Yahweh.

*   *   *

The time arrived at last when the inhabitants of Tarshish, by the Pillars of Hercules at the opposite end of the midland sea, came to encounter God with the same literal intimacy of Abraham and his children, although ages later and in a distinctly different fashion. The modern Iberians are generally considered to be an admixture of west European races, yet there are significant remote connections with the Semite and Hamite peoples of the Near and Middle East which cannot be discounted. Spanish savants themselves hold that the earliest immigrants to the Iberian peninsula came from the Atlas Mountain region in extreme northwestern Africa—tribes from an Oriental pastoral people whose other descendants are the nomadic Berbers across the Straits of Gibraltar.

Their blood stemmed from that of Abraham's fellow Semites and their Hamite kin, perhaps his own ancestors also, for their original home had been the same uplands of the Near and Middle East. From there, in ages past, their forebears had wandered ever westward, driving their flocks in centuries-long stages past the green Nile Valley, and all along the African Mediterranean coast, to the barren stretches south of Gibraltar. In time, as one measures prehistoric time, some of their descendants crossed the straits northward to find another familiar landscape, if considerably more fertile.

It was like the case of Israel moving northward from Sinai to Palestine, to what a desert people might consider a land of milk and honey compared with what they had left behind. This makes prehistoric Spain match Palestine, its Mediterranean counterpart, in the blood and living habits of her earliest people as well as in her landscape.

In time, again measuring time as just before, Celtic tribes came down into the Iberian peninsula from the green Atlantic coastlands of Gaul, not only to mix with these people, particularly along the northwestern litoral, but also to acclimatize themselves to a warmer and drier landscape. To be sure, Gaelic traits survive in the foggy vales of northwestern Spain called Galicia, and in Portugal. But for the rest the dominant Iberian strain took over completely, and landscape did the rest—especially in the central plateau. And thus the resulting Celtiberians continued being more East Mediterranean or North African than West European. This was helped along in no small measure by the frequent arrivals of Phoenicians from Tyre and Sidon, descendants of the Canaanites and other Semites of that region, blood cousins of the forebears of Abraham himself. Then came the Carthaginians, likewise of Phoenician derivation.

Of course, there were also Greeks who settled at various points of the Iberian coastline, but their numbers were not enough to ruffle racial patterns and the pastoral outlook in the interior uplands. And finally there came the legions of the newest world empire, Latin Rome, who by now had become the mistress of all the lands encircling the Mediterranean, and far inland in several directions from its shores.

It was not so much her blood that Rome left in so many countries that she conquered as her genius. Roman aqueducts and bridges are still in use today. But what is much more evident, the languages of its peoples are thoroughly done over by the Latin. In this one respect did Rome thoroughly conquer Spain, displacing her ancient Celtiberian and other dialects (except the unique language of the northern mountain Basques) with the rustic Latin of her legionnaires.

But this Latin the Iberians managed to transform with the nuances of Near East speech, tempering the clipped Latin consonants with those of

Canaan. At the same time, Latin replaced the Near East gutturals with its clear open vowel sounds.

2. The Western Canaan

We do not know exactly what forms of worship those early Iberians had. Very small fetishes or "idols" have been uncovered, many of them in connection with coins and costume jewelry, but no really great temples or statues—nor a profusion of inscriptions and literature proclaiming a highly developed polytheism as in Babylon and Egypt, or as in classic Greece and Italy. What little has been discovered of classic temples and large statuary pertained to the Greek and Roman invaders themselves, not to the natives as a whole, especially in the interior highlands.

Hence one likes to assume that in the periods of Greek influence or Roman occupation, the interior Iberians themselves, for being an upland pastoral people at base as part of their landscape, had preserved the tradition of a single Deity, though considering his spirit-*elohim* as minor gods as did the Canaanites and other Near East kin of Abraham's ancestors. And these minor deities could well have become identified with northern forest spirits introduced by the Celts. *Había duendes en España,* goes a saying; that "there were elves in Spain" cannot be denied. This goes along, too, with any traces of witchcraft that remain, as they do in any country, for sorcery is universal.

But surely the Phoenicians could well have strengthened or prolonged the Iberians' basic though imperfect monotheism with the knowledge of El-Elyon. It was El-Elyon whom the famed Melchizedek, priestly king of Salem, had invoked ages ago when blessing Abraham, and Abraham had returned the favor by calling upon his own beloved Yahweh, as if both understood that they meant the same Supreme Being.

Landscape and blood, then, prepared the Iberians for a deeply personal covenant with God which was soon to come, although in a different fashion from the one of Abraham and his children. In old Palestine itself, many centuries had gone by since the early development of the Hebrew people. They had suffered many reverses as the result of recurrent infidelities against Yahweh; but they had also enjoyed successive spurts of vigor and glory brought about by great prophets inspired by the Lord to keep his promises to Abraham alive—when an altogether new kind of prophet arose in the ancient lands of Judah and Israel.

His name was *Yehoshuah,* which means "Yahweh saves." It was not an uncommon name, but what its bearer did and said made it most distinctly unique thereafter. It became known to posterity as "Jesus," from the Greek and Latin rendering of the Semite word. Not only was this Jesus intent on purifying the cult of Yahweh among his people, but he claimed to be someone very special from on high whom Isaiah and other prophets had described. He had a fair following at first, but the greater number of his people tended to reject him for not fitting in with their picture of a powerful messianic Son of David coming to deliver their land and temple from the yoke of the Romans.

Nor did Jesus himself encourage this idea, preferring to stress instead a most particular sonship with God as his beloved Father. But what drove the leaders in Judea to fury in this regard was the way he said it. It is related that he told them one day that Abraham ages ago had rejoiced at his coming; when they derisively pointed out the vast disproportion in the time element, he brazenly told them: "Before Abraham ever was, *I am!*" This bold expression, in both its sound and its connotations, clearly evoked the now-unutterable Holy Name of Yahweh in the ears and minds of these students of the Law.

They immediately picked up stones to kill him, this being their Law's punishment for such blasphemy, yet he escaped them somehow. But the hour came not long thereafter when he allowed them to get hold of him, and they delivered him to the hated Romans to have him crucified. Soon the faithful disciples of Jesus began proclaiming that he, by his predicted death upon the cross and resurrection from among the dead, had established God's kingdom at last. It was the one promised to Abraham because of his faith, and for which he had been told that all communities of men would forever bless him.

The disciples' own mission now was to spread this evangel or gospel—words meaning "good news" in Greek and Anglo-Saxon respectively —to each and every nation beyond tiny Palestine: the news that Yahweh had wondrously set up his tent among his upland shepherd people, and that this Jesus would return to gather the faithful flock into the Father's eternal fold. For this reason they now began proclaiming their "Good Shepherd" as the long-expected Messiah or "Annointed One" of God. Greek being the *lingua franca* of Asia Minor at the time, Semitic "Messiah" became Japhetic or Aryan "Christos," and the new chosen people came to be known as Christians.

Foremost among the propagators of the Christian gospel was a man named Paul, a former Pharisee and persecutor of what had appeared at first to be a wayward Jewish sect. Paul himself, extremely proud of being a Jewish descendant of Abraham, chided the converted but coldish Galatians with these telling words: "Scripture foresaw that God was going to use faith to justify the pagans, and proclaimed the Good News long ago when Abraham was told: *In you all the pagans will be blessed.* Those therefore who rely on faith receive the same blessing as Abraham, the man of faith!" By faith, of course, Paul meant the Hebrew *hesed,* which at the moment seemed beyond the grasp of these more prosaic Grecian *goyim,* or "gentiles."

Paul continued spreading the same Good News throughout all of Asia Minor and Greece and the many isles of the Mediterranean, then along its northern coastline as far as Spain at the opposite end of the inland sea. For the fame of Spain, under her more modern Greek and Roman names of *Hesperia* and *Hispania,* was already known to Jewish patriots two centuries before Paul's time, as noted in the first book of the Maccabean wars of liberation. Paul, in his letter to the Romans, twice mentioned his intent to visit Spain.

The gentile natives of the Iberian peninsula, *goyim* for not being direct descendants of Abraham, yet ultimately kin by several counts to his own pastoral ancestors of the Near and Middle East, took Jesus of Palestine most ardently to their hearts. If the Greek and Roman pantheons had left them as cold as were their marble statues, the Semite Yehoshuah found here a *hesed* worthy of Abraham and of the land of its birth. Many centuries later it was to find expression in a sonnet so typical of the Hispanic soul as to be anonymous, as are indeed most of the Psalms. Yet at the same time it has been attributed to this or the other of Spain's most famous saints and poets:

> No me mueve, mi Dios, para quererte
> el cielo que me tienes prometido;
> ni me mueve el infierno tan temido,
> para dejar por eso de ofenderte.
>
> Tú me mueves, Señor, muéveme el verte
> clavado en una cruz y escarnecido!
> Muéveme el ver tu cuerpo tan herido,
> muévenme tus afrentas y tu muerte.

Muéveme, en fin, tu amor de tal manera
que aúnque no hubiera cielo, yo te amara,
y aúnque no hubiera infierno, te temiera.
No tienes que me dar porque te quiera,
porque aúnque cuanto espero no esperara,
lo mismo que te quiero te quisiera!

Briefly translated: Neither the promise of heaven nor the threat of hell can make me love you, my God, as much as your cross and sufferings and most especially your love; were there no heaven or hell I still would love you as I love you.

This is pure *hesed.*

3. The Castilian Landscape

Although the converted Iberians dwelt far away from the eastern Canaan, they daily saw Zion and Golgotha close to home at every rock-strewn hill. It was a landscape made for similar visions. Here the Lord came down to converse with their mystics in clear star-spattered nights, like the one over Bethel when ascending and descending choirs of Yahweh's *elohim* knit heaven and earth together for Jacob the shepherd—like the one over Bethlehem when hosts of them warbled the Good News to some of Jacob's descendants tending their flocks on the Judean hills. All this was to find unusually strange expression, not only in the Palestinian sad lands of Castile—so sad as to have a soul, as one of her poets put it—but in a similar New Mexican landscape far across the western ocean.

None other than Miguel de Unamuno, that most sensitive child of Iberia, has given us so full and vivid a picture of the *anima hispanica,* the Spanish soul, against the landscape that helped to make it what it is:

From whichever coast one goes into the Spanish peninsula, the terrain appears greatly varied. One then enters a maze of valleys, gorges, draws, and *encañadas;* and finally, after a long or shorter ascent, he will arrive upon the central plateau, criss-crossed by the naked sierras which furnish the large basins for its great rivers. Across this tableland stretches Castile. . . . One may range at times for leagues and further desolate leagues, and scarcely see a thing except the endless stretch of plain where wheat shows green or stubble yellow, some monotonous grave procession of drab oaks promenading by slowly, or of sombre pines holding up their heads as one. From time to time, fringing a skimpy half-dry creek or a clear stream, a few *álamos* within the infinite solitude put on a vivid and intense vitality. These shade trees, as a rule, announce man's presence; yonder lies some *pueblo* on the flatland basking in the sun, toasted by it or blasted by the frost, of *adobes* more than likely, graving the outline of its church's belfry upon the blue of sky. . . .

What beauty, that of a setting sun upon these solemn solitudes! It swells on touching the horizon as though hungry to enjoy more of the earth, and sinking it leaves a golden dust upon the sky, and on the earth the life's blood of its light. The infinite dome grows pale apace, gets swiftly dark, and, following a fleeting dusk, a night profound drops down upon it tremulous with stars. These are not at all the sweet and long and languid twilights of the northern countries.

Broad is Castile! And how beautiful the sadness in repose of that sea of stone so full of sky! It is a landscape uniform and monotonous in its contrasts of light and shade, in its unblended colors bereft of intermediary tints. . . . Gentle transitions are lacking, nor is there any other harmonic continuity than that of the immense plateau and the density of blue which spreads over it and gives it light.

This landscape does not waken sensuous desires of *joie de vivre*, nor does it summon feelings of voluptuous ease and comfort; it is not a green and luscious turf inviting one to tumble on it, nor are there folds of land enticing one as to a nest. Musing on it calls not forth the beast which sleeps in all of us . . . as when confronted with the luxuriant fields of opulent vegetation. It is not the type of Nature that pampers the spirit.

Rather, it detaches us from the impoverished ground below to rap us up into the pure, unwavering, naked heaven. There is no communing here with Nature, nor does she absorb us in her exuberant splendors. This infinite countryside is, if we might put it so, a landscape which is monotheistic instead of pantheistic. While not losing himself in it, man is diminished by it, and in it he experiences amid the dryness of the land the aridity of his soul. . . .

Always, whenever I contemplate the Castilian plateau, two paintings come to mind. The first consists of a desolate landscape, dry and hot beneath a vivid sky; one space of it is filled with a multitude of kneeling Moors, their muskets on the ground, their heads buried between their hands . . . and standing at their head a sun-burnt leader with his arms stretched up to the infinite blue, his vision lost upon it as if saying: "God alone is God!" The other painting shows . . . an immense lifeless plain in the dusk's melting light, and in the distance the silhouettes of Don Quijote and Sancho stark against the dying sky.

Leave out the word "Castile," and it could be Palestine—and also the central portion of New Mexico far across the western ocean in a newer and vaster world.

This word picture of a landscape and its people was painted several decades ago, before our present technologies began altering the Iberian landscape to some extent with lakes from dammed-up rivers and with networks of highways, and the people's way of life through modern appliances—just as the present-day Israeli have been changing the face of biblical lands, or the American engineers the old visage of New Mexico. But the total picture remains valid. The eternal aspect of mountain and plain, the very atmosphere, are much too big to be done over in a day; so, also, the deeps of the human spirit they have nourished.

4

Same as Jerusalem's

The eyes of Arabs and Israeli from the Near East, and of Spaniards from the Iberian peninsula, quickly light up with mingled joy and nostalgia when they first behold the landscape of New Mexico. This is most true of the north-central Rio Grande watershed which is its bosom. How very much like home, these visitors feel themselves compelled to tell you.

Other interior parts of the great North American Southwest, which are similar in general aspect, fail to elicit such a spontaneous response. Westward from the watershed of the Rio Grande, the continent begins showing the characteristics of northern Arizona's endless complex of colorful deserts and mountains all the way to the incomparable Grand Canyon. But the contrasts are much too violent. The landscape seems newly created and untried by man. Somehow, the atmosphere of New Mexico is missing.

In the opposite direction from the Rio Grande, across the great Rocky Mountain cordillera, begin the famed Great Plains which once upon a time shook under the thundering hooves of countless bison. Their western fringes keep New Mexico's own aura for as long as mountain ranges and their foothills remain in view. But these pleasant bays of undulating grassland soon give way to the nation's Midwest prairie ocean, rich in economic possibilities but devoid of character.

To the north, where the adolescent Rio Grande threads its way down from its high mountain sources in Colorado, the sierras soar mightily with truly Alpine splendor; but then, again, the land and sky no longer are New Mexico. And to the south, which finds the slanted river hurrying faster toward the Gulf of Mexico, after mountain range and level stretch have sold their birthright of pine and juniper for a mess of drab mesquite, the whole terrain takes on more and more the bleaker look of the Sonoran desert, the New World's wilderness of Sinai.

In short, New Mexico has no deserts and canyons as grand and as colorful as those of northern Arizona, or dry stretches as wide and as bleak and as hot as the Sonoran plateau of northern Mexico, western Texas, and southern Arizona. Her rolling plains, shrunken as well as ennobled by small wooded ranges and tablelands scattered among them, and by blue sierras visible along the horizon, cannot compare in size and fertility with the oceanlike prairies of the North American Midwest. Nor are her highest mountains as widespread and majestic as those that fill the Colorado country to the north.

But the New Mexican landscape has something that they all lack. It is Holy Land.

What is Palestinian and Castilian New Mexico cannot be platted in surveyors' squares; nor are there any sea boundaries, as with Spain, to trace its limits. It is simply an uneven area determined by mood as well as by topography, or rather, by a certain landscape subtly affected by a mood that can be felt.

It is true that the general region is many hundreds of feet higher above sea level than the Holy Land or the central Castilian plateau; hence the reason for this atmospheric similarity must be New Mexico's precise altitude in conjunction with just the right distance away from oceans and other sources of moisture. And so, to the Mediterranean visitors at first glance, the hunched junipers and piñons on every side begin to look much like stands of olive trees in Samaria or Extremadura. Barer hills and plains bring up memories of Carmel and Esdraelon, or of the countryside of La Mancha south and west of Toledo all the way to the Portuguese border. Dry washes are familiar *wadis* to one group of visitors, *arroyos* to the other.

The gentle yet majestic rise of the Sangre de Cristo range and other lesser sierras like the Jemez evoke visions, not of Alps, but of Lebanons and Sierra Morenas back home; and the not too wide or deep Rio Grande, green only for short distances along its meandering banks, is a Jordan or Guadiana flowing with ancient life-giving purpose past countless buried ruins of human habitations, prehistoric homes that once so much depended on its waters as do living towns and villages today.

This comparison with upland Spain is not new by any means. It was already a common notion in earliest colonial times both in Europe and in the New World. Friars and soldiers returning to Mexico City used to regale their fellows in convents and barracks with their descriptions of this still mysterious northern land, and these descriptions were picked up by local historians or by travelers from Europe who kept journals. One of them wrote in 1774: "The climate is like that of the two Castiles: it has its seasons of snow and rain, is mild in spring, and extremely hot in summer." And a friar-historian of Jalisco made this remark about New Mexico: "It is current belief that this territory is the one most similar to the Spanish peninsula."

Other such comments could no doubt be found by further research, but a very much older phrase that prods the mind at the moment is that promise made to Abraham in Genesis 15:

> To your descendants I give this land
> from the wadi of Egypt to the Great River.

1. The Ancient Dwellers

Palestine and Castile, of course, were landscapes ancient with people when men first settled on this their New World counterpart. But it is this same fact of continuous human habitation through so many centuries which also contributes much of that mood we spoke of to New Mexico's particular atmosphere. To start with, there are all the prehistoric ancestors of this land's Native Americans who lived in and off the very landscape, from the time they honeycombed tall sandstone cliffs for dwellings, walling up the larger natural openings like swallows' nests for ceremonial chambers (reminders in a crude way of Qumran and Petra), to a later period when they built horizontal imitations of them upon the valley floors.

The very soil is more than the scoria of ages of geology because it is also made up of human stuff that once breathed and loved, and everywhere it hides combsful of hearths which once warmed and nurtured human life for centuries. The occupancy of these *Anasazi*—the ancient people—does not go nearly as far back as the ruins of the primitive Iberians of Spain, and much less of the pre-Hebraic Semites and Hamites of the Near East, but its subtle effect on the landscape is exactly the same.

Then there are their living descendants, the "Indians" whom the first Europeans found living here in the same type of houses. These had cozy rooms of compacted earth and flagstone rising out of the landscape as an integral part of it—as they had done elsewhere millenniums ago to shelter the peasantry along the Nile and the Euphrates. For these people were likewise agricultural. They eked a bare living from the same kind of soil in the exact manner of their Anasazi forebears, since they lacked the abundant waters of the Egyptians and Mesopotamians. It was a hard life of meager corn-planting and some hunting of wild game by the most primitive means in an upland country which Nature had really intended for grazing.

However, North America had no domesticated sheep or goats, or cattle and horses; otherwise these people would surely have been a pastoral folk as the land itself called for. Is this why, also, they never came to discern some sort of Elyon or Shaddai as had the shepherd people of the far more ancient Near and Middle East across the world? At least we know that, as tillers of the soil, they became spiritually ingrown by tying man's primitive urge for religion to the cycle of the seasons, as had the much more ancient and progressive farmers of Mesopotamia and the Nile. But, since tillable land was confined to small patches along their only river and its tiny tributaries, the population remained very small, and thus unable to emerge from the Stone Age into such populous civilizations as were made possible by the bounteous silts of the Nile, the Tigris, and the Euphrates.

And so their mythology also remained as simple as their lives. Pinned down to their small section of earth by their daily limited round of occupations, they could not visualize a universal myth of Creation. Their sight peered no further than the immediate horizon and an ancient time when their primeval ancestors emerged from a sacred hole in the earth as from a womb, much like the shoots of maize upon which they so much depended. By that same opening dwelt the Mother of all beings (whose symbol was the phallic sheathed cob of maize) with her two constant companions, the twin warrior–medicine men—a neat, compact bisexual concept which had not developed into the Mesopotamian and later Graeco-Roman mythology of gods gamboling among themselves in what we might call a "civilized" manner.

Theirs were not gods in this sense. They were the male-female principle of life without a starting point of creation, but ever creating with the seasonal cycles. And so their ancestors had emerged from the vulval depths as full-grown adults, yet as ignorant and helpless as newborn babes, and in darkness since so many human births take place at night.

But there were also certain beings (like the Old World *elohim*) waiting to nourish them and train them as parents and relatives do their children. These were solid terrestrial humans and animals who had somehow gotten the "know-how" of tapping that mysterious Power which all men come to observe in Nature. One lit the sun for them, another the moon. Others brought the rain clouds from the horizon's rim, and the rest taught them how to build earthen homes and to grow maize and squash from the same earth. Those which were animal-beings taught them how to hunt wild beasts for food and clothing, as well as the use of wild herbs for curing all kinds of sickness.

Those benign human and animal "ancient ones" stayed with the first people until skepticism reared its ugly head, as it also must have happened in the history of much older rituals in Babylon and Egypt, and even among the primitive Hebrews, not to mention our own Christian forebears and our contemporaries. Some more sophisticated individuals began laughing at the rest of the people for believing in the ancient ones since these, they said, were nothing but ordinary folk wearing masks and paints and feathers. This made the ancient ones so angry, the story goes on to say, that they vanished from among men forever. But in their mercy they taught certain of the faithful how to wear their masks and other paraphernalia, and how to chant the right songs, so that they also, by assuming the persons of those knowledgeable beings, could make the clouds bring rain, the sun insure good crops, and wild herbs cure their sick. This sacred know-how was then passed down the generations through societies of medicine men under the watchful eye of each community's chief shamans.

To sustain all this ritual, *kivas* of caked mud partly buried in the maternal earth's bosom served these people as had the lofty and massive stone or brick temples of Mesopotamia and Egypt served their much more sophisticated builders in their more highly ritualized magic ceremonial. For, basically, the religious outlook was the same.

2. The Oñate Expedition

Into this dry upland landscape and the humble stone-age religious and social milieu of its aborigines there came, in the springtime of 1598, that first Spanish colony under Don Juan de Oñate which was introduced in the beginning, and with its own intense feeling of evangelical purpose along with its oft-expressed biblical self-identification.

Most significantly, in the opening canto of his epic *Historia de la Nueva*

México, Captain Gaspar Pérez de Villagrá, the self-appointed bard of the expedition, noted with pious pride how this greatly desired Promised Land of "the New Mexico" lay

> At thirty-three degrees of latitude
> below the Arctic Pole, the very same,
> we know, that is Jerusalem's the Holy.

Villagrá did not remain with the colony, yet he did it a finer favor by returning to Spain and publishing his thirty-four classic cantos at Alcalá in 1610. His enthusiastic epic poem, sometimes faulty as historical narrative from too much poetic license, is still priceless for many reasons. It not only brought the attention of the mother country to a new daughter far across the ocean sea, but started off the latter's history with her very own Genesis and Exodus in verse. And the poet-captain was so correct in his geography at this point, just as we are delighted by this observation of his after having drawn such a detailed parallel between New Mexico's landscape and that of Palestine.

Then, the prose of Oñate's Act of Possession at La Toma by the lower Rio Grande, which the poet was careful to insert among the cantos, reflects the same attitude. It is a civic-religious ritual forged by Spain's more than seven hundred years of battling the Moors, and exalting Christianity as Spaniards saw it under the leadership of their own monarchy. In fact, Spanish writers in past decades had boldly referred to the late Emperor Charles V as holding the office of Moses in the new dispensation, while the Pope in Rome merely exercised that of Aaron. In other words, Spain was Judah, and the rest of the Christian nations, including the Papal States, were the less important tribes of Jacob.

It is in this flamboyant spirit that the Act of La Toma spells out the expedition's main intent of christianizing the natives of this land as subjects of the Spanish king. They are to be made his subjects, and Christ's own in the bargain, through the teaching of God's Spanish Levites, in this case the Franciscan friars accompanying the colony. And there is a decidedly scriptural undertone throughout as the general claims the new country "for the royal Crown of Castile and the monarchs who have ruled over it . . . relying and standing on the one and absolute power of the eternal holy Pontiff and King Jesus Christ . . . foundation and cornerstone of the Old and New Covenants, the beginning and perfection of the Scriptures. . . ."

High above Oñate's bare head the new country's standard hangs from its mast-piece topped by a shining cross. Its front displays the embroidered image of the Virgin of Remedies, celestial patroness of the Spaniards in the city of Mexico as she is now of the ones entering a new land named after it. The reverse shows the quartered gold castles of Castile on red and the red lions of León on white. All emblems together portray the *anima hispanica*, the Spanish soul, coming upon new pastures.

The audience of four hundred armed settlers standing at parade attention at La Toma, and of more than a hundred and thirty brave women with their many children, must have listened with the same elation as those ancient Hebrew shepherd families who, upon leaving the desert of Sinai for good, paid excited heed to Joshua's proclamation by Jordan's waters as they prepared to enter the Promised Land.

We might also compare the occasion with a much later one in Scripture, when Ezra read the Book of the Law all morning long to the Judaic remnant just returned to Jerusalem from Babylonian captivity. For this return under Ezra and Nehemiah around 538 B.C. marks the birth of Judaism as we know it today. And our own era's famous year of 1492, when the various old Iberian kingdoms had become united at last under Ferdinand and Isabella—who in that same year underwrote the discovery of America by Columbus—signifies the birth of Spain's own national identity as well as the beginning of her Golden Age.

So can we also say here that April 30, 1598, was the birthday of the Hispanic people of New Mexico as a cultural unit apart from Spain herself, and also from what are now Mexico and other Spanish-speaking nations on this side of the globe. Here, for the space of three centuries and a half, until its fast disintegration in our day, a small Spanish enclave existed humbly with its archaic southwest Castilian rural customs, language, and feelings, as nurtured and modified in complete isolation by its own Palestinian-Castilian landscape.

3. The New Upland People

One is tempted to idealize the occasion and romanticize those pioneer pilgrims themselves, as Christians have the ones in the Bible. Other people have done the same for their own ancestors' landing on other American shores. As one of our latter-day American historians observed, "History is a mass-invention, the day dream of a race."

Except that the Spaniard, like the ancient Semite, does not really romanticize; he takes the real as it is and exaggerates it. Even in their dialogues with divinity, the biblical patriarchs foreshadow Don Quijote and Sancho Panza in their stark humanity. And so one feels no embarrassment in bluntly saying that these first Castilian migrants to our New Mexico were neither suave saints nor scholars, but rather a cantankerous lot for the most part. Nor were they the flower of Iberian aristocracy, which would neither change their character nor improve their quality, although several in their surnames and confident attitude betrayed a remote genteel ancestry or a lapsed pedigree. But now they were a plain and mostly unlettered countryfolk.

However, they were not plodding peasant farmers who have little to say. They were stockmen—*ganaderos*—madly avid to possess their own pastureland, and voluble with vain-boasting and with the droll refrains with which Cervantes was just then mentally forming the rustic characters in *Don Quijote de la Mancha*. Realists and idealists at the same time, they were like Don Quijote and Sancho who, as Unamuno put it, "travel together, help one another, quarrel, love each other, but never fuse."

For, as a whole, they originated in that same central highland of La Mancha and the similar countryside next to it, in Extremadura. Some were Creoles born in the New World, true, long before there ever was a Mexico, but they still bore the characteristics of their compatriots who had recently crossed the ocean sea. The roster of their surnames, and of those in the large contingent which arrived two years later, makes up a litany of the high Castilian plateau.

There were other types represented by single individuals. Among those who stayed to occupy the land was a Basque, and also a handful of people from the Portuguese, Galician, and Catalonian litorals whose remote antecedents included ancient Celts, Goths, and Greeks. In fact, there was a Greek among them, a contemporary of El Greco from the same birthplace on Crete. And a couple of them brought along some Tlascaltec Indian women, two or three of whom some bachelors eventually took to wife.

But the majority were from the Castilian uplands—*extremeños* and *manchegos*—"semitic" Iberians in blood and pastoral tradition speaking the *castizo* Castilian of the high plateau. A trio of Canary Islanders shared the same language and mannerisms, since their recent forebears, who in latter times had conquered and settled those islands, were from Extremadura. Lastly, those who had been born in the New World of Spanish parents were of the same blood and tradition.

This showed on their lean and leathery faces—high forward cheekbones, lantern jaws often, and nose sharply defined—of Semite and Hamite ancestors from a long-forgotten Iberian past, not necessarily from more recent Moorish times, although strains of Arabic and Jewish cannot altogether be disregarded. Most had black hair, either straight or wavy, or with that frizzle which is peculiarly Levantine. Others were described as having either reddish or blond hair, very likely showing strains of Celtic or Visigothic, although such characteristics were not unknown among the Near East ancients.

One prominent individual appears to have been a scion of the famed Jewish family Carvajal in Mexico City, which had borne the brunt of the Inquisition there. Another who came later, a Gómez from Lisbon, also passed under the tribunal's shadow as a *marrano* falsely suspected of practicing Judaism in secret. And both are my direct ancestors on both the paternal and maternal side.

One can see why, surrounded by their flocks and herds and straining to enter and possess a vast virgin pastureland, they fell in love with its arid edges at La Toma. For these already began reminding them, if only spiritually of Palestine, altogether physically of that old landscape in central Spain south of Toledo which stretches westward to the Portuguese border. Truly, it was like a return to their ancient home, except for the single and most important fact that this land would be their own, not those old feudal estates of dukes and counts where their forebears had lived as serfs through recent generations.

Here they themselves would be the dukes, as Don Quijote was at this time promising Sancho Panza if he fared forth questing with him across the wide, wide world.

The thought which most of them relished was that they would become acknowledged *hidalgos* at long last. Don Juan de Oñate carried a royal decree to this effect. They would be "somebodies" as the lineal descendants, which some of them considered themselves to be, of provincial heroes who had been knighted during the centuries-long Moorish wars, and whose surnames they proudly bore. At the same time, they would have laughed with hearty humor had some wag brought up an irreverent refrain which went: *Entre criados, putas y frailes se buscan linajes—*"Among servants, whores and friars, the search for noble forebears."

This overriding desire for an estate akin to nobility, or *hidalguismo,* has been Spain's chief malady, as her writers have observed. It is this very same quirk which had already gained so much of the New World for her, and not any mere thirst for gold for its own sake. Inca and Aztec gold were for buying titles of nobility, as well as ships and armies for further feats of derring-do that promised higher titles still.

While Don Juan de Oñate and the captains of his staff—none of whom cared to remain in New Mexico—did dream of finding rich new realms for this purpose, the others who came to stay, and those who periodically followed them thereafter, sought only the minimum of *hidalguía,* so long as the ownership of pastureland went with it. Here, very much like the Israelites under Joshua, they hungered for the extensive grazing lands which lay open before them and for the taking, where their sheep and cattle and horses could multiply themselves into infinity with the least labor on their owners' part, thus bringing these owners not only ease and leisure as befits true *hidalgos,* but full independence from all the pharaohs, kings, and dukes of the world.

But there is a more serious feature to be reckoned with, as there was with the Bible folk under Joshua. The formal Act of Possession at La Toma had been preceded by a solemn mass chanted by the Franciscans, one of whom preached a stirring sermon on the colony's spiritual purpose. Then the soldiers staged a play which a captain by the name of Farfán had composed for the occasion; its theme was the martyrdom of those three simple friars who had entered this land some twenty years before and given it its name, and whom the colonists now regarded as "heralds" of their present enterprise.

"The Evangelical Conversion" is what they were actually calling their entry into this Promised Land, for with the Spaniards of that day as with the Israelites of old, eager expectations of land and freedom could not be divorced from a deep sense of divine commission. It can also be seen in Oñate's address to the Holy Cross at the end of his proclamation: "Open the door to these heathens, establish the church and altars where the Body and Blood of the Son of God may be offered, open to us the way to security and peace for their preservation and ours. . . ."

All the sufferings which these people had endured in order to reach the

Promised Land, and whatever hardships were to come, as many would, were deemed a most welcome penitence if it brought down God's aid and blessing on the missionary enterprise. And fanatical as these folk were in their intent to impose the worship of their own Deity upon the natives of this extreme western Canaan of the New World, it implied a common sharing of economic destinies as well as of worship according to the fraternal code of their own Covenant.

5

Into the Promised Land

Many years ago, at the time I was beginning my documentary researches on my people's imprint upon our landscape—and the landscape on them—I made my first trips down to La Toma country, either by car upon the older modern highway which followed the winding Rio Grande for a greater part of the way, or on the train which took off midway from the river valley near San Marcial to follow the old Jornada del Muerto and then join the river once more at Rincón.

Each route complemented the other from Albuquerque south to Socorro, and from Rincón down to the historic kingdom's northward passage of El Paso del Norte. Thus, in between, the railway's lengthy wayward swerve east of the barren flanks of the Fray Cristóbal and Caballo ranges completed the tracing of the ancient Camino Real, or King's Highway if in name only, which had begun with the initial entrance of the Oñate colony far back in 1598.

1. From Sinai to Jordan

For me, after the train pulled out of Albuquerque's old Alvarado station, the itinerary presented much more than fleeting views of the river valley's narrow greenery, hemmed in on either side by monotonous rolls of desolate plain with bluish mountains in the distance, or the scant series of villages and towns along the way. Behind my eyes there unfolded a vivid map of old and venerable historic places, some of them now long forgotten. Before my gaze, in successive motion picture frames, there passed a northbound troop of many horsemen escorting eighty loaded ox-drawn *carretas*—"like ants hauling wheat," Villagrá put it—Arabian steeds and lumbering carts on which I also rode within the travelers' weary loins.

Albuquerque was not merely the villa of this name founded late in 1706, but the mid-1600s Trujillo estancia of San Francisco Xavier close by and the Chávez estancia of Atrisco across the river from it, both of them pastoral establishments of my own direct forebears. Just as much were the later ranchos and plazas of the 1700s, like Armijo, Pajarito, and Los Padillas down the stretch. Then came the ancient Tiwa Pueblo of Isleta which once gave its name to the civil magistracy of further ancestral places like Los Lunas, Los Chávez, and other such communities named after families in the area later called Belén—and east of the river the seventeenth-century estancia of Tomé Domínguez de Mendoza, then its contemporary estancias of Romero and Robledo at the long-deserted Piro pueblo of La Joya de Sevilleta.

Farther south, after another desolate stretch relieved only by the sharp Ladrones peak on the west and the wavy Manzano ranges to the east, there came the 1815 town of Socorro, in whose wide area Oñate's people of 1598 first saw the now long-vanished Piro pueblos of Teypana and Pilabó—and which Oñate gratefully named Socorro after the friendly natives "succored" his vitamin-starved colonists with generous supplies of maize.

And farther down along the actual bottomlands had stood the estancia of Luis López, the modern ranches still bearing the three-hundred-year-old name, and after that the little hamlet of San Antonio, patron-saint of the long-vanished Piro pueblo of Qualacú—the first of the many Indian pueblos of New Mexico which the Oñate colonists came upon.

Then before one knew it, after penetrating its marshy edges of salt cedar for a spell, the train had crossed over the Rio Grande to the ancient Paraje de Fray Cristóbal on its eastern bank; it was never an actual settlement, just a stopping point where Father Cristóbal de Salazar, Oñate's favorite chaplain, must have died while returning to New Spain. The naked stone sierra receding steadily to the right had also become his monument by acquiring his religious name. As in Genesis and Exodus, death was very often the christener of places.

Here began the now famous Jornada del Muerto, meaning the day's travel route that recalled a dead man, a corpse—and therefore "the Dead Man's Route" and not the "Journey of Death," as often mistranslated. This flat and desolate Negeb desert of La Jornada bore no vestiges of human habitation. Nor did it have any signs pinpointing certain place-names in my mental map like La Cruz de Anaya, El Alemán, and El Perrillo. The first must have been a wooden cross marking the spot where a seventeenth-century settler named Anaya had succumbed along the route or had been killed by Apache arrows. The second recalled the discovery by those early travelers of the sun-dried corpse of an itinerant German trader, Bernardo Gruber by name, who had been jailed in Santa Fe for practicing the black arts and, when escaping south, had here perished from the desert heat, thus naming the Jornada itself through his misadventure. Lastly, El Perrillo called to mind a little dog which had strayed from some Apache hunting party and had come wagging its friendly tail among the sun-parched colonists of 1598. In return for bits of food and fond pats it had led some of Oñate's horsemen to a most welcome water spring not far off the route.

Such were the action scenes unreeling within my skull when the chair cars started to shake and groan as the train wound its way slowly down into the river valley once more, to the little depot of Rincón, originally called El Rincón de Fray Diego. Here an early seventeenth-century Franciscan had died coming to or returning from the pueblo missions. From Rincón there was the final stretch of both the steel tracks and the modern valley highway, the latter having come down well away from the river's left bank from Socorro.

And for this last space there was a pair of other names to ponder— Robledo and Doña Ana—before the naked stone gateway of the kingdom hove into view at last. Every return trip, whether by train through the Jornada or by automobile up the more direct stretch of highway, used to renew all these visionary tableaux in reverse order. Or in direct order, rather, as we now go back to the birth of a new people and to their subsequent plodding northward into their Promised Land.

*   *   *

When the entire colony proceeded upstream along the Rio Bravo del Norte, which we now call the Rio Grande, the expedition's chronicler recorded how it reminded some individuals of the Guadalquivir, which in Moorish Arabic also means "Great River." For those of the colonists who had come from Spain, besides the one or more who were natives of Andalucía, had spent months or even years around Sevilla awaiting their call to the port of embarkation at Sanlúcar de Barrameda. Besides, the great Guadalquivir was not too far south from the others' Extremaduran hometowns that lay just north of the Sierra Morena which divided the two provinces.

They now crossed this great river at the pass between those pyramidal hills of bare stone which they named "El Paso del Norte" by combining, as we have seen, the two ideas of fording the river and passing through the narrow defile in their journey northward. This spot, the area of modern El Paso's Smeltertown, was considered thereafter as the gateway to the kingdom of New Mexico. Incidentally, as the chronicler wrote somewhere, the wild Indians of the region already had a name for the pass in their language, and the writer rendered it into Spanish as "Los Puertos." This term likewise means a gateway as well as a mountain gap, and so the newcomers were not so original after all in naming El Paso del Norte. But this goes very well with our recurring scriptural allusions, for the many spots in Exodus which the Israelites were naming as historical landmarks of their own adventures in Canaan were often their own later interpretations of already long established Canaanitic place-names.

Symbolically, this was also the crossing of the Jordan opposite Jericho, and had the ancient Hebrew settlers been with the colony now they would have noticed a remarkable resemblance between this winding stream and the Jordan's own meandering course—not so much in the swiftness of the brown torrent as in the grassy banks in narrow strips much of the time or else spreading outward in small meadows with clumps of olive-hued osiers along the edges. And beyond them on either side were the rolling stony hillocks and higher mounds of naked earth or stone also proclaiming themselves Holy Land. To these Spanish pilgrims at the moment, and as they trudged farther onward with their sluggish two-wheeled wooden carts amid their browsing livestock, it began to look more and more like the central and southwestern Castilian hills of home.

One particular incident, which occurred three weeks later, highlights such impressions in three and a half centuries of retrospect. It was the late spring festival of Corpus Christi when the colony halted to set up its tabernacle of boughs once more, just north of the present city of Las Cruces and the older town of Doña Ana. The Ark of the Eucharist was borne around in customary procession in celebration of the feast. It also happened that here a sixty-year-old ensign named Pedro Robledo died and was buried, and in remembrance a great bare roundish mountain on the river's west bank has borne the name "Robledo" to this day.

This was the first death in the Promised Land. The deceased and his large family had originally come from Toledo and its countryside. He is the oldest ancestor in that pioneer expedition of both my parents by several lines. Hundreds of other living New Mexicans could say the same if they traced their own ancestry. But to me, because of this very knowledge, the sight of Mount Robledo is always a thrill.

It also reminds me of the fact that it somehow resembles the great tawny mound on which the ancient city of Toledo has stood for many centuries; except that Toledo's mound is almost surrounded by a horseshoe bend of the Rio Tajo, while our Rio Grande passes Mount Robledo only along one side. Moreover, it evokes in its round bareness certain photographic views of Mount Carmel and Mount Thabor in the Holy Land. And yet, Mount Robledo is very much larger and higher than the Castilian and Palestinian places it calls to mind; hence it has to be something other than mere measurements that makes them so akin.

*   *   *

Soon the travelers found the river winding closer between steep banks continuously split by traversing gullies. They were either shallow or very deep wadis and arroyos, which would bog down the carts at every few turns of their solid wooden wheels. Besides, they provided ready-made blinds for ambush. For here any old Israelites present would have likened the terrain to the land of Edom, since the advance scouts of this Hispanic Exodus had reported seeing bands of sneaky native Edomites (the Apaches) which could seriously harass the colonists' progress towards their goal. This forced them to climb eastward onto flat desert country at the place later called the Corner of Fray Diego, as we have seen.

The route over this Negeb was most tedious, but of necessity it became the regular one for reaching or leaving the kingdom. This is that Jornada del Muerto on which the heat-buffeted men, women, and children had that cute and hope-restoring adventure with the little stray dog; and following authentic biblical procedure, they called the spot "El Perrillo." Once this evil stretch was conquered, there was the final return to the ever-welcome Jordan in wider valley terrain, when the colony entered the settled areas of their Promised Land.

First came the Piro pueblo of Qualacú, and then its sister pueblos of the Socorro area with its new Spanish name extolling native Indian charity and good will. From a distance these Indian villages would have looked to some like Semitic mud towns of the Near East, had any biblical people been with the colony. To these Spaniards they appeared like hamlets in Morocco or the southern rural Spain of their day. Scores of tiny emerald fields of spouting little green fountains of maize along the river bottoms lent an air of placid contentment. These were the first civilized structures and cornfields they had seen for hundreds of miles since they had left the Spanish and Indian settlements in southern New Spain.

For the natives they had encountered thus far in the Sonoran wilderness had been miserable nude bedouins without stable habitations. Here, however, the general scene was most pleasingly familiar. They were *pueblos*, or well-ordered "towns," in contrast with the *despoblado* or uninhabited and forbidding Sinai they had left behind. And so began a designation for these Indian villages and their inhabitants which is current to this day also in the English language.

2. Canaan and Castile Again

The face of the landscape, too, had come into focus in familiar features and complexion. Now even the rolling hills on either side of the widening valley, not to mention sharply cut embankments of earth and stone, wore the gentle pastel hues of chalky white with canary and roseate ochres, the very ones of Extremadura and contiguous highlands of the Sierra Morena. Some hills and mesas even showed crenelated castle ruins on their tops, not those castles of Castile built in medieval times by the Spanish or Moorish nobility, but fortresses more elaborately carved by wind and rain through the ages out of the craggy sandstone caps.

More and more the rounded hills appeared dotted with piñon and juniper, gray-green in the bright sun, which one could swear were extensive olive groves. (While traveling in like sections in Spain, a person from these parts is liable, at unguarded moments, to take such olive groves for stands of piñon and juniper.) These two trees they called *sabina* and *piñón*, for resembling certain evergreens back home. Several kinds of low silvery bushes which they brushed through at every turn they named *chamiza*, for looking from a distance like rushes of this name in Spain.

Then there was the low slender-spiked yucca which they named *palmilla*, for resembling the head of a tiny palm. Its root would for many generations provide housewives with a foamy soap. But at this time none of them dreamed that the thin spikes, razor-sharp along the edges, would in much later times provide a stinging whip for certain bloody penances; nor that the *nopal* or low-lying pear cactus, and the *entraña* or taller cactus branching out like stiff "entrails," would also serve the same sinister purposes. Nor yet that such lovely hillocks and their cover of *sabino* and *chamiso* (as both were later masculinized) would be silent witnesses to many a penitential procession of blood—the blood of some of their descendants some two centuries thereafter.

*   *   *

Beyond all this on the horizon all around, but especially toward the north, high mountains nibbled at the sky like blue and purple Hermons and Sierras de Gata, yet unable to diminish the turquoise firmament which kept on drawing the eye to infinity—by ancient primitive tradition the dwelling place of the God of Abraham and Jacob and Moses, and of Muhammed —and, in the lively imaginations of these new Castilian upland folk, also the mansions of the Eternal Father which Jesus had prepared for those who love him.

As for the native Canaanites they now encountered, these proved altogether friendly, although some at first fled to the nearby hills, dismayed by the apparition of people so different from themselves. Once reassured by friendly overtures, however, they offered the strangers gifts of maize sorely needed as a relief to a diet of beef and mutton. This maize was very much their providential manna, since the wheat grains and legume seeds they brought along had to be hoarded for the next year's planting.

Village after village, as the expedition kept advancing, made pledges of friendship in the same way, also by making acts of reverence to the crosses in the friars' hands. This caused the naïve missionaries and colonists to interpret them as acts of fealty to Christianity and the Spanish monarchy.

Poet Villagrá had a good word for these natives, describing them as handsome and healthy with not a cripple in sight, not given to drunkenness like the Indians of Mexico, and devoted to the art of painting. As an example of the latter, he says that during their brief stop at the pueblo of Puaray (north of present Albuquerque) the Spaniards were led into a ceremonial chamber to see murals depicting the martyrdom of the three Franciscan heralds of 1581. But the official chronicler, who surely would have noted down the fact had he seen something so extraordinary, says never a word, except to remark that they stopped at Puaray where the three friars had been martyred. Nor does it seem likely that the natives of Puaray would have disclosed something so incriminating.

Finally the months-long trip came to an end when the colony made its last halt at the northernmost Tewa pueblo of Okeh, which they promptly christened San Juan in honor of John the Baptist. Villagrá, ever whetting his poetic fancy, said it was called "San Juan de los Caballeros," ascribing this knightly title to the three little Franciscan heralds who had lain down their lives as Knights of Christ twenty years before. The poet must have recalled how St. Francis himself had romantically called his first band of friars minor the Knights of the Lord's Table. Anyway, if the poets's title is factual, it could be that Don Juan de Oñate, in selecting the name of St. John in his capacity of patron saint of the famed Knights of Jerusalem and Malta, was honoring himself and his staff as proper "gentlemen," while casting a sop to his commoner followers who now could pick up the crumb-designation of *hidalgo.*

At San Juan the first church was built with the very first *adobes* made in the new land—the large and substantial sun-dried mud brick of the houses of ancient Ur and Harran and Canaan, of Egypt and the North African litoral as far west as Morocco, from where it had passed on in prehistoric times across Gibraltar's narrows into Spain. Once more there were festive religious rites, with readings from the consecration of Solomon's temple when the church was dedicated, followed by a comedy by the thespian group among the soldiers, and "tilts of Moors and Christians" put on by the cavalry, for the entertainment of the happy families and their amazed Indian hosts of San Juan.

The newcomers soon proceeded to build their own Shechem with its shrine to the true Lord at San Gabriel, within the triangle formed by the river Chama running into the Rio Grande. It was an ideal spot for the necessary planting which had to be done to supplement the people's flesh diet, and the digging of irrigation ditches to bleed off the precious fluid from the adjoining streams was the first order of the day.

The Franciscan padres were apportioned among the various linguistic groups of pueblos, so that the heathen peoples of the new Canaan might soon become true and equal brethren of the new dispensation. For as Jesus had taught, and the Spanish Crown had most strongly specified through its viceroy in New Spain, there was to be perfect peace and brotherhood under the one Father and Lord, not the most unchristian slaughter and slavery which had most shamefully taken place when the Indians of New Spain and Peru were conquered without royal authority by those two Extremaduran countrymen of theirs, Cortés and Pizarro.

Nor were the natives to be shorn of their customs and languages, or their farmlands taken away. Moreover, since there was grazing land in abundance for all, as soon as the precious livestock brought by the colony and friars had well multiplied in a country so evidently destined for grazing, these kindly people could then join the pastoral fraternity as well, to enjoy luxuries in food and clothing which they had never experienced before.

With regard to farming, it is not surprising that a pastoral *and* masculine Castilian trait betrayed itself from the start. In return for their own magnanimity, the Spanish males expected the Indians to share their agricultural products with them in the future, as they had generously done in the summer and fall after their arrival. The land itself would take care of the livestock. This attitude was imbedded in their language. In Castilian, *labor* is used exclusively for farming and for farmland; hence the farmer is a *labrador,* a laborer plain and simple, at the bottom of the social scale. Next comes the artisan or shop worker, the *obrero,* the operator who "makes" things, but still a common lout because he is engaged in long hours of manual work. But the stockraiser, the *ganadero,* he is the one who makes Nature do most of the work whereby he "gains" a livelihood. This stockman, therefore, is closest to the nobleman who doesn't have to work at all. Thus a pattern was being set for subsequent New Mexican history.

The friars soon put an end to this exploitation of the Indians of San Juan. At first, while Oñate's long forays of exploration were going on, the Spanish women had to cultivate and harvest the crops of native maize and whatever European seeds they had brought along. And sturdy women they must have been, especially Luisa Robledo, as shown the first summer when wild Indians from the eastern plains came to attack San Juan when her husband and the other men were away exploring.

She was the daughter of the old ensign from Toledo who had died along the trail, and the wife of Bartolomé Romero, likewise a Toledan who was one of Oñate's best captains. Brave Luisa gathered all the Spanish and Indian women on the flat rooftops to pelt the invaders with stones while taunting them with screeching female invective. The ruse worked, for the enemy, a small band most likely, gave up and left.

I identify this valiant and inventive Debborah because she is my direct ancestress by several Romero, Lucero, Roybal, and other lines on both my mother's and my father's sides. I would not doubt that, like the brave prophetess in early Judges, she burst into triumphant song from the roof-tops after the baffled foe had slunk away.

3. Battle of Jericho

All this notwithstanding, matters had to turn biblical with regard to violence and bloodshed upon the poor native Canaanites. The early Hebrews had appropriated interior Canaan by divine sanction when this sometimes meant the extermination of entire towns and tribes. The "ban" of Yahweh, they called it. While a similar sense of manifest destiny lurked deep within these just as determined shepherd Spaniards—professedly bent on friendly evangelization yet triggered for just as drastic action when provoked—their monarch had laid down stringent rules barring such conduct. The misdeeds of Hernando Cortés, Francisco Pizarro, Nuño de Guzmán, and other such maverick plunderers in New Spain and Peru still hurt the royal conscience; in fact, the cruelty displayed in this very land by some of Coronado's men a little more than half a century before, in 1541, had halted all authorized entries until now, except for the harmless one of the three little martyred friars midway in 1581.

But then, there stood Ácoma, a pueblo proudly and confidently perched high on its great rock in the midst of a large desert west of the Great River. It was a most unfortunate incident at this soaring cliff pueblo which started it all, even if it gave the new *hidalgos* a taste of quixotic knightly tilting and furnished Captain Villagrá with an epic climax to his poem. The great mesa of Ácoma, its beetling sides rising four hundred feet sheer on most sides, lent itself dramatically to the impending events.

To any of the Spaniards who had ever seen the massive bluff of Ronda near Granada, where a fabled Moorish caliph had built a city complete with an ornate harem—only to lose it all eventually to the conquering Christians —the sight of Acoma could well have conjured up those storied memories, except that this natural fortress in the New World and its aerie town were completely bare of greenery. But to a Jew of the first century of our era, Acoma would certainly have brought up a startling image of Masada across from the Lisan peninsula above the Dead Sea, where close to a thousand starving refugees from the razed city of Jerusalem elected to die rather than surrender to a besieging Roman army.

It so happened that Oñate had left San Juan with his staff and part of his troops to explore the uncharted continent southwestward to the South Sea. The other contingent under his nephew, Captain Juan de Zaldívar, while on its way to catch up with the leader, stopped by at Ácoma to gather extra provisions for the expedition. But the Indian headmen refused to barter their pueblo's cornflour and cotton blankets for proffered hatchets and other metal items which their people lacked and very much coveted. Under the pretext of leading the Spaniards to different storerooms, the Indian leaders separated Zaldívar and the eighteen men who had climbed the mesa with him; then the pueblo's warriors pounced upon the unsuspecting visitors and killed most of them, including Oñate's nephew.

Five of the captain's companions, desperately swinging their swords as they were pushed back to the precipice's rim, dropped backwards into thin air. Among these were Pedro and Francisco Robledo, two young sons of the ensign who had died when the colony first entered the Promised Land. Four of the men landed on a thick slope of powdery sand at the cliff's base and walked away alive, but Pedro Robledo, who fell off to one side, struck flinty ground and was killed. The four survivors and the other men waiting below galloped away to overtake their leader and break the disconcerting news to him.

Blinded by grief and rage, the more so because of his own nephew's tragic death, Oñate brought his men back to San Juan in order to plan an assault on the sky pueblo and what he considered a much-deserved punishment. The father superior of the Franciscans, when consulted according to royal protocol, averred that Oñate had a right to reimburse himself and others for any damage suffered from the Indians "as did Moses in the defense of the Hebrews when they were maltreated by the Egyptians." An obvious if well-meant sophism it was, there being no parallel at all between the tyrant Pharaoh and these natives whose privacy had been invaded. Furthermore, the good padre warned, all killing had to be avoided as much as possible "because it is repulsive to God, as may be seen when he would not accept a temple or house from the righteous David because he was a murderer." Again, a farfetched example. But, Scripture or no Scripture, and despite whatever explicit royal instructions he had received, Don Juan had already made up his mind.

Captain Vicente de Zaldívar, brother of Oñate's slain nephew, set out fuming for the cliff pueblo with seventy fully armed men and some artillery pieces. An orderly siege was set at the single approach to the top. This started as a steep sandy slope, then went straight up in a narrow winding trail against the walls of a gigantic fissure in the dizzy declivity, ending in a series of handholds and toeholds gouged out of the rock.

First overtures for a peaceful parley were shouted up to the defenders, but these, peering confidently down over the edges above, shouted back their defiance and dared the enemy to scale the cliff at their own peril. Without further ado, the more adventurous Spaniards began climbing the precipice under a hail of stones and arrows. To the Indians' amazement, they all managed to reach the summit, if with battered morions and cuirasses. What had made this possible was the steady firing of harquebuses and the small cannon from below. Captain Romero, husband of that Debborah back at San Juan, was later commended for his accurate aiming of the field pieces.

Poet Villagrá minutely describes the total assault, citing the brave deeds of his onetime military associates, from Zaldívar down to the humblest militiaman, as they join in hand-to-hand combat with the desperate chieftains and warriors on their lofty home ground. There are touching tragedies, as when the Basque Archuleta accidentally shoots his army buddy, the Portuguese Rivadeneira, wounding him mortally.

But the highest drama is reserved for the Toledan Diego Robledo, Deborrah's younger brother and sibling of Pedro who had been killed days before in his leap off the cliff. Diego's fierce sallies to avenge his brother's death look more reckless than brave, as when he nimbly leads the first ten men unscathed to the top, thus making it easier for Zaldívar and the others to do the same. At this point a burly chieftain lurches at him, and Diego runs him through the chest with his sword; but instead of dropping dead, the Indian tries to grapple with him and gets another thrust through the thigh. Then, having fallen down on the rock floor as if dead, the Acoman suddenly clutches the unsuspecting Toledan by both ankles, stands up straight and whirls him around over his head, and sends him flying several feet away. Only then does the huge Ácoman collapse in death. This humiliation spurs Diego to madder feats of valor, which inspire the rest of the Spaniards to total victory.

How factual this and other incidents are, and how much embellished by a poet's fancy, we cannot tell. But many such feats must surely have been performed for those few colonist-soldiers to take such an impregnable natural fortress which was so well defended. In this respect, our poet, who patterned his epic on Vergil's Aeneid—even starting it with "I sing of arms and the man"—has to bring in the gracious intervention of the gods.

In his case it is the traditional Hispanic divinities, as it were, who appear in the clouds aiding the Spaniards: Santiago himself, or St. James the Apostle, riding a white charger as he is said to have done during the Moorish wars back home in Spain, and also the Virgin Mary who for centuries has been Spain's conquering queen. The battling Spaniards were too busy to have seen them, of course, and so the poet has the captured chieftain of Ácoma relate the celestial vision which made his people give up the fight.

With this grandiose gesture to national Spanish piety and pride, followed by an address directed to his sovereign as he begs him to consider the valor of his subjects in a strange new world, Villagrá ends his Aeneid about a newborn people—but ever with emphasis on his noble master, Don Juan de Oñate, and Oñate's two nephews. Villagrá gives no hint of this master's terrible and inhuman vengeance upon Ácoma: how he ordered a foot cut off from all male Ácomans twenty-five years old and older, and condemned the rest of the inhabitants to penal servitude.

This we get to learn from the records of Oñate's trial on his recall to Mexico City. Evidently the enslavement of all the people was not carried out, thanks to the friars' intervention, but the cruel mutilation was something that could not be undone, nor the bitter memory it left on Ácoma and the other pueblos.

*   *   *

Here we can very well turn the tables around on my Bible-conscious forebears by comparing the natives of Ácoma with the besieged Jews on the heights of Masada in the year 73 of our era. Our Indian "Eleazar Ben Yair" on his lofty cliff city had seen the lowland villages of his fellowmen succumb shamefully one by one to the advancing strangers from the south; they had been overawed by the fearsome beasts the bearded palefaces rode and by the magic sticks which spewed forth lightning on command. But mighty Ácoma, with her ample stores of provisions and her great natural cistern filled with sweet rainwater, had always withstood all attacks from the wild enemy hunters of the western desert and the eastern plains.

Ácoma could do it again and show the other pueblos that the much fewer "Kashtéra"—"Castilians," as the Keres still call the Spanish New

Mexicans—were not invincible. The trouble was that this brave man knew nothing about European military tactics, nor did he have any idea of a spirit of manifest destiny which most often has the edge in such matters. Had he known of the cruel vengeance which was to follow his defeat, he and his men might well have put all their people to death, as did the Jews of Masada, rather than surrender to such a fate.

It was a bad start, indeed, for the colony and its sincere evangelical purpose. Still, this or any other isolated instance of its kind is a far cry from those ancient divine bans; or from the later decimation, if not extermination, of eastern North American tribes by others who likewise gloried in the Christian name.

6

The Miserable Kingdom

Toward the end of New Mexico's first century, Don Fernando de Chávez II, when referring to a political fracas of 1643, called the land *"este miserable Reyno."* Much later, in 1718, one of his seven sons, Don Antonio de Chávez, used exactly the same phrase on the occasion of his marriage. These are the only occurrences of the expression in the reams of colonial documents that have survived, hence it could well have been a term passed down in the family from father to son.

Not that these men despised their native land when they called it "this miserable kingdom." Their grandfather, Don Pedro Gómez Durán y Chávez, who had come from Llerena in Extremadura in 1600, had worked for the formal establishment of the colony on a local civic basis at the time it was in danger of being abandoned. His eldest son, the first Don Fernando, had fought long and hard against wild tribes, which were assailing the young colony on every side, in order to preserve it. And the latter's eldest son, the second Don Fernando just mentioned, had strongly urged the return of the colonists to their homeland after their fatal defeat and exile following the Pueblo Revolt of 1680, when other leaders preferred to move back down into New Spain. This Fernando's seven sons knew no other country with which to compare the extensive grazing lands they had inherited through their first ancestor's love of the landscape, and through his son's and grandson's own struggles to keep it theirs.

What these my direct name-ancestors were decrying as a miserable kingdom was not their native landscape which they so much loved, but certain adverse circumstances which had come to make it so. The second Don Fernando was recalling the arrogance and misdeeds of too many of the royal governors whom the viceroy had sent on the average of every three years since Grandfather Pedro's time. His own son Antonio, in command of the small garrison in Albuquerque, was showing how a whole century's isolation and abandonment by the mother country now forced him to marry a close Baca relative because the smallness of the Hispanic population left him no other choice.

1. The Kingdom of the New Mexico

Some will say that the misery had begun with Oñate's terrible revenge after the battle of Ácoma. This is true as an isolated instance with regard to the colony's evangelical hopes. It was only one phase connected with the general attitude and conduct of Don Juan himself and those of his nephews and staff officers, who were not interested in establishing either the simple pastoral colony or the missions among the Indian pueblos—unless they encountered a chimera which had already disappointed and ruined Francisco Vásquez Coronado sixty years before.

In his vain searching for the latter's mythical golden cities of Quivira far out on the eastern plains, or a fabled lake-city of Copala and a river of pearls across the western deserts and mountains—and the equally nonexistent Straits of Anian across which lay the storied wealth of India and Cathay—Oñate had left the women and children in San Gabriel at the mercy of enemy tribes. Except for a handful of men left with them, these had to work their small fields as well as care for, and guard from theft, the precious livestock on which the pastoral colony's future depended entirely.

Consequently, the male colonists who had at last found their dukedoms of grazing land resented being taken away continually in such mad ventures. The friars, moreover, knew that the incident at Ácoma had turned the other pueblos against them, and they were hearing disturbing rumors concerning their own safety. A clamorous mutiny ensued, led by the more scared among the friars and a few of the weaker-hearted stockmen. What they were demanding was the return of the colony to New Spain. There the fleshpots of Egypt lay beckoning to the less dedicated.

This is when, in 1602, Don Pedro de Chávez and his father-in-law, Captain Cristóbal Baca, persuaded others to sign a petition to the Crown through the viceroy, requesting that the unstable colony be declared a *"re publica,"* as they put it. This meant an official civic entity with its own local officials independent of such uninterested adventurers as Oñate and his staff had proved to be, and different likewise from the feudal structure back in Spain. Significantly, Chávez and his cosigners, although ignorant of the early Hebraic government which gave its name to the Book of Judges, were asking for a similar system of popular magistrates. It was an idea inherent in the pastoral mentality since time immemorial.

But at the same time some friars wrote to the King, begging him to take the missions directly under the royal wing, and to support them financially for God's greater glory and the spiritual and material good of the native Indians. They, too, wanted no more of men like Oñate and his ilk; but, like the later Israelites clamoring to Samuel for a king, they little realized that their king's periodic representatives as royal governors would be no better. For it was this friars' request which was granted seven years later, in 1609, well after Oñate and his henchmen were gone. By this time the King's royal censors were reading the manuscript of Captain Gaspar de Villagrá prior to its publication the following year. As we have seen, the poet-captain had written his cantos with the purpose of bringing his master Oñate back into the royal graces. What his epic descriptions accomplished was to renew and perpetuate in royal administrative circles the legend of "the *new* Mexico" as a fabulous Shangri-la where the wealth of Far East Asia might still be discovered any day. Like Spain herself ages ago, New Mexico had become a Hebrew Tarshish, or a Greek Pillar of Hercules, to the people of Europe.

*   *   *

In this year of 1609 the crown sent Don Pedro de Peralta to establish the "Kingdom of New Mexico," with instruction to found a capital city worthy of so grand a title. This word, *reyno,* as it was then spelled, had been used by Oñate and previous explorers in different parts of the New World in the very general sense of "realm," or royal possession, as it is also done in English today. But here it meant a real kingdom, one on a par with those very old ones of Castile, León, Aragón, and others like them, all of which had been brought together into one single Spain by Ferdinand and Isabella. But very often they were still being called "the Spains."

Now New Mexico was one of them, even if at present she had no resident viceroy. The only reason for such a supreme title was that this frontier Spanish enclave, a world apart from the New Spain of Cortés south of it, would soon develop into a royal entity by far superior in wealth and importance to it and to Peru still farther south.

This obsession at the Court is further brought out in a book which was printed in Madrid twelve years after Villagrá's epic poem. Francisco Murcia de la Llana was a professor of the classics in Madrid who also dabbled in Pindaric and Sapphic odes himself. His imagination was saturated with all kinds of nonsense about New Mexico and about the deeds of Oñate and his young son Cristóbal there, no doubt fed to him by Oñate's vainglorious relatives at the Court. In 1622 he published an anthology of classic-style poems in Spanish along with some Latin acrostics, by himself and other Court litterateurs, glorifying the supposed heroism of a lad who actually was too young, and sickly at that, to have performed any of the heroic deeds attributed to him.

No specific ones are mentioned, naturally, but throughout the classic paeans of mournful praise the land of New Mexico stands out repeatedly as a veritable Shangri-la. Time and again it is called a promising "other Spain," or "another still more distant Spain."

Don Pedro de Peralta, the Kingdom's first Governor and Captain-General, must have felt extremely disappointed when he was confronted by the first and only puny settlement at San Gabriel; it seemed lost in a vast region of mountains and plains and deserts which boasted of no other "cities" than the humble mud pueblos of the local Indians. And yet—he very likely was thinking to himself—who knew what lay over those sierras farther on, *más allá,* especially toward the north, which was still terra incognita? The Straits of Anian! And perhaps almost visible across them, the great trade cities of India and China! Whereupon he proceeded to choose the site and lay out the plans for a royal capital.

The leading *ganadero* self-made dukes also savored their own disappointment when Governor Peralta came. Their new country, its landscape and atmosphere so much like that of their ancestral Castilian plateau, was now their own land—perfect in every detail for their leisurely raising of sheep, cattle, and horses without any obeisance to, or influence from, the old feudal nobility back home. But now their newly found pastoral dukedoms were being brought closer to the old system they had left behind in viceregal New Spain hundreds of leagues across the wilderness of Sinai, in feudal Old Spain still more leagues beyond the ocean sea. It was indeed a miserable thought, to start with.

2. Villa of the Holy Faith

Governor Peralta named his new capital *La Villa de Santa Fe,* after having marked out the customary *plaza de armas* or parade ground as its center. Then he ordered the erection on its northern flank of the *casas reales* or royal governmental buildings with their inner courtyards, which would also serve as his residence as well as headquarters for the colonial militia. For in his title of Governor and Captain-General he was the King's alter ego, both as supreme civil magistrate and as military commander-in-chief.

For being the capital of an officially designated kingdom, the Villa was indeed a "royal" city, if in adobe embryo, and the governor's residence a "palace," although these two regal terms were not employed until much later times. And no less important in the Spanish municipal scheme was the parish church, which stood on the eastern side of the plaza. It was named for the Virgin under her title of the Assumption.

The original inhabitants, who were transferred with their chattels and herds from San Gabriel, did not use any of these high-sounding terms except the one of "Kingdom." This they always emphasized. When referring to the capital they merely said "la Villa," and to this day in Spanish the Santa Feans have been called "Villeros." Or else they said "Santa Fe de los Españoles," for its being the only Spanish town in that century.

In fact, it was the royal will that all the colonists were to reside there, both to give it civic substance and for their families' protection. Also, the few Tlascaltec Indians which some of them had brought from New Spain were settled on the south side of the Villa's clear mountain stream, in a *barrio* or ward which these people named Analco in their own tongue.

To be sure, it was a very small capital city of adobe, Peralta must have thought, but destined to be a great metropolis someday. He had purposely placed it on a most prominent location which also happened to be one of the prettiest in the world—like Granada's by the Sierra Nevada. No doubt, he had also chosen the site because of its elevated central position overlooking the Rio Grande pueblos to the north and to the south, as well as those closer ones directly south in the Galisteo basin, and the great pueblo of Pecos to the southeast. The great queenly sierra behind it, and the spacious apron of high plateau towards the front, offered sufficient protection from marauding wild tribes from the deserts and plains beyond.

All this might well have inspired Captain Villagrá to call the new capital "Jerusalén," but in 1610 he was back in Spain receiving the adulation of his friends as he passed out the first copies of his poem fresh off the press at Alcalá.

The name "Santa Fe"—Holy Faith, as anyone can guess—whether chosen by Peralta himself or by royal authorities higher up, went well with the colony's and the friars' evangelical purpose. Actually, it followed a tradition whereby other towns in Spanish America got the very same designation. It was in remembrance of the first Santa Fe, the royal encampment of Ferdinand and Isabella outside Granada from where these monarchs had supervised the capture of the last stronghold of the Moors in 1492. This makes one wonder if landscape had also inspired Peralta, for if you look from the original Santa Fe towards Granada and the beautiful Sierra Nevada behind it, you cannot help but notice a good resemblance between that snowclad range and our Santa Fe's Sangre de Cristo.

Yet Villagrá's likely choice would have been just apropos. Just as everyone speaks in the Bible of "going up" to Jerusalem, no matter from which direction, so have folks said this about Santa Fe since its founding. As with Jerusalem, there is no other way.

*   *   *

It is hard for us to believe now that the Villa of Santa Fe, as a Spanish church-state seat of government, was actually expected to grow into a lively center of civic-religious power and influence, like Sevilla or Mexico or Lima, like the ancient theocratic Jerusalem shedding divine grace and royal favor from her holy height. Nevertheless, this was the unrecorded dream of the authorities at the royal and viceregal courts. All this depended, of course, on the fast commercial development of the new Kingdom itself.

But, as we see it now, this obviously could not happen. For none of those fabled cities of Quivira and Copala were ever found in all the region around it, only vast empty continental sweeps of mountains, plains, and deserts in the four directions of the compass. The legendary Straits of Anian connecting the South Sea with the coast of Labrador, thus opening new and closer routes to India and Cathay on one side, and to Europe on the other, proved to be only a map-maker's fantasy. Under such adverse circumstances of geography, commerce of any worth was a total impossibility, and therefore also any civic-cultural growth which depends upon it wholly.

In short, the Kingdom of New Mexico was to remain an isolated frontier post of adobe for centuries to come, despite its grandiose name.

But let us suppose that a navigable arm of the Gulf of Mexico had reached at least as far as the gates of the Kingdom at El Paso del Norte. Not only would La Toma have become a busy Vera Cruz shipping out enormous quantities of livestock, of wool and hides and the more prized cured skins of deer, elk, and bison, but new people with greatly varied knowledges and skills would have poured into the northern interior to develop further sources of wealth in ores and timber.

Santa Fe would have blossomed out into a veritable new City of Mexico with its own elaborate churches, palaces, schools, and commercial houses, while other later towns like Santa Cruz and Albuquerque would have been other Pueblas and Guadalajaras. Then the Kingdom of New Mexico, under her very own viceroy with limitless resources at his command, would have eventually extended her borders at least as far north as the present Canadian border, and certainly westward to the California coast and eastward to the Mississippi. The subsequent history of western North America would then have been altogether different.

However, this could not have happened, for all the reasons just given. Moreover, the Bacas and the Chávez and the Montoyas, and their interrelated fellow-conquistador clans with their narrow *ganadero* outlook, would not have wanted it that way—even if an *elohim*-angel from heaven offered them a choice. It would have cramped their pastoral life style, as one gathers from an early incident when these people destroyed some mining equipment brought up from New Spain.

For rich gold discoveries would have brought back royal and feudal authority still much too close for comfort, as we can see from their desultory treatment of successive governors sent them from Mexico City every three years. The competition inherent in the trades and professions of an expanding commercial culture would have wrought havoc with their pastoral dukedoms, and left them serfs once more—as it actually came to pass in our own times at the hands of other barons of industry and commerce with a totally alien racial outlook and background.

Hard upon the capital's founding, the leading settlers had thumbed their noses at the royal will by getting away from governmental headquarters and taking their families and livestock to their allotted grazing lands up and down the basin of the Rio Grande. Exposure to enemy Indian raids and any other dangers was a price worth paying for the freedom of movement and full enjoyment of possessions as befitted true *hidalgos.* And this was doubly so because no higher noble ranks stood between them and any king.

And so the Villa with the holy and historic name, no matter how great its implied title and how queenly its setting, remained a small adobe town for three centuries. The Kingdom itself continued as a vacant adobe empire of magnificent distances sparsely dotted with Hispanic and Indian villages made of mud, and all completely isolated from the rest of the world. In time the people were to become strangers even to the rest of the Hispanic world, and so provincial in their isolation as to regard all other lands as *tierra afuera,* the outer world.

One cannot help but think of the Rechabites, a small clan of Judah described by the prophet Jeremiah. These folk deliberately clung so strictly to the original pastoral life of the patriarchs when the Jews were developing into a prosperous commercial nation that, in spite of the prophet's religious admiration for them, they eventually became lost from the mainstream of Hebraic evolvement. In much the same way was my New Mexico eventually cut off from the subsequent history and development of Spain and other Spanish lands in the Americas. The people became a lost tribe within their very own Holy Land.

Part Two

THE
NAZIRITE

Zain

Once her nazirites were brighter than snow,
whiter than milk;
rosier than coral their bodies,
their hue as radiant as sapphire.

Beth

Now with faces darker than blackness itself
they move unrecognizable through the streets.
The skin is shrunken against the bones,
dry as a stick.

—Lamentations 4:7–8.

7

Blood and Sand

As the last anxious weeks of gestation wore on—of my people and my own self shortly before the Oñate Expedition reached the Rio Grande for the birth at La Toma—two incidents were recorded by the keeper of the colony's log which have a heavy bearing on our general theme. The first and most important event was the colony's ritual celebration of Holy Week's end out on the bleak Sonoran desert throughout the days and nights of March 20 and 21 of that year of 1598.

The minor second one occurred the following day, on Holy Saturday, when the thirst-haunted people and livestock literally stumbled upon what the pilgrims named Los Ojos Milagrosos—The Miraculous Springs—when one of the horses' hooves sank through a bit of boggy ground. Then, as the chronicler puts it, a waterspout about the thickness of an orange shot up into the air nearly the height of a man, and then continued flowing about a span high. "We spent Easter Sunday at this place," the day's entry ends laconically. It's a wonder that neither the chronicler then, nor the poet-captain a dozen years later, seized upon this small but most welcome incident to compare it with Moses striking water out of the rock. But the scriptural allusion does bubble underneath the text.

1. Whips and Holy Week

What had taken place in the two preceding days, however, is of much greater significance. The laconic log-keeper merely states that on Holy Thursday, March 20, "we adored the Most Holy Sacrament," and on Good Friday, March 21, "we went to the Descent from the Cross and Holy Sepulcher." It all means that the Franciscan padres set up a makeshift altar where the Toledan-Roman liturgy of Holy Thursday was celebrated in the morning. At its close, the consecrated Host was exposed within a linen-enshrouded chalice upon the altar, for the colonists' eucharistic worship throughout the rest of the day and all the following night. Thus they "adored the Most Holy Sacrament."

Next morning the Good Friday liturgy observed the consummation of the wafer by the priestly celebrant, along with the ritual "denudation" of the purple-wrapped crucifix and the stripping of the altar's every covering — all as a symbol of Christ's death and burial. The small articulated image of Christ which they evidently had, after being detached from its cross, was laid out like a corpse upon its burial slab. All this constituted the "Descent from the Cross and Holy Sepulcher." Here the colonists prayed in mournful silence before breaking camp, to come upon the miraculous spring the following day.

But for Captain Villagrá more than a decade later, all this was much too tame for his epic poem. Besides, not only the soldiery as a lot, but most especially Don Juan de Oñate and his two Zaldívar nephews, had to play a more personal role which as laymen they could not have done in the liturgy proper. Readily at hand for Villagrá's purpose was a well-established Spanish penitential feature of Lent—self-flagellation—which would help him vest his heroes with extraordinary Hispanic piety while toning down those most unsavory reports which had reached the royal throne in Spain following Oñate's trial in Mexico City. The blood of Ácoma had to be covered up by Oñate's own, as it were.

The universal medieval Holy Week liturgy of Tenebrae—Latin for "darkness" and las tinieblas in Spanish—commemorated Christ's Passion and Death with dramatic intensity. It consisted of the chanting of mournful psalms and prophetic lamentations in Latin by the clergy as thirteen candles were extinguished one by one until total darkness. This rite was just then being observed in the choirs of the great friary churches of the Dominicans, Augustinians, and Franciscans, and equally so under the supervision of the chapter canons at the cathedrals of Mexico City, Puebla, Guadalajara, and other pioneer dioceses of the New World.

Each of the twelve candles which represented the apostles, flickering in the otherwise darkened church upon a great Menorah-like candleholder that stood prominently in the middle of the chancel, was snuffed out at the end of a psalm and its prophetic lesson; then the middle (and thirteenth) candle, which represented Christ, was solemnly carried behind the main altar and there extinguished as a symbol of his agony and death. In the darkness that fell upon Jerusalem at that earth-shaking moment, the thundering earthquake was dramatized by a hellish clatter of wooden clappers, the rasping of revolving ratchet drums, and the rattling of chains.

In the black sepulchral silence which followed, both the clergy and the faithful fell on their knees and spread out their arms in the form of the cross for the space of a dozen or so paternosters, avemarias, and as many doxologies which they muttered in secret. But soon the silence was broken by muffled slapping sounds made by some fervent participants whipping their backs over their clothes, and sometimes on bare skin.

This last act obviously commemorated the previous scourging of Christ in Pilate's guardhouse, but among Spaniards it was also considered one of deep personal penitence. Hence the flagellant was called a *penitente*—"penitent," pure and simple. Ordinarily it was the masculine members of local parish confraternities, or lay male affiliates of the friars like the "Third Orders" of the Franciscans, Dominicans, and Carmelites, who practiced this token flagellation in groups.

But just as often, unaffiliated as well as affiliated individuals, when carried away by their Lenten fervor, stripped off their shirts and covered their bare backs with crimson stripes for that given period.

No one took it amiss—it was the Spanish soul at its most fervent. Back in Spain, in the period following the discovery of America, it was not uncommon for such pious societies, or even the whole male congregation of a parish, to go on public processions of blood even outside of Lent, as when plague or drought struck the countryside. The purpose was to placate what was considered to be God's anger, and as a result bring down his merciful blessings in the form of health or rain. The custom had come to the New World, and its excesses had later been proscribed on both sides of the ocean by combined royal and ecclesiastical decrees under heavy penalties.

But it cropped up sporadically thereafter, if in lesser degree, as in such occasions as the one just described. To repeat, it was the Spanish soul at its most fervent, and its spirit had come down in a direct line of blood and landscape from dim antiquity in the Near East to the bleak hills of upland Iberia.

*   *   *

Now, it is quite possible that some of Oñate's male settlers and soldiers did bare their backs to lash them with strips of rope, or with their leather

belts, out in their bleak and starry desert of Sinai on that Holy Thursday
night of March 20, 1598. It would have taken place right after the friars had
ended their chanting of Tenebrae in a much more humble and primitive
situation. But, had they actually done so, the chronicler would have
recorded it in his characteristic brevity with something like "we took the
discipline." For this was something routine which bore no stigma at all. But
he said nothing.

However, poetic license not only looks for the dramatic but loves to
stretch out time and multiply numbers, and this is how Captain Villagrá
years afterward put real red meat into his cantos:

> The friars there upon their knees
> all kept a wake the whole night long;
> there was a big and gory scourging, too,
> by much grief-stricken penitents
> who begged of God in tearful prayers
> to save us all and show the way
> across those desolate desert lands,
> just as his grandeur plowed a path
> right through the waters when, dryshod,
> the sons of Israel came forth free. . . .
>
> The women and the children all
> now begged his mercy in bare feet;
> as one, the soldiers with both grips
> gashing their backs from either side
> with cruel lashes, bade him hasten
> to their aid; and Francis' humble sons,
> devoutly wearing their hairshirts,
> kept up their clamoring and prayers
> for God to heed and bring them help.

The first two lines depict the night-long liturgical vigil of Holy
Thursday correctly, when friars and faithful alike took turns in groups
while the others took their night's rest. But if any bloody flagellation did
take place on this occasion, one has to doubt very much that there were that
many extra-pious souls among those rough soldier-colonists whom I have
come to know like my own hand. Nor would the scourging have lasted
more than a brief period, according to custom.

Meanwhile, the poet's reference to Exodus, about the Israelites crossing the sea to freedom, does reflect the motives of the people in their desperate straits along with their scriptural consciousness throughout their difficult pilgrimage. However, Villagrá's own motives for all this grand penitential exaggeration are revealed in the passage about Oñate and his nephews which immediately follows:

> The General at a place apart,
> which he wanted me alone to know,
> while flexed upon his knees turned on
> twin-fountains from his eyes, and then,
> tearing both shoulders open, spilled
> a sea of gory crimson as he prayed. . . .
> also his two nephews at their posts
> with whipping cut themselves to pieces
> til the light of dawn appeared. . . .

Here is Villagrá's fancy at his maddest, yet there is method in it. The honor of his beloved master Oñate, and that of the Zaldívar brothers, had to be restored in the family annals back home in Madrid. The combined Spanish colony and Franciscan mission had to survive and flourish by means of direct royal aid in order to wipe away that blot on the Oñate family crest. And so, along with them, both the friars and the settlers must be made to glow with what was then considered to be the epitome of Hispanic piety. This very description, when relayed by the royal book-censors to his Majesty, influenced his decision to continue the colony along with the Franciscan missions.

Not content with this, the poet interrupted his verse cantos with prose by inserting a copy, as drawn up by the official notary, of his master's Act of Possession at La Toma three weeks later. It signified, as we saw long ago, the colony's divine commission of bringing the Good News to all the natives of the Promised Land. And at the end of it the notary attests how Don Juan de Oñate, after the proclamation of royal possession had been read to all the people, personally nailed a cross onto the bole of a live cottonwood and then knelt down to declaim in a loud voice:

> Cross, holy Cross that you are, divine gate of heaven, altar of
> the one and essential sacrifice of the body and blood of the Son of
> God, way of the saints and means of attaining his glory, open the

door to these heathens, establish the church and altars where the body and blood of God's Son may be offered, open to us the way to security and peace for their preservation and ours; and give to our King, and to me in his royal name, peaceful possession of these realms and provinces for his blessed glory. Amen.

The subsequent actual possession of the land did not turn out so peaceful, as we have seen. But here we have a solemn reassertion of the colony's own sincere evangelical feeling. It is expressed by means of a symbol which had become the combined Spanish national and religious standard at the end of a centuries-long struggle between the Cross of Iberian Christianity and the Crescent of Moorish Islam.

What had happened toward the end of that Holy Week out on the desert, if it did happen at all outside of the poet's mind, stands forth as a vivid symbol of the Spanish soul groping its way into one more frontier of empire in the New World's terra incognita now being penetrated. It was most certainly not the introduction of a specific society of "Penitentes," as many would write someday with so much bland assurance. For behind all this lay a peculiarly universal Hispanic preoccupation with the material cross on which Christ had bled and died. The ritual personification of it, as just seen in the Good Friday liturgy and in the official acts at La Toma, seems almost to overshadow the main Christian object of worship himself.

It is this material cross, grown far beyond the symbolic, which was behind it all. Crude wooden forms of it would soon be dotting the landscape, to the wonder of uncomprehending strangers centuries later. The idea of intense personal suffering which the cross represented would ever afterward continue simmering here in the racial blood which those first settlers were bringing into a landscape so much like the one that had nourished it for ages.

It is a long story of blood in connection with landscape—a shepherd blood and its hesed upon upland landscapes of severe bright colors, crystal skies, and sparse rains.

2. Ritual and Holocausts

A little book of Bible stories which I knew as a lad contained many line-drawn illustrations based on nineteenth-century German engravings.

Naturally, the figures of Adam and Eve and all other biblical characters were purely Teutonic types, while the landscape background was more north European than Palestinian. The Christmas picture, for instance, showed the Holy Family inside a cozy wooden stable in a fairyland forest, while the Crucifixion drawing presented an unsullied blond Christ in muscular repose upon a neatly planed cross overlooking a Rhineland valley.

Such first impressions etch themselves so deeply on the virginal matrix of the young brain that better-informed images acquired later on in life fail to erase them altogether. At times they reassert themselves against all reason, specifically the Nativity tableau which was further grooved into the mind by similar Gallican-designed crèches or mangers in the parish church, and under the Saxon-inspired Christmas tree at home. To this day, I find it hard to see that the authentic Bethlehem scene which Luke imagined was actually more like a small sandstone cave around Abiquiú, or else a simple flat-roofed adobe hut in Chimayó, than a gabled wooden stall in the Argonne Forest or in the Schwartzwald.

But for me the romantic Teutonic Calvary view in that boyhood book did not keep the same indelible hold. The Crucifixion had much stronger suitors for my eye in certain local *Cristos,* or native-carved crucifixes and "Ecce Homos"—all gaunt and gory, almost frightening at first sight, and always most fascinating. There were many of these in the adobe chapels of outlying villages where my pastor used to take me to serve as his acolyte. They displayed the saddest of suffering and dying Christs, ugly to me at that time with their sharp-limned black beards and locks, with blood-smeared ribs and limbs that reminded me of a flayed jackrabbit.

But they did make me realize that Jesus' passion and crucifixion might have been an ugly thing, too, not what the pretty German pictures said, or the trim crucifixes of French manufacture in our parish church, or the effeminate "holy cards" then being printed in New York's Barclay Street which the school nuns meted out by way of scholastic prizes. It must have been the same, I started thinking even at that tender age, and decidedly worse for the stench, when the Aaronic priesthood sacrificed so many sheep and cattle daily in the temple of Jerusalem. The periodic slaughter of a calf, a lamb, or a kid in our own little town's private corrals and backyards always brought these things to my mind. Somehow I also felt by some unerring instinct that all this had come to pass, not in pleasant grassy glades and dense woods like those in the Grimm Brothers' tales, or in Robin Hood's greenwood forest, but in a land very much like mine.

All this, no doubt, had everything to do with what I once regarded as my "call," a bittersweet *hesed* urging me as a lad to leave my father's house and a landscape which was my life, and to forego all future normal contacts with men and women, in order to go into a different world which the Lord would show me. Specifically, it was to become a Franciscan friar like those early ones who had led my people into our own Holy Land, sensing somehow that their ideal held the secret to this mystery of blood and landscape. It was a decision which gradually began acquainting me with more mature books—and with the Book itself which dwelt more at length on such matters—which were to revive memories of a cobbler complaining to my mother one spring day, and visions of bleeding figures on Good Friday wending their tortuous way up to a gaunt Calvary cross upon a piñon-studded hill against the sky.

*   *   *

Blood sacrifice in homage to a Supreme Deity, or to any number of gods and spirits, has been a hallmark of religion ever since man can remember. It follows more or less the same pattern everywhere, but the mood or expression of it is decidedly affected by landscape. There is a world of difference between the dank and dark Druidic ritual of the shadowy forests of northern Europe, as also the voodoo-type rites in the dense jungles of tropical Africa and Asia—and those of the open arid or semiarid lands of Hammurabi, Abraham, and Ahkenaton.

Dense vegetation and gloomy rain-skies breed sagas of frightful witches and eerie hobgoblins along with dark portents of festering pain and decaying death that fill the soul with dread. This spirit persists in what we call the "gothic" literature of the dark northern countries, along with a preoccupation with such ghoulish fantasies as haunted houses and polter-geists, Frankenstein monsters, and the vampires of Transylvania.

Contrariwise, in the almost treeless regions colorfully bright with sun all day and stardust-dappled all through the night, the gods take on a nobler cast while pain and death look more like casual acquaintances. Witchcraft also, which is just as universal, differs as much in atmosphere from the northern kind—as much as the Arabian Nights differ from Faust and Macbeth.

The bright and dry Near and Middle East also had their blood sacrifices. But even here there is a marked difference between the worship of the upland pastoral people and that of the agricultural and urban dwellers of the lowlands. The early Hebrew scriptural tradition attests to both, and the various disciplines of archaeology are ever bringing more details to light. Among the early Hebrews, the need for contact with the One God, whether to acknowledge his supreme sovereignty or to placate his anger or to obtain his favors, is expressed by means of the slaughter of a prized domestic animal which is then completely destroyed by fire. The smoke spiraling heavenward in that spotless air carries the "message," so to speak, and is regarded by both human and divine parties as "a pleasing odor"—if only relatively so because of the dry land and climate.

It is as though the one sacrificing his precious hard-earned lamb or heifer were saying: "Lord, if I could do it or if you would allow it, I would gladly immolate my own self or my own child on this altar, to prove my obeisance to you as the author and giver of life and every good thing." But, of course, the Israelite's God has strictly forbidden human sacrifice, even the least bit of self-mutilation, according to the pastoral lore of his people. In this case, the lamb or calf took the place of the human offerer; and of this sort, it came to be written in due time, was the acceptable sacrifice of the righteous Abel, the prototype of the pastoral worshipper.

Despite the Hebrew writers' disdain for the neighboring pastoral Canaanites or other such Semite folk as being rank idolaters, these people also strove in the same direction; only that in worshipping the single Deity, they incurred the unhappy if blameless fault of mistaking his *elohim* for lesser gods. Nor were they averse to cutting and bleeding their own bodies in times of grief and remorse. The Hebrews had to be restrained from doing the same, and so they tore their garments symbolically and sprinkled ashes upon their heads.

All this was much more pronounced among the lowland agricultural-ists of the eastern great rivers and of the great Nile, and especially among their more sophisticated fellowmen dwelling in the commercial centers athwart the Green Crescent from Babylonia to Ugarit and down into Egypt. Here matters were not so simple. Civilization, then as now, meant complication and multiplicity in every facet of life, including worship. To the primitive pastoral Hebrews, all that pagan worship was like the unacceptable sacrifice of Cain, the tiller of the soil and subsequent seeker of the big cities.

As agriculture in vast feudal proportions expanded the material wealth of those fertile areas, creating the commercial cities which in their turn wondrously produced the various arts contributing more and more to human pride and comfort, the mythology so intimately connected with this progress became all the more demanding by way of sacrificial ritual and the erection of great temples. In these architectural triumphs which at least figuratively sought to scrape the very heavens by means of brick and mortar, each god and goddess dwelt within its particular idol; upon its altar parents finally came to sacrifice their own children, as in the case of Moloch, while men and women flagellated each other in the fanes of whichever god or goddesses of carnal love they adored. Obviously, this kind of mutual scourging to hone the passions was hardly sacrificial or penitential.

Still, whether in the purer monotheism of the upland pastoral Hebrews and the tainted one of their shepherd neighbors, or in the ultimately gruesome polytheism among some of the highly civilized lowlanders, the open landscape and clear skies quickly purified the air of the stench of fresh slaughter and burnt flesh while quickly drying up the offensive sight of spilled blood—just as such landscapes and climates are known to stem the spread of microbes and hasten or obliterate the processes of decay.

In much the same way with regard to the human spirit, personal pain and suffering, here so thoroughly drycleaned like shed blood by sun and sand and air, took on the language and visage of one's most intimate contact with divinity. Death itself, free of the morbidity of damp darkness and long festering, assumed the noble aspect of a person's supreme moment of truth.

All this not only served to set the Semite-Hamite peoples distinctly apart from those of rainy lands in their mental and spiritual approach to death and suffering, but was the long preparation, not to say the very foundation, of that stupendous phenomenon and mystery whereby divinity itself, according to the proclaimers of the Christian Good News, could salvage mankind's poor condition through one individual's gory passion and death upon a cross.

All this could have only come to pass upon a dry upland landscape.

3. The Sacrifices of Abraham

As the first historical personage to walk across the Bible pages, Abraham was a true creature of that arid landscape and clear climate with its native idea of blood sacrifice. Despite his enlightened *hesed*, he could not escape being influenced by his Elyon-worshipping pastoral neighbors who

also harbored lesser gods, but even by those of the crass idolatry of the
agrarian lowlands from which his father Terah had fled. This can be seen in
connection with Yahweh's double promise which entailed two pacts or
covenants, the covenant regarding land and the covenant concerning
offspring. Upon entering Canaan, Abraham compacted the land-covenant
by slaughtering three of his domestic animals, which he then slit down the
middle, placing the halves of each carcass opposite their partners. Then, so
went the ancient legend, he fell into a trance and, when darkness fell, a
smoking fire-pot and a flaming torch passed up and down between the
slaughtered halves as a sign that both sacrifice and pact had divine sanction.
Now the land of Canaan was legally his.

Many centuries later, when the compilers of this tradition wrote down
this very odd incident, they minutely described every detail as it had been
passed down, little realizing that Abraham had carried out a magical
formula of the ancient pagans whereby two chieftains sealed a business deal
in which the gods played some hanky-panky with smoking braziers and
flaring torches.

Abraham's second pact with the Yahweh of his *hesed* was the better
known offspring covenant. It took place when the Lord ordered him to
circumcize himself and all the males of his household, at the same time
specifying circumcision as the perennial sign of the paternal covenant
between himself and Abraham's descendants. But this, too, had long been a
puberty or premarital rite among the Egyptians and among neighboring
tribes like the Moabites. By the time the incident was recorded, this ritual
was believed to be exclusively Israelitic. Here, no matter what its origin, not
to mention its being an act of mutilation, it was a truly personal act of blood
sacrifice for Abraham and the males of his household.

But the supreme trial of Abraham's faith came when Yahweh
commanded him to immolate his own son Isaac, the very offspring of his
promise, in the way that he had sacrificed many a prized lamb in the past.
He must have thought right away of how the lowland pagans sacrificed their
children to their gods. However, here Isaac was the one and only fruit of his
long union with Sarah, and this only by God's miracle in their advanced
years. Of course, as we are told, Yahweh held back his hand at the crucial
moment and provided a ram in Isaac's stead. Nevertheless, Abraham at this
moment did offer a personal blood sacrifice, the blood of his heart.

This long prehistoric tradition of vicarious offerings of one's blood, and
the personal kind displayed by Abraham in his many acts of self-abnegation

over and above the bloody one of circumcision, set the pattern for Hebraic life and worship for scores of generations to come. There was the daily burning of livestock, the choicest heads of the tribal flocks and herds. Some victim-oblations honored and thanked God for his divinity as well as for his benefits to his chosen human kinsmen; others were expiatory ones for the sins of the people in general. Besides these, purification rites for individuals breaking numberless Semite and Hamite taboos much older than Abraham, but which now had the sanction of divine law, also kept the blood of lambs and heifers flowing and the altar fires burning.

And there were also those happy festive sacrifices throughout the year which celebrated the seasons—another borrowing from the agricultural lowlands—but not so much in observance of the harvest cycles as for recalling the outstanding favors of Yahweh's *hesed* since the days of Abraham and Moses. The best loved of all these feasts was the Pasch, or Passover, when each family slew a spotless lamb, roasted it whole, and then partook of it along with the unleavened bread and blessed wine in total sacramental gravity. For this ceremonial of the Paschal Lamb reenacted that momentous night when, at the Lord's command through Moses, the head of each family slaughtered a lamb and smeared the doorjambs of his house with its blood; God's angel of death then slew all the firstborn of the Egyptians because their own doorways were not thus marked, and skipped or "passed over" the children of the Israelites. Meanwhile the Hebrew families, dressed and shod for a long journey, prayerfully ate of their viaticum which took them through a saving sea and set their sights back toward their native landscape.

Like the Sabbaths and all the year-round sacrificial rituals, Passover was more than mere nostalgia for the Lord's storied manifestations in the halcyon days of Abraham and Moses. It was a "making present" of Yahweh's *hesed* among them in their own generation. Other peoples in later ages, and in other distant places and climes, would do something very similar if in different forms, making present in their own divine yearnings, and in the context of their own racial lore, what had been promised to all the tribes of earth because of Abraham's faith.

8

The Consecrated Ones

It would seem necessary, at this particular stage, to remind ourselves again that the Hebrews who have been so thoroughly treated all this while in connection with landscape, faith, and sacrificial ritual—and their adventures so frequently alluded to in connection with those of a pastoral folk being born in a much newer world—were the primitive and exclusively shepherd people of the semiarid uplands of Palestine, and not their more settled and sophisticated descendants of the later kingdoms of Israel and Judah with their expanding economies of agriculture and trade.

Much less can one force any parallels with that vigorous remnant of Judah which, following its return from Babylonian captivity under Ezra and Nehemiah, developed into that most extraordinary people known thereafter as the Jews—and for whom *hesed* has been the main living source of unity despite worldwide dispersion, and of vigorous survival through ages of direst persecution to this day. All the way to this point we have concerned ourselves with the primitive Semitic *hesed* of Abraham and his immediate shepherd children while they were one with the landscape. Naturally, we follow its progress as manifested in later times as it informed the aspirations of the kingdoms of Israel and Judah.

1. The Nazirate

Within that primitive Semitic *hesed* so intimately connected with so much blood sacrifice, there appears a distinctive feature, one which is most personal and penitential in essence, and which seeps down into subsequent Israelitic life. The phenomenon in question is that of the *nazirites,* meaning "consecrated ones."

Only a very few persons in the Bible are described or at least mentioned as being such. But most of the great prophets, from what we gather from their personalities, appear to have belonged to this category. Consequently, one cannot help but wonder if such wandering groups as the "sons of the prophets" and the "companies of prophets" did not themselves, as nazirites, constitute early ascetic brotherhoods within the Hebraic religious way of life.

This mysterious institution, itself called the Nazirate, has its regulations minutely outlined in Numbers 6 as Yahweh's own instruction through Moses:

> If a man or woman wishes to make a vow, the vow of the nazirite by which he is pledged to Yahweh, he shall abstain from wine and strong drink. . . . As long as he is bound by his vow, no razor shall touch his head; until the time of his consecration to Yahweh is completed, he remains under vow and shall let his hair grow free. For the entire period of his consecration to Yahweh he must not go near a corpse. . . . on his head he carries his consecration to God. Throughout the whole of his nazirate he is a person consecrated to Yahweh.

This quasi-penitential phenomenon in ancient Hebrew religion is in itself most fascinating. But it becomes more so when tiny flashes or echoes of it appear later on, not only in subsequent Bible pages but ages afterward among other peoples and in other distant climes among the bare hills of La Mancha and the olive-studded slopes of the Sierra Morena in Spain, among the chamiso-clad and sabino-flecked foothills of the Sangre de Cristo range in northern New Mexico. The story is a long and tenuous one.

As we have just seen, the three essentials of the nazirite's vow were total abstention from the fruit of the vine, leaving the hair uncut, and avoiding all contact with the dead. By refraining from wine and strong drink, the nazirite spurned a life of pleasurable ease in order to become more sharply aware of God's promptings. By leaving his hair untrimmed, since the hair of the head was the magical symbol of strength among all the Near East ancients, he placed all his reliance on God as the source and giver of all bodily and spiritual vigor. Lastly, his consecration to God was about as sacred as that of the Aaronic priesthood, the members of which were forbidden to become contaminated by contact with the dead.

Of course, there is no such thing as self-flagellation or any bloody form of torture mentioned here, for any mutilation outside of circumcision was most strictly forbidden; but the idea of personal sacrifice and abnegation as signs of special divine consecration stands out most clearly.

Two famous early heroes are pictured as true nazirites. In Judges 13, Samson is described as being a nazirite to his barren mother. As we know from his fantastic career, he did not fully observe all these fine points, except for the mat of uncut hair which is the burden of his adventurous story. But this is because his own identity as a pious consecrated hero had become mixed up with that of a mythical titan-god with long hair who, as a model for the later Greek Hercules, had all kinds of gigantic tasks to perform. But at least the more authentic annunciation of his birth as a nazirite would someday inspire the Evangelist Luke to describe the ones of John the Baptist and of Jesus. Then there is Samuel, at the start of the first book bearing his name, likewise described as a nazirite when promised to his barren mother Hannah. Here there is no admixture with pagan myth, and the grateful song of Hannah finds very strong echoes in the Virgin Mary's "Magnificat" as written by Luke.

Even in the later Judaic period, when the Torah was being put together, the Nazirate was held in such high esteem that the editors honored their beloved patriarch Joseph with this designation, evidently in retrospect— unless these more ancient traditions in Genesis 49 and Deuteronomy 33 suggested the nazirite idea itself in the first place. In the oracle-poem attributed to the dying Jacob when he addresses his twelve sons, Jacob calls down a blessing "on Joseph's head, on the brow of the dedicated one [nazir] among his brothers." And again, in the very ancient Blessing of Moses, the same well-wishing is repeated on the twelfth tribe: "May the hair grow thick on the head of Joseph, of the consecrated one [nazir] among his brothers."

Finally, the Nazirate is still in existence as late as the liberation wars of the Maccabees shortly before the Christian era. It is recorded that the embattled Jews, when mustering the people against their Greek oppressors, "marshalled the nazirites who had completed the period of their vow." They will even be met within the Christian Testament, as in Acts when Paul and some others cut off their hair at the conclusion of vows they had made.

This beautiful term and idea of self-consecration to the divine rings out plaintively in the old prophetic writings; or rather, it has become beautiful to the prophets in retrospect. These inspired visionaries in the midst of the commercial and agricultural Judaism of their day looked back nostalgically to the strictly pastoral past of their forefathers, and it is under these

circumstances that Lamentations 4 recalls a former state when Zion was all
fidelity to Yahweh:

> Once her nazirites were brighter than snow,
> whiter than milk;
> rosier than coral their bodies,
> their hue as radiant as sapphire.

Amos, more matter-of-fact, is no less nostalgic when he quotes the Lord
berating the northern kingdom of Israel:

> I raised up prophets from your sons
> and nazirites from your young men. . . .
> But you have forced the nazirites to drink wine
> and given orders to the prophets,
> "Do not prophesy."

The much earlier pastoral people's final decision on having, not the
Lord himself directly as their shepherd, but earthly kings after the manner
of the lowland tillers and city dwellers, had brought the once free upland
folk closer to the life pattern of the pagans, and great numbers of them
followed their dissolute royal houses into the sensual abominations of
pagan cult and life. This had eventually brought on the Assyrian and
Babylonian invasions, as God's way of punishment, which permanently
exiled some tribes and drove the rest into extinction.

A fitting punishment for the many, it was at the same time a most
painful sacrifice and penance for the faithful minority which someday
would come back to the Promised Landscape where Abraham's *hesed* had
flourished, and where it must continue to live on for all communities of
men.

3. The Nazarene

The descendants of the remnant which returned with Ezra and
Nehemiah were the Jews in Palestine chafing under Roman rule when
Jehoshuah or Jesus of Nazareth appeared upon the scene. In recent decades,
Greek and Syrian despots had ravished their thrice-holy land and made a
laughingstock of its inhabitants. Now Rome, the most powerful empire of
them all, foully crouched upon their sacred ground. A sense of prophetic

timing, heightened by wishful thinking, told them that now was the time for the appearance of a Messiah who, by somehow expelling the mighty intruder, would reestablish David's kingdom.

From scattered hints throughout their holy writings, some expected him to be a conquering king, others a miracle-working high priest, or else a "prophet-like-Moses." Others combined all three ideas in one and the same person. There was an ascetic Jewish sect of Essenes upon the desert cliffs of Qumran by the Dead Sea who had cherished such hopes for a wonder-working high priest, while the more numerous folk in the rest of Palestine envisioned a victorious king. Another much more ancient group in Samaria also awaited a conquering Messiah; known more charitably as the kindly Samaritans in Christian annals, they had been rejected by the Restoration Jews for having intermarried with their pastoral neighbors who were not pure enough in their worship of the One God.

At this time, also, there was a man named John—a true nazirite and prophet he appeared to be—who since his early youth had been living in the desert near Qumran and was now proclaiming that the kingdom of God was at hand. Clad only in a cutty sark of camel's hair, he came by the Jordan preaching a bath or baptism of repentance as the most fitting way of receiving the Messiah with a pure heart. He subsisted solely on locusts and wild honey, and presumably abstained from wine and carried a bushy head of never-trimmed hair. For he had been born of a barren and aging mother, and under circumstances which leave no doubt that Luke had the births of Samson and Samuel before him when he composed this account.

And it was Jehoshuah of Nazareth whom this John was pointing out to his listeners as Yahweh's-Salvation, as the Passover Lamb of God about to take away the sin of the world. Here John the Baptist could well have called Jesus a fellow nazirite, had he been aware of a tradition that was to be found many years later in the Gospel of Matthew. After Mary and Joseph brought the boy Jesus back from Egypt—itself a symbolic borrowing from Exodus —this author wrote that they settled in Nazareth, adding: "In this way the words spoken through the prophets were to be fulfilled: He will be called a *Nazarene.*" But, strange to say, no single Hebrew prophet had ever made any such prediction in these very words, much less in connection with a town called Nazareth. Evidently the writer was thinking about the expected Messiah in Isaiah 49, the "suffering servant" whom Yahweh *called by name from his mother's womb, formed him in it, and became his strength;* he was the one whom the Lord in a very special manner *consecrated for himself,* as in Jeremiah

1. These phrases also bring to mind Samson's and Samuel's predicted births as most especially consecrated nazirites.

Hence that phrase in Matthew can also read: "He will be called a *Nazirite.*" The original Greek rendering suggests it, and the English Geneva Bible translated it almost literally: "Hee shall be called a Nazarite." Formal nazirite or no, Jesus of Nazareth did seem to those who knew him as an extraordinary holy and consecrated man of God, as when he fasted for forty days and often went into the hills to pray alone. He expounded the Law and the Prophets as one having authority, they said, and many began believing that the Messiah had arrived at last. But their religious leaders in Judea could not stand one claim he made, and so they looked for ways to get rid of him.

It was Passover-time, the year their chance was thrust upon them. Upon an evening, Jesus celebrated the memorial Pasch with his family of the Twelve, in a borrowed upper room of a friend's house in Jerusalem. With them he partook of the sacred roasted lamb as one preparing to make a most important journey. Recalling, according to ritual custom, the steps by which the Lord had delivered their forebears from Pharaoh's bondage, he gave them to understand that he himself was the paschal lamb of a new and everlasting Passover.

The sacred supper over, Jesus went sadly out into the night, down to an olive orchard where he passed through the red sea of his bloody sweat and agony, and there the temple guards arrested him. After having been tried as a blasphemer against Yahweh's holy Name, he was delivered to the hated Roman governor, for him to crucify as a rouser of the populace against Roman law and order. Pilate's soldiers flogged him most cruelly, and then loaded him with the crossbeam of his wood of immolation, leading him like another Isaac, "as a lamb to the slaughter," to the mount of execution just outside Jerusalem. A silent nazirite he went, "like a sheep to the shearer," like Samson to be shorn for a time of his mortal strength.

Late Good Friday afternoon, his stark cross stood high against the Palestinian sky and landscape, crossed post and lintel smeared with the blood of the lamb.

*   *   *

This is how his faithful disciples, and the first generation of converts, related it afterward through hindsight, after recalling his command to "search the Scriptures" in order to establish the divine credentials of his mission. It must be remembered that those first believers were not so much from among the Pharisean and Sadducean Jews of Judea proper as from the northern Galileans and a motley assemblage, all recorded in Acts, of dispersed Jewish peoples who were mostly Greek-speaking. Also, from the most favorable tone with which the Samaritans are treated within the gospels, and from the quoting of their own version of Torah in the speech of Stephen in Acts, it is evident that Samaritans constituted a goodly quota of first converts; and from the ideas and expressions peculiar to John's Gospel, many of the Essenes of Qumran and Ephesus must have embraced the Good News.

All this sacred-scroll searching helped them reconstruct their picture of Jesus within the olden Scriptures' "penitential" context all the way from Genesis to the last of the Prophets. The conclusion was that Jesus had filled the triple office of Messiah as king, as high priest, as the prophet-like-Moses. And the weapon with which he had conquered death itself was the cross of his personal, not a vicarious, sacrifice.

This marvelous systematic borrowing was altogether within the traditional pattern of textual evolution found in the older Hebraic Scriptures themselves. These had started out with a step-by-step adaptation of an ancient pagan Sumerian myth of Creation in six days. In like manner were the Creation and Fall of Man borrowed, even down to the last detail of a cherub flashing his threatening sword at the gates of Eden, in the very land of the myth's birth. Such "cherubs," by the way, were sphinx-like Babylonian monsters representing some of the pagans' deified *elohim*, not the pretty winged "angels" of our Christian artists' romantic fancy. So were the "seraphs" heathen representations of fiery-winged serpent-gods, and Moses himself set up the bronze image of one in the Sinaitic desert for the worship of his people sorely beset by snakes—and this an evangelist startlingly referred to as a prototype of the crucified Christ.

All this is purposely said here to point out how, in spite of our carnal and spiritual ancestors' human stumbling in their search for divinity, they so wonderfully managed to pass down the pure *hesed* of Abraham to posterity. It is also brought in here to illustrate how monotheistic orthodox worship can often take on strange and even barbaric aspects that seem to overwhelm its inner core of spiritual devotion. This is especially true with regard to penitential practices—and in some cases, blood sacrifice —which seem to be a compulsive adjunct whenever *hesed* has become a bittersweet obsession.

It is no wonder, then, that the Cross, once such a shameful vehicle of Roman execution, should become a symbol of triumph over sin and death, and a sign of personal dedication. In the eyes of a fast-expanding new people of God, it embodied in poetic figure as well as in stark reality the devout consummation of all the divine promises made to Abraham because of his faith. A renewed *hesed* had sprung from the root of Jesse which was to color the story of man's search far beyond the lands of Shem and Ham and Canaan.

Those first Christians had no idea, of course, how all this was to shape and color the doings and thinking of men in centuries to come, and in lands far away from the Palestinian landscape. Sometimes it would take on very unusual forms around the inner core of faith—as when in Spain, and later in the Spanish New World and specifically in New Mexico, the cross-bearing image of a red-robed Christ with long blood-matted hair would be known, to the exclusion of all other titles, as *The Nazarene.*

9

Way of the Cross

In the decades following the annexation of New Mexico by the United States in 1846, some of her leading native citizens, along with many Anglo-American ones who had been settling in the territory in ever-growing numbers, kept petitioning Congress in Washington to have their beloved land declared a state. They were repeatedly turned down, however, and statehood did not arrive until relatively recent times, in 1912.

The reason given for one summary rejection was an indiscreet gesture by New Mexico's territorial congressman, an Anglo-American by the way, when he shook the hand of a solon who had just helped defeat some measures proposed by legislators from the Deep South. These southern gentlemen took their revenge by defeating his own bid for statehood. But years ago I read somewhere that one southern legislator remarked in his speech before Congress that most of New Mexico's population still consisted of savage Indians and ignorant Mexicans, and that the latter were so much steeped in superstition that they studded all their fields and hilltops with crosses. For this one reason, he argued, they were neither ready for nor worthy of American statehood.

The few scattered timber crosses seen on northern New Mexico's hilltops nowadays are now mistakenly referred to as "Penitente crosses." Some are admittedly such in origin, but the countless ones of prior times, two centuries before there were any such Penitentes, and others down to our day, were simply evidences of the Spanish soul's hold upon the landscape. No owner of a rancho, however small it might be, ever thought of *not* erecting a large cross in the middle of his property; if there happened to be a sandy or rocky hill on it, or nearby, so much the better. Nature herself provided a handy Calvary.

To that man and his contemporaries, such an image of Cross and

Calvary held profound meanings which they felt in their blood much better than they understood with their minds. Now too many of their own descendants, and more so the outsiders who have come since then to develop that same cherished landscape, or else ruin it in the attempt, do neither for the most part. This is why the Cross's long story in its relation to landscape and a very special heritage calls for detailed treatment, as did the faith and sacrifice of Abraham which went before.

1. The Royal Road

The fortunes of the Cross have been as varied as the material forms it eventually took wherever Christianity spread. Because human nature is basically the same when it comes to fidelity or laxity in worship, no matter among what peoples or in what climes or situations, those fortunes parallel those of the Hebrew Ark of the Covenant. At first, as may be gathered from Paul's letters, the Cross was an Easter sign of triumph over death and evil that was to be gloried in by every disciple. Like the wooden Mosaic Ark to the early Hebrews, which was said to contain the stone tablets of the Law given on Mount Sinai, it was valued much more as the Lord's mercy seat whereon his glory became manifest than for its material associations.

The Cross was therefore a cross of light, primarily, and not a mere one of wood. It was the Christian sign of *hesed.* It remained so during the initial centuries of pagan persecution when the material emblem of the believer was not its very simple physical delineation as was that of the fish, or else the "Chi-Rho." The Chi-Rho itself was a combination of the first two alphabetical characters in "Christos." These two cryptic codes appear much more often in catacomb and other early inscriptions and grafitti than the too-self-evident outline of the cross.

What brought the Cross to the fore, and to the crossroads of its subsequent history, as it were, was the cessation of persecution in connection with the conversion of Constantine, an upstart Roman emperor. Specifically, the whole concept is embodied in a double mother-and-son legend; namely, Constantine's vision of a cross during a famous battle, and his mother Helena's subsequent discovery of the very wood on which Christ had died.

Early in the fourth century, so the first story goes, when Constantine was desperately hard pressed during crucial combat, a great cross of light appeared high on the sky bearing the phrase, "In this sign you shall conquer." One version held that it was the Chi-Rho that he saw, not the cross, but the latter version prevailed. At all events, a general amnesty for Christianity was Constantine's gesture of gratitude for the victory that ensued, and the once-persecuted disciples of Jesus crawled out of their catacombs and secret ghettoes to begin leavening the then-known world with their Good News, or triumphant message of the Easter Cross.

The second story relates how the queen mother, when making a pilgrimage to Jerusalem, found three crosses buried in the vicinity of Calvary. Two of them were first applied to a dying man, but it was contact with the third cross which immediately restored him to health; hence this third cross had to be the holy rood on which Christ had died while the other two had held the thieves who were crucified with him. Whatever one may think about this test by threes, this legend of Empress Helena would someday shunt the believer's regard of the Easter Cross onto pathways other than the one opened by her son.

It should be noted here that Christianity had also spread far north of the Mediterranean countries even before Constantine's conversion. Our traditional preoccupation with the Greek, Roman, and Levantine martyrs under the Neros and Diocletians makes us forget that the Cross had quietly found its way into Gaul and the Germanic northlands, and even as far as the British Isles. Along pathways of conquest and commerce long ago established by the Caesars, the Good News reached such old Roman colonies as Lyons on the Rhone and Cologne on the Rhine, as also smaller centers inside Britain and Erin.

Even though the majority of these far-scattered Christians, particularly their hierarchical leaders, were Mediterranean folk originally, the vast hordes of so-called barbarians in those faraway lands could not help but see and feel something entirely new lighting up their dark forests and bringing warmth into their cloud-swept heaths and valleys. The ground was being prepared for the day when universal amnesty came, for the people of those so very different climes and scenes to begin imparting their own tinge and flavor to a *hesed* which had long been prophesied for them as well.

What Constantine's conversion and act of amnesty did was to bring the Cross into instant royalty, so to speak, as had the Ark been regally enthroned after its poor desert wanderings when David became Israel's king. However, this was no small Semitic nation in tiny Palestine over which it began to hold sway, but all the civilized nations of every racial derivation which were then under the imperial rule of Rome and Byzan-tium. Now the provincial governors and magistrates throughout the Empire began proclaiming the Good News as the state religion, and their people turned their backs on the old graven gods to embrace what formerly had seemed to them a mysterious Jewish sect of cross-worshippers.

Now the self-styled new People of God could not help but think that Yahweh's promise to Abraham had at last come true among all the tribes of earth, and all mankind was now coming to bow down in his presence from Sabbath to Sabbath. For they did write that their sacrifice made once and for all upon the Cross, and now being constantly commemorated in their "breaking of bread," fulfilled a prophecy about a clean oblation being offered to the Deity from the rising of the sun to the setting thereof.

Meanwhile, the material blessing (or curse) accruing from royal favor kept burgeoning apace. Where King David's son Solomon had built a sumptuous temple for the Ark and its Shekinah of the Lord, Roman-Byzantine imperial power now caused thousands of them to rise up everywhere for the glorious Cross as the universal mercy seat. Following the example of an emperor who gave his *basilika* or royal palace to the current pope in Rome, provincial rulers everywhere in the world empire erected further basilicas and churches in all the cities and towns of the various patriarchates and bishoprics, from Toletus in Spain to Byzantium by the Dardanelles, from Ephesus and Antioch and Jerusalem in the Levant to Alexandria and Carthage on North Africa's shores.

And the Cross itself began appearing fast on each of their apsidal half-domes, emblazoned in giant proportions in gold mosaics upon fields of mosaic cerulean blue; fashioned out of gold and silver, and studded with rubies and emeralds, it topped tall staffs which headed the most imposing of ritual processions; embroidered black on white for greater contrast, it covered the long liturgical palliums and omophorions of the high priests of the new order of Melchizedek.

Not to be outdone by the priesthood, royalty itself adopted the golden bejeweled emblem to adorn kingly crowns as well as the brocaded bosoms of palace lords and ladies.

*   *   *

But that such a symbol of shameful death should have so fully captured the nations upon its release from the darkness of persecution—no matter how great the might of imperial influence now aiding it—seems no less fantastic than Constantine's vision or Helena's discovery.

From the start, Paul himself had been obliged to acknowledge that to the Jews the Crucified Christ was an obstacle, and to the pagans madness; yet it was from among the hot-hearted Jews that the cult had arisen, and it was the cool-minded Greeks and Romans and other northern *goyim* who were embracing it in the face of direst persecution. Those who came after Paul wrote that it was the blood of martyrs which had been the seed of Christians, and this is very true, when we keep in mind that those *martyrs* (Greek for "witnesses") had not rushed to their painful torture and death for any love of suffering or dying, but as witnesses to something most extraordinary.

This something which so strongly captivated the minds and hearts of the children of Shem and Ham and Japheth indiscriminately, no matter what their landscape and the temper of their blood, was a desire hidden deep within the human heart—the wish for a blessed immortality as a reward for *hesed* or, better still, as that divine love's natural consequence.

No previous religion of any stature had ever made such a promise. It is true that many of the pagan worshippers of ancient Akkadia, Sumeria, Babylon, Ugarit, and Egypt had harbored the idea of an underworld, a *Sheol* in the Semitic tongues, where one eventually might arrive to join the nether gods and meet the shades of loved ones in some shadowy undefined existence. But since their Semite-Hamite mentality could not conceive of a person's *life* (soul or spirit) existing apart from his body, that idea of immortality was a very much confused one, particularly when they saw the body inexorably crumbling back to dust.

An effort to solve the problem was made by the Egyptians when they took so much pains to mummify and entomb the dead, even though mummification and protective tombs and pyramids offered no final solution. The more intellectual Greeks had come to distinguish "soul" from "body" as a philosophic possiblity, but even this did not make their Elysian Fields in the netherworld any more appealing.

Not even the ancient Hebrews who, as ultimately Semite-Hamites also conceived man as one living whole who was inseparable in his flesh and life, had any better assurances. Even their Torah with all its wondrous spiritual insights provided no definite answer. For them there was only that vague primordial notion of Sheol, or they said that their loved ones in death had been gathered to their fathers, or they had gone to Abraham's bosom. But if the body went back to dust, and what had once been a living thing was indivisible, where was the afterlife and when did it start? Or, in what did it consist?

Because of this, the Sadducees in Christ's time denied the immortality of human life. On the other hand, the Pharisees leaned in its favor, and this was because Greek ideas of the separate existence of soul and body had begun to influence Jewish thought. In fact, the clearest ideas on the subject appear in the Greek version of the Old Scriptures which the Jews of Alexandria had translated for themselves and added thereto, parts which the Palestinian Jews later rejected. It is this Greek version on which the Christian Testament is based, not the Hebrew canon which was drawn up well after Christianity was born.

Consequently, when Paul wrote his doctrinal letters and when the gospels and other parts were later compiled, all with Christ's resurrection from the dead as their main focus, it was a similar resurrection promised to each faithful believer which drew all and sundry to the Cross. By the time Constantine was replacing the Roman Eagle upon his imperial standard with the Easter Cross, it already meant to all who accepted the Good News a sure promise of everlasting bliss in the mansions of the Eternal Father for those who loved the Lord.

*   *   *

It was indeed a triumph for a sign that had once been a shape of death and shame. But gradually those same royal heads and breasts of the Roman-Byzantine Empire, like those of Solomon and so many of his successors, began whoring after other gods. Royalty and nobility began handling the established religion for their own ends while scandalizing the faithful with their licentiousness. Now *goyim* Isaiahs and Jeremiahs arose to hurl their warnings in the persons of some zealous bishops, but most especially through many a hermit who had fled into the wilderness to do penance in preparation for his prophetic mission. The days of the martyr-witnesses were gone, and these Gentile nazirites were now the witnesses of faith for the common people. The earnest Christian turned to them for guidance and, in contrasting their self-abnegation with the license of those in high places, began looking more upon the actual wooden cross of Christ's suffering and death as the one sign of hope and redemption than on the cross triumphant.

Now the legend of Queen Helena's finding of the true cross of wood began overshadowing in earnest the ideal one of her son's vision. The fastings and vigils of ascetics like St. Antony in their desert caves, or of those strange individuals who displayed their asceticism on the tops of pillars like St. Simon Stylites, further created the impression that sanctity and salvation lay more in such penances than in the Resurrection Liturgy being celebrated with the pomp and panoply of royalty. Eventually, these solitary nazirites banded together like the ancient sons of the prophets, and their monasteries became the centers of religious inspiration for the masses.

Once again, the northern Assyrians had to come down like the wolf on the fold, but this time it was the Hun from the steppes of northwestern Asia, and the Visigoth and Ostrogoth and Vandal out of the cold dark forests far north of the Mediterranean's sunny shores. The great Roman Empire, for a while glorified with a light its pagan Caesars had never dreamed of, fell mortally wounded. For the Cross, the Dark Ages had begun in more ways than one.

But things took a different turn from those heathen invasions in the Bible. The north European barbarians had no ancient civilizations for their background as had those of Assyria and Babylonia. Having no kingdoms or great cities whither to lead their victims into captivity, they stayed among the conquered. Besides, they liked the milder climate of the southern coastlands and were attracted by what little was left of the old Greek and Roman civilizations. Inevitably they intermarried with the inhabitants, adopting as well as influencing their languages and their way of life—and their religion.

As a result, instead of being obliterated like many of the early Hebrews in Palestine, the Christians of Europe received a great increase in numbers along with a renewed vitality. It was a new and promising start, even if at the cost of untold suffering, of the destruction of antiquity's accumulated sum of knowledge, and—for the Cross—the further dimming of its character as a beacon of pure light. The blood of Japheth had as much to do with it as did the European landscape, so different from the Palestinian one of Christianity's birth.

And over in those very dry and sunny uplands of Abraham's *hesed* a new star was rising—or rather a crescent moon—which would present a new and ferocious foe even while it claimed the same One Lord whom both the Jew and the Christian cherished as their own.

2. Abraham's Other Children

Wherever Spanish is spoken, in every Castilian household and, in America, from the southern tip of Chile to the northernmost villages of New Mexico, a common daily expression to be heard is *ojalá*. It is something like "would that" in English, as when we say, "Would that this or that happened." Actually, it is the adaptation of a Moorish Arabic phrase meaning "May it be the will of Allah." For that matter, when the Spaniard at the bullring shouts *olé*, he is unwittingly saying "Praise God" from the same language. It is a grammatical brother of the Hebrew *hallel*, as contained in the familiar term "hallelujah."

Of course, there are all kinds of words and expressions in Spanish which have the same Semite origins, but these two have a very strong religious one, as is most evident. Furthermore, they both speak for a great harkening to the One God's voice which took place in Arabia long ago, when an extraordinary man named Muhammed stirred up a world which the Cross had taken to its own since Constantine's day. What Muhammed did has to be considered in some depth, both in relation to the Crusades which were to stir Christian Europe for centuries, and for its impact on the Spanish soul along with its language.

Now, the average Christian today would be loathe to share the *hesed* of Abraham with the Muslim, just as the strict Jew might not care to do so with either. But the fact is that Muhammed also fell genuinely in love with God. It might appear like a strangely harsh brand of love to the unbeliever, yet his religious experience also had its roots in Abraham's mystic story, and in a number of ways.

In his day, the big Arabian peninsula dangling below Palestine and alongside Egypt, of itself a great forbidding desert land especially when contrasted with the Promised Land of milk and honey or the fertile valley of the Nile, was inhabited mostly by nomadic tribes considered idolatrous by both the Jews and the Christians of the times. These people of Arabia, however, were the mixed descendants of several small Semitic nations which since dim antiquity had been worshipping the Deity under the Canaanite name "Eloah," but had long ago misconverted his *elohim* messengers into minor gods.

From the north had come the blood and lore of Edom, the general area which had furnished the biblical writers with the original theme for the book of Job, and had also contributed the sayings of such sages as Agur and

Lemuel to the book of Proverbs. The original Edomites, furthermore, were supposed to be Abraham's children through his grandson Esau, Jacob's cheated elder brother. Incidentally, the form "Eloah" in the Hebrew Scriptures appears only in the poetical works, and mostly in Job; in the current dialect of Arabia the Name was being pronounced "Allah."

Also in the north were the Ishmaelites, whose own traditions—likewise corroborated by biblical lore—held that they were the progeny of Abraham through Ishmael, the rejected son begotten out of Hagar, Sarah's maidservant. From here on southward, Hamite blood and tradition had filtered in from Egypt, presumably bringing with them other pagan deities or *djini* to swell the ranks of the deified *elohim* among Arabia's people.

These largely nomadic folk the Hebrew Scriptures likened to the wild asses of that vast arid wilderness; it was an indirect compliment, since the true ass, now so often confused with the lowly donkey, was a spry and intelligent beast most highly prized by the mounted gentry of the Near and Middle East. In the droll tale of Balaam, the animal is made to speak most sagaciously. All in all, it was a most apt description for a people honed and toughened by their harshest of landscapes.

*   *   *

Muhammed was a true son of this wild blood and landscape, but with an inner sensibility which, like Abraham's and his father Terah's before him, saw into the "abominations" in the native worship surrounding him. These filled him with uttermost disgust, as if the mystic strain in Abraham and the original author of Job had not quite become extinguished among these bastard desert children of the Promise. During his initial unrest Muhammed began looking about for enlightenment among small Jewish synagogues strung along the Red Sea's coastline of his country, and likewise among some little churches of the Nazarenes, as these Christians were known in that general area.

His heart must have thrilled with joyous pride upon discovering the beautiful story of his remote Father Ibrahim among the Hebrew "People of the Book," and especially as to how Ibrahim had wondrously found the love and identity of the One Lord of the universe in his beloved Yahweh-Eloah. From many passages in their holy writings, the forerunners of his rabbinical informers had long formulated Ibrahim's great message in their *Sh'ma:* "Harken, O Israel, to Adonai [Yahweh] our Elohim, Adonai is One!"

Here in ancient text and traditional ancestry he had his answer. It became the rallying cry he himself began shouting to his fellow tribesmen of Arabia, and later to the world: "There is no God but Allah, Allah is One!"

The *hesed* of Abraham had taken hold of Muhammed in all its beauty and strength. But because Muhammed was made of much sterner stuff, for ages forged and tempered in the heat of his bleak native landscape, his grasp of it had to be told in his own word for it, *al-islam,* which means "surrender." Whereas Abraham's *hesed* had meant tender submission to Eloah's love, Muhammed's *islam* was harsh surrender to Allah's will. He who so surrendered was henceforth a *muslim.*

This rigidity showed its effects on the penitential aspects of worship. While bypassing vicarious animal sacrifice and its priesthood—was it because Jerusalem's temple had long been destroyed, or because lambs and kids in the sparse desert were much too precious to annihilate by way of worship?—Muhammed did sanctify circumcision, which had been in vogue among some of his ancestors even before Abraham. Fasting, long a painful acquaintance by force of circumstance among the desert nomads, he enjoined strictly for the entire month of Ramadan; other voluntary fasts as a remission of sin he strongly encouraged. To the total prohibition of pork he added that of wine, inspired by the example of the nazirites in their total consecration inasmuch as he considered his own dedication to God more perfect than that of the Jews.

This naziritic preoccupation, along with the Book's mention of the "sons of the prophets," ultimately prompted some of his followers to lead ascetic lives in groups, and many individuals to go about as holy men with such odd practices as we associate with the storied dervishes. Others later on, instinctively recurring to the self-mutilation of pagan ancestors, took to self-flagellation in times of sorrow or remorse.

Strictly adhering to the detailed Hebrew first commandment regarding graven images, and because of his own zealous proclamation of Allah's Oneness, Muhammed condemned all images of any kind. This was to inspire the birth of that severe but beautiful style of decorations called arabesques, which in turn would become part of the Spanish soul and landscape.

Since the Jews, whom Muhammed so much admired because of their written records, taught that Moses himself had composed the Torah word-for-word at God's dictation, he himself—as the Prophet-like-Moses promised therein for a new dispensation—felt obliged to write his own Law in Arabic, the *al-Koran.* For this he did not claim direct divine dictation, but had it done through the double agency of the Angel Gabriel and "the Spirit." Here appear the ideas which he had derived from the Nazarene Christians whom he had interviewed. While he could not accept Jesus as the Son of God, since this seemed to violate Allah's Oneness, he could not help but marvel at his virginal birth as announced by the Angel Gabriel to the Virgin Mary, and made possible by the power of the Holy Spirit. For him, Jesus had indeed been the priestly and kingly Messiah. But he, Muhammed, was definitely greater than the Nazarene because he himself was the predicted Prophet sent to God as the other, the final, Moses.

From the Nazarenes he also borrowed the doctrines of bodily resurrection for all faithful followers as well as an everlasting bliss in a wondrous paradise, except that this heaven of his would contain pleasures of the flesh, which Jesus had categorically denied. But the nub of his rigid outlook was the idea of inexorable fate, the *qisma* (later called *kismet*), which held that all future events were preordained, no matter what a person might do about it. It was derived as much from the astrological theories of some of his star-gazing forebears as from his own emphasis on God's unbending will.

To sum it all up, it was Islam which insured immortality for those who enbraced it. The Ark of the Jews as a symbol of God's nearness had long disappeared. And the vaunted Cross of the Nazarenes was all vanity because, as these semiheretical Christians of his country had told him, Jesus had not actually lived and died in the flesh but appeared only as a phantasm. Muhammed's own Koran was therefore God's very last word to man.

*   *   *

Because the Israelites of the Torah and their Jewish progeny were hardly ever proselytizers, wishing to keep their Adonai and his Promise to themselves, they had never been able to do what the Ishmaelites of the Koran accomplished for their Allah within a relatively short span. They conquered the entire Semite-Hamite world with the message of Islam; for it caught on like fire, whether or not assisted by the sword. The one minor Semitic dialect called Arabic, which in time had spread all through Arabia and given the peninsula its name, not only made them all Muslims but eventually imposed the Koran's language on all other tribes and nations throughout the Palestine and Asia Minor of all Canaanites, Jews, and Syrians.

As for Christianity, while it struggled to flourish anew in Europe among the motley "sons of Japheth" under the newly invigorated patriarchate of Rome, the weaker Christian patriarchates among the "sons of Shem and Ham" shrank under the shadow of the various caliphates of Islam. The Cross was enjoying new life from the Mediterranean strand of Spain, Italy, and Gaul up to the misty isles of Erin and Britain, then throughout the dark forests of the Teutonic peoples. But the Crescent now ruled over the once great churches of Jerusalem, Alexandria, Antioch, Armenia, and Chaldea. From Egypt westward along Africa's northern coastline it finally swallowed up the great Roman churches of Carthage—to gaze at last upon the last "orient" landscape across Gibraltar's Straits, the Tarshish of antiquity now Spain the Catholic, whose love for the Crucified Jehoshuah was as passionate as the Muslims' own for Allah.

But here we must once again take up the fortunes of the Cross in the twilight European landscape of fairy dreams and witches' brews, and see how the conquest of the Holy Land by the Crescent affected its peoples through the Crusades and their aftermath.

3. Danse Macabre

One or the other *morada* chapel of the Penitentes north of Santa Fe still has a "Carreta de la Muerte." This is a small, crudely fashioned cart with two solid wooden wheels, modeled after the big clumsy ones which were the only vehicles in New Mexico since Oñate's times until the first dray wagons and carriages arrived from the eastern States in the last century. Seated on the miniature cart is a figure of Death, what looks like a much-shrunken skeleton about to discharge an arrow at the onlooker from a bent bow.

The one at Trampas is usually kept in the little baptistry of its quaint village church of San José de Gracia; here the figure is entirely draped in fustian black, showing only a white ghoulish face with staring shell-eyes and, of course, the bony hands. Another one at nearby Córdova is still more fearsome; undraped, this articulated wooden carving looks like the misbegotten hybrid of a bantam skeleton and a giant praying mantis. A stranger stumbling upon the thing in the dark might well die of heart failure.

Such death carts used to be dragged by the Penitentes in their Holy

Week processions through their particular towns. They proclaimed not so much Christ's death as the certain uneasy fate of Everyman.

The whole macabre idea is not Spanish at all. It harks back to other darker landscapes in medieval times when the triumphant Cross had lost its Easter brightness, and a starless night stretched like a pall all over Europe north of the Pyrenees. It is the very same spirit which produced the Danse Macabre of Gaul and the Totentanz of the Germanic countries, what has been rendered in English as the Dance of Death. Here in New Mexico there are also later dark undertones from Indianic Mexico which will be pointed out in their turn.

*   *   *

The assimilation of the northern Gothic and related invaders with the Mediterranean folk of southern Europe produced a definite change in the climate of the Cross even when the sunnier landscape of the Greeks and Romans remained the same. This climatic change became complete with the Middle Ages. For centuries now, invigorated Mediterranean Christianity had been sending missionaries, mostly Benedictine monks of this mingled northern and southern Aryan blood who had become the founts of its vigor, all through the Frankish and Germanic forests and valleys. Gaelic monks who had meanwhile flourished in the misty glens and dells of Erin and Britain had also entered the field from their direction. Countless monasteries had gathered those once savage barbarians into well-ordered towns and cities, mostly by fostering a prosperous agriculture for which these lands and peoples were so well suited.

Both the missionaries who were afire with St. Benedict's basic motto of *Ora et Labora,* and the new converts whose tough instincts had been bred into them by ages of grim struggle against severest cold climates in order to survive, could not help but make the best of the rich black loams of the rainy northlands. All this eventually promoted a lively commerce all over the continent under remarkably stable forms of feudal government. Learning and the arts began to flourish along with it, even if ever so painfully slow, having to start from scratch because their invader forebears had practically destroyed the human fund of knowledge assembled by the old Greeks and Romans.

Like peasants and merchants everywhere, the peoples of this new civilization—pushed much more strongly by their peculiar vitality than those of warmer lands—began evolving a passion for work itself, a sense for the many advantages accruing from law and order, and a curiosity for thorough inquiry into the deep mysteries of life and of thought.

The north European work ethic, afterwards religiously mislabeled, had begun. So had the notion of supermen, whereby the huskier, fair-skinned industrious man of the northlands—now imbued with a facsimile of the *hesed* from a different dry world—began deeming himself superior in every way to the smaller and darker one of the southern sunnier scapes. At first it was not so much directed at the fellow Christian to the south as against those people among them in whose ancestor *hesed* itself had been born. Someday this animosity would sound the very depths of human savagery in the ovens of Nordic Superman.

Thus in due time a new Christian Roman Empire was able to function all over Europe, and this time with the heart of empire well away from Rome and Byzantium. Materially, it was very much like the ancient agricultural and urban civilizations of Mesopotamia and the Nile, by now long buried and forgotten. They were the same except for the rainy landscape, frozen cold through the long winter but all the more lush in summer with no need for artificial irrigation. Spiritually, however, the empire happened to be built on a monotheism born of Abraham's *hesed,* from a drier and sunnier landscape as it had been lived and taught by the followers of his descendant, Jehoshuah of Nazareth.

Yet the leaden skies and shadowy forests kept a hold on the inhabitants they had nourished from time immemorial. Their dark and somber landscape had inspired for their Druidic forebears an underworld of lurking woodland gnomes and witches seldom up to any good. The tangled roots of ever-present trees in blackest loam, however so rich in the foods and fodders it produced, spoke to the senses of dark decay. If now a sun-filled resurrection was promised as a certainty through Christ's Cross, it had to be reached laboriously through life's dreary tunnel, where grinning Death waited with ready scythe at every turn while mischievous devils in gargoyle shapes harried each one of life's pilgrims.

It is true that the magic of the Near East's gods had not succumbed altogether before the tablets of Sinai, nor the *djini* and evil eye before the scimitar of Islam; nor had Pan and the auguries of the classic Mediterranean coasts faded completely before the light of the Cross. But the dry landscape of the Levant and the sunny shores of southern Europe gave them a less menacing aspect.

Not that the northern medieval soul did not struggle hard to pull itself out of the slough of its native surroundings. The resurrectional power of the Cross, no matter how much shaded or hidden, still drew it upwards from this morass towards the light. The fruits of this desperate response can be seen in the great romanesque and gothic abbeys and cathedrals of the times, in the romantic songs of the minstrels, in the brighter features of the Crusades. In other words, the fears engendered in their zone of twilights found refuge in romanticism.

Although the churches' soaring stone columns and leaping vaults and arches could not avoid repeating the landscape's theme of tall dark forests and gloomy skies, their builders succeeded in giving them the fantasy of rare sunny days by capturing, in prismatic glories of stained glass, the essence of the meager sunlight which their climate allowed them. It was purest romanticism summoning forth verities which could not be seen or felt firsthand. There was, for example, the Christmas crèche, born in a gush of poetry through St. Francis in sunnier Italy, now brought to loveliest perfection through the crafts and carols of the snowlocked northern forestlands; and with it the legendary Magi of the East now elevated to tinsel royalty. The winter carols, the sweetest folklore music in the world, were followed by the songs of knighthood in the spring.

Chief among the romances which brought knighthood into flower were those legends which strained towards the sunlit source of their beliefs through the Holy Grail. Some said it was the plate of Christ's last supper which had held the consecrated bread of life, and on which Joseph of Arimathea had collected some drops of precious blood from the cross; others, that it was the very cup of that last Passover which had held the Lamb's royal blood in the first wine thus consecrated.

Both versions of the legend had it that either vessel had been brought to those dark lands by the same Joseph himself, the very man who had donated his own rock tomb to receive the Master's slain body. Here even death intruded fully into the mystic story, by the emphasis laid on the blood from the cross and on the sorrowful tomb; its resurrectional glory was exchanged for the Grail's sad glamor. For this glowing vessel kept ever receding like a dark fen's will-o-the-wisp; those worthy to encounter it had to rest content with a mere glimpse of it.

It was the same with the Crusades, a yearning towards the sunny landscape of faith's birth, but still a desire not so much to behold the Easter light as to see the Holy Sepulcher itself and wrest the empty relic from the

Saracens. Occasional triumphs each time that the Holy Tomb was won for a time from the foe shed some welcome rays when victor or straggler returned home with deeds of pious valor in behalf of the true Cross of wood and the authentic Sepulcher of stone out on the sacred sunlit soil of faith's birth. Such figures as Richard the Lion-Hearted, Godfrey de Bouillon, and St. Louis of France were the Davids of the latterday wars of Yahweh. But the glory emphasized was still the one of grim suffering and painful death for a holy cause.

The Holy Rood or actual wood on which Christ's life and blood were spilled, not the shining symbol of eternal victory, was the main object of devotion when pieces of the purported True Cross were brought home to be enshrined in the major churches, as also the supposed Holy Nails which had pierced the Master's body, and no less the Holy Shroud in which it had been wound when laid in the now all-hallowed Tomb. A mere shred of the Crown of Thorns inspired St. Louis to build that matchless jewel of stone and rainbowed glass, La Sainte Chapelle.

The actual wood of the cross had become more important than its meaning, the empty grave more significant than the resurrection it implied. As the *Golden Legend* claimed, in a romanticism gone wild, a slip of Eden's Tree of Life which had been planted in Adam's mouth after his death was the ancestor of the tree from which the cross was made. Together with Helena's finding of the True Cross after it found its own way into the liturgy, such medieval fantasies were more familiar to all and sundry than Paul's message of the immortal Cross of triumph. Yet even all this managed to produce true holy saints and nazirites, as sincere as those among the early martyrs, but one cannot look back on them as being brighter than snow and whiter than milk, or their personalities rosier than coral and more radiant than sapphire.

*   *   *

In keeping with this worship of romantic sorrow, and ever so morbid, was the practice of dissecting the bodies of fallen Crusaders in order to return their bones, surrounded by sacred Palestinian soil, back to their dark homeland. All this was further heightened by recurrent plagues more terrible than any pestilence recorded in the Bible. Invisible phantoms of evil air periodically carried off lives in droves to cast futher gloom on every side. The swarms of locusts in the lands of Genesis could at least be seen and understood for what they were, but the invisible viruses of bubonic plague and other dread diseases, devourers of human life instead of pastureland, were plainly insects out of hell. This happened mostly in the closely packed towns and cities where the countryfolk had flocked because of economic changes, or as a result of invasions from without, not to mention the constant wars between castle lords of which the common serfs and their crops were the principal victims.

Increasing commerce with other lands, especially those mysterious kingdoms in the tropical underbelly of Asia, brought all sorts of disease-bearing vermin in the holds of ships and the clothing of voyagers. While the clean dry climate of Palestine and the pastoral way of life had preserved the ancient Hebrews and other Semitic folk from such widespread devastating pestilences, the dank north European climate over a dense population promoted the spread of deadly viruses in rats and lice. Nor were the people protected by the salutary Hebrew laws of diet and purification. No rules of hygiene prevailed. Street gutters were open sewers. The populace lived close to swine and ate them indiscriminately, along with various rodents and other "unclean" animals of field and stream. When people died by the thousands, the familiar sight of charnel pits and houses made Death a dreaded if familiar figure.

In worship itself, Death climbed upon the Cross to show Christ in a grip that seemed never to let go, as when a legend from the Balkan countries, that the Cross had stood above the tomb of Adam, caused a skull to be added to the base of crucifixes. The Holy Week liturgy with its three-day Tenebrae or "dark hours" for mourning Christ's death drew more worshippers than the happy vigil of Easter. The *Dies Irae* recalling the fears of Doomsday drowned out the Easter hymn. Black vestments and palls, these often decorated with skulls and crossbones that must have inspired the Jolly Roger of pirate lore, replaced the white raiment of resurrection at funerals. They were in turn the inspiration of a grim form of architecture when charnel bones served as groins for the vaults of graveyard and monastic crypts, as may still be seen in those of the Knights of Malta and a friary of the Capuchins in Rome.

Even the forms of popular entertainment and instruction, like the Miracle Plays performed in church or town square, dwelt mostly on the theme of man's Fall and Christ's Death, and then went on to depict the transcendental presence of Death itself for Everyman—the grinning skeleton on its cart or in a portable cage, ever menacing the beholder with a poised scythe or with an arrow pointing from a taut bow. The macabre Dance of

Death was for long the favorite performance, graphically portraying the skeleton beating his drum and dancing at man's every stage of life, from birth until death, even at christenings and weddings where joy was supposed to reign. Engravings and woodcuts of it, like the famous ones by Holbein the Younger, illustrated the secular as well as the devotional books of the times.

Nevertheless, the faith and piety of the medieval Christian European were genuine. With all his growing anti-Semitism, he sincerely blessed the name of Abraham for a gift that had reached him across sea and landfall after so many centuries. Yet his faith fell short, somehow, of being *hesed*. The translation of the word itself into the languages of Japheth, the so-called Aryan tongues, either had to do with the processes of the mind or with romanticized feelings. It could not exactly be the *hesed* of the Palestinian landscape.

10

Flagellanti versus Francis

In *The Land of Poco Tiempo*, Charles F. Lummis began his chapter on the Penitentes of New Mexico by berating the Encyclopedia Brittanica of his day for not including them in its article on flagellation. But then, before telling about his own experiences with them in 1888, he launched on what he deemed a scholarly treatise on the subject in general by copying, point by point, from the learned work he was castigating. It ranged from the rites of most ancient pagan times to medieval practices in Europe which reappeared there sporadically even into his own century.

As the Brittanica stated, the Egyptians flogged themselves in honor of Isis, Spartan boys were whipped before the altar of Artemis, and during the Roman Lupercalia the bystanders felt themselves privileged when caught by the whips of the Luperci. Of course, one can see that such tortures endured in honor of manifestly erotic gods and goddesses were more for heightening the passions than to express sorrow for sin. These were among the abominations which Yahweh condemned among the lowland dwellers of Mesopotamia and Egypt, and among the Greek chamberers to whom Paul denied the kingdom of heaven.

With regard to Christian medieval practices, Lummis could not distinguish between their motives and those of the pagans who preceded them. Much less could he discern what blood and landscape had wrought in a remote corner of a modern world that he had stumbled upon.

1. Taking the Discipline

In Christian records, flagellation dates back to the Dark Ages in connection with law infractions, as when bishops and abbots made use of it to discipline wayward monks and clergy. In time the word "discipline," which originally meant "the training of disciples," became the term in church parlance for penitence, whether meted out or self-applied. Finally it became a synonym for self-scourging and for the scourge itself, when pious individuals in monasteries, and also outside of them, began "taking the discipline" as a means of curbing the sensual passions or to make amends for past sins.

Soon self-flagellation also became an act of loving empathy for the stripes which Christ had undergone at the hands of his executioners. It was not uncommon for a pious king or duke in his privy chapel, as well as the lowly peasant out in the woods or in some hidden shed, to vie with holy monks in their cells or anchorites in their caves in expressing their devotion to the Cross of suffering in this manner.

These latter penitents had never heard that self-flagellation had been a ritual practice among those pagans in the Bible who were there painted as the despised foes of God and his chosen people. Much less did they realize that it was a demonic feature very dear to certain deviates in Greece and Rome to whom Paul denied salvation. All they saw, in their innocent fervor, was their beloved Christ bound to a column in Pilate's praetorium, and being flogged unmercifully for Everyman's sins by the Roman soldiers.

The times were those when the light of the Easter Cross had been veiled by the blood of the Cross of suffering; it was the era when Death danced at christenings and weddings as well as at wakes and funerals. Hence, what a better act of loving gratitude could there be than to undertake the same kind of torture for love of Jesus? Had not he himself said that any disciple who did not take up his cross to follow after him was not worthy of him? Did not St. Peter write in his first letter that when Christ suffered and bled he left an example for every Christian to follow in his steps? And, of course, the great St. Paul himself had practiced self-flagellation, for did he not acknowledge at the end of First Corinthians 9 that he chastized his body and brought it under subjection lest he himself became a castaway?

It did not occur to them that Jesus and Peter might have been using figures of speech, or that perhaps the gospel editors decades afterward, influenced by the fact of the crucifixion, could have inserted that matter of taking up the cross into the actual sayings of Jesus. And there was Paul's declaration about disciplining himself, when he had no scourge in mind but was merely employing a picture and terminology which were most clear to his sports-loving Greek audience—that he was like an athlete at the stadium who trained and toughened his physique by avoiding ease and soft living, thereby evading the possibility of his being disqualified from the Olympic games.

Such widespread devotion had to burst out into the open streets and countryside. Medieval Europe, bled by futile Crusades which still left the Holy Sepulcher in Muslim hands, and spent from piling up sky-seeking gothic spires like Babylonian ziggurats that brought heaven no closer to relieve man's miserable estate, broke out in a ferment of religious movements that went past what was then considered the orthodox thing. Frequent petty wars between rival cities and castle lords all added to the restlessness, as did in too many instances the luxurious and scandalous living of the higher clergy.

The people's one recourse was the gospel in its pristine simplicity as they saw it. However, they could not help but color their fervor with the dark shades of their own landscape, which had inspired the Danse Macabre, the Totentanz. Besides those movements which vociferously challenged the accepted Christian tenets of the times, like the peasant Albigenses, the Poor Men of Lyons, and the Anabaptists, there were those which adopted public flagellation as the sole means of saving the world, and which are now generally referred to as the Flagellanti. It is to these that latter-day writers like Lummis have linked the Penitentes of Spain and consequently of New Mexico.

In externals they are very much the same. Blood and landscape, however, make a difference which will become apparent when we come to the Spanish soul.

Ever since the eleventh century, even church leaders had begun to encourage public self-flagellation as a means of penance for sin, so long as the scourging societies did not deny doctrine or ecclesiastical authority. But quite often they ended up by denying both in the spirit of the Albigenses and others who preached their own theories about salvation. Like them they summarily damned to hell all those who did not follow their example, confident that Doomsday was close at hand. Led by fanatical monks and friars in many instances, such groups spread from Italy into most of northern Europe. They flourished especially during great pestilences such as that terrible plague called the Black Death.

We in our enlightened age can be as quick in looking down upon all these Flagellanti, whether orthodox or heretical, as were the contemporary popes and princes in condemning and persecuting the latter. Yet they were doing in public and in common what had been admired all along as salutary penance among private individuals, some of whom had even been raised to the altars. It had been the accepted way of the Cross. If their stance was so fanatically gloomy, it was the temper of the times as well as landscape that made it so. However, any traces that persisted as accepted practice, particularly among the religious orders, have to be understood within their own context.

2. Sweet Saint Francis

Well over forty years ago, on the Friday following the happy day when my youthful classmates and I had been solemnly invested with the brown Franciscan habit, and given a new name as friars, our novice master passed around to each one of us a small scourge made of ordinary cotton sash-cord. It was some fifteen inches long, consisting of a loop handle which ended in six tails knotted at the end, all of the same material. He called the thing a "discipline," as he explained to my puzzled companions how "taking the discipline" was a very old penitential custom in monasteries.

Every Wednesday and Friday evening after supper, he said, we novices would all repair to our individual cells reciting the Psalm *Miserere* in unison. Once all cell doors were closed, a bell would give the signal for each friar to scourge his back over his thick woolen robe for a minute or so, when the bell gave another signal to stop.

It was only a small token act of self-flagellation; nor were the scourges themselves so formidable. Yet our mentor, upon noticing the continuing shock of disbelief on the young American faces before him, thought of adding a final word of solace. "It is not nearly as bad," said he—pausing to glance over at me with a twinkle in his eye—"as that of the Penitentes of New Mexico."

This last remark sped high over the heads of my companions, as had much of the preceding instruction. Those young fellows from "ethnic" immigrant families of the midwestern and central States were much better versed in the baseball scores of the current season than in any useless details from medieval history. Nor had they ever heard of any such thing as the Penitentes of New Mexico. To them, New Mexico was a hot desert state in the Southwest where one of their classmates had come from, while their very provincial parents and relatives at home persisted in regarding it as a foreign country.

Besides, this was almost the third decade of the twentieth century in Ohio, not the thirteenth in the Germany or Ireland or Poland of their forefathers. Yet even I myself felt a bit disturbed. When the bell rang that first evening, I picked up the scourge in my cell and promptly started to giggle like a girl. What came to my mind at the moment was a certain verse about a stolen cow which I had long forgotten. Then I heard the same giggling in the cells on either side of mine, followed by muffled whacks that could be none other than those received by a mattress.

Comparing notes afterwards, we novices were hilariously relieved to discover that most of us had been identically inspired. Thereafter, come Wednesday and Friday eve, our narrow cots were the scapegoats for our sins. Our novice master was no fool, not to know what went on, and must have harbored the same low regard for this medieval relic kept embalmed in the Order's constitutions by diehard old Italian friars at headquarters back in Rome. For the good St. Francis had no such thing in his simple rule of gospel counsels, nor was it in the spirit of the *Fioretti* and other contemporary accounts of his life.

*　　*　　*

One bright and tender glow lights up medieval Europe's murky scene of the Dance of Death and the Flagellanti in the person of St. Francis of Assisi. The hold that his extraordinary loving personality has had on all peoples to this day prompted G. K. Chesterton to say that there have been many great Franciscans but only one Francis, just as there have been countless good Christians but only one Christ. With no intention of placing Francis on a par with Jesus, this writer of paradoxes wanted to get at the core of his lovable uniqueness, which had also escaped the admiring efforts of non-believers like Renan and Sabatier, not to mention Francis' own faithful disciples like St. Bonaventure and others.

Their search for his secret had been carried on by means of grave philosophical and theological dissection, or through the misty veil of romantic poetry, or by a tricky combination of the two. It was simply the Japhetic or Aryan way of looking at things.

The fact is that Francis, although an Italo-Provençal, happened to be thoroughly imbued with *hesed*. And only God knows how it happened. As a result, he is the one and only saintly person among thousands of such sainted ones in Europe's history who successfully combined within himself the realistic Semitic faith of Abraham and Jesus with the poetic romanticism of his own Aryan nature. For who else, without appearing maudlin, could say that he had wed Lady Poverty because she had been Jesus' companion from the day he was born poor in a stable until the hour he died upon the Cross?

Up until his time, man in general had looked upon Nature, animate and inanimate, as something mysterious to be dreaded or else adored in the personages of gods and spirits; and those who believed in Genesis, which taught that God gave man complete domination over all things, looked upon creatures as objects to be exploited without either sense or mercy. Francis, however, considered them all his brothers and sisters for their having come from the Creator's hand just like himself.

The Cross, to him, was indeed that all-hallowed instrument of Christ's death, as all his fellow Christians believed, but first and foremost it was the splendorous symbol of life and resurrection. He did weep because men did not fully appreciate the price that had been paid upon it, but he also burst out in song because the price had been paid. Like Paul long before him, he trained his body for the spiritual contests of life on this sin-filled earth, but he did it with the humor of heaven—"Brother Ass" he called his sometimes stubborn little frame, recalling the gentle donkeys which had warmed the poor Savior in Bethlehem and also carried him on many a journey until his final entry into Jerusalem.

In short, Francis through his person and brief sojourn on earth gently but firmly chided his fellowmen about the follies of what we now call the rat race of human pursuits—when men trample on their brothers and foul their terrestrial nest in their mad hunger for money, luxury, power, and vain self-esteem. Yet, while utterly poor by choice, he did not rant against the person of the avaricious and luxurious merchant, prince, or churchman. While cherishing chastity as a pearl of great price, he did not damn the libertine, even going out of his way to kiss the hand of a priest living in unholy concubinage. Humbly obedient to the laws of God and of the land, he pardoned and blessed the robbers who beat him because he had nothing they could steal.

The penitence that he took upon himself, then, was not the self-righteous scourging of the Flagellanti. His own penance was the reaction of his fellowmen, whether lay or clerical, to the apparent foolishness of the *hesed* within him, a reaction he could easily understand; it also came by way of pain and sickness from the backhand of a Nature he loved so much, and this perhaps he could not understand. But *hesed* does not question, as Abraham knew and as Job painfully learned. As Paul wrote much later, *hesed* bears all things joyfully and patiently until truth shows its face.

In time, when the truth of it did appear blurredly to them, people of every station in life came to admire and love Francis most dearly. Many tried to be like him by becoming part of a happy band which gathered around him. And to this day everyone holds him in loving reverence for his Canticle of Brother Sun and all the Creatures; it is his life's song which ended, as was to be expected, with kindly Sister Death leading the world's Sweetest Nazirite by the hand into paradise.

But few in his own pleasant Italian landscape or the darker northlands of Europe could see clearly beyond the romantic poetry of it all. Even those who were justly proud of being called his Franciscan disciples, so many of whom attained the heights of spiritual greatness, merely lent substance to Chesterton's sage observation.

The case was somehow different in the dry and sunlit upland landscapes elsewhere. The clear Palestinian one saw Francis once, when he visited the Sultan in a naïve peaceful Crusade of his own; this Muslim ruler was so charmed by the poor little man's goodness that he treated him with every kindness and let him return home unharmed. And ever since then his friars have tended the Holy Places in an affectionate atmosphere among Christians and Muslims alike. It was the same with Spain. When he made a brief pilgrimage to Compostela, the Castilian landscape became Franciscan almost at once, and this spirit later filled a newly discovered world all the way to its utmost recesses in a similar landscape called New Mexico.

For all these dry upland landscapes and their peoples, the romantic poetry in Francis was a bit beyond their ken. Or rather, because of this, they saw more clearly into the core of his being, his *hesed*. This is why the Franciscans here appear more starkly penitential, let us say, than the ones in the pages of the *Fioretti*. Finally, the influence of his clerical and lay disciples on the Castilian–New Mexican landscape cannot be rightly understood without some grasp of their origins and organization.

*   *   *

Once the benign example of Francis had caught fire among his countrymen, all sorts of people wanted to enter more intimately into his sphere of joy. Those men who were free of family obligations he accepted as the "lesser brothers" among God's people—hence the official term "friars minor" as taken from the Latin and the Italian. Some of them were ordained priests and the rest were unordained "lay brothers," but all equally Friars Minor wearing the same gray rags and a knotted rope which had become their dear founder's badge of identification.

Because this was his initial group of followers, it came to be known as the *First Order*. Of these were the gray-robed missionaries who accompanied the Oñate colonial expedition into New Mexico, and who sometime later changed the gray to blue in honor of the Virgin Mary.

A second group formed around Francis's ideal. For women also begged to join him, and he could not refuse them. Among the first were the noble Lady Clare and her sister, and other good maidens of lower estate, whom he formed into a community of "poor ladies" who provided an example of evangelical detachment to the traditional big nunneries which had become rich and often meddled in secular matters. These humble women came to be known as "Poor Clares," but officially they were subsequently designated as the *Second Order* of Francis. None of these came to New Mexico in colonial times, except for giving a name to the Indian Pueblo of Santa Clara.

Finally, there was the *Third Order*. It has caused much confusion simply because Francis himself happened to call it "The Order of Penance." (In Spanish it is *la Orden de Penitencia*, and this misled Lummis and other writers after him to misapply this phrase often found in old New Mexico documents to something entirely different—the Penitentes.)

This third group of Franciscans consisted of men and women who were tied to family and other social obligations, and these duties Francis would not allow them to shirk by becoming Friars Minor or Poor Ladies. But because his heart could not refuse them either, he assured them that they could be just as much his affiliated brethren if they remained in their homes and occupations while leavening society with his message. This was their "penance," in the word's original and truest sense, a complete turnabout for the good in their relationship with God and their fellowmen.

In New Mexico, while one or the other of the original colonists might have been such a Tertiary, conditions were such that no fraternities of the Third Order of Penance were established until the eighteenth century, following the reconquest and recolonization by Don Diego de Vargas.

*   *   *

With regard to medieval penitential practices, here it is most important to know what changes the three Orders of Francis underwent after his death. Bereft of his personal élan on the one hand, and influenced by ecclesiastical rule and customs on the other, the First and Second Orders eventually simmered down into monastic institutes like the other orders of the times. There was always a "Franciscan" difference, naturally, for the legacy of Francis was much too rich in itself to be diluted altogether. One of the monastic influences consisted in the observance of stock penitential practices imposed by communal rules, or else self-imposed by individuals. These were stated periods of silence, prolonged and frequent ones of vigils and fasting—and self-flagellation. The latter was performed on stated days by the community, either in the convent chapel or in each individual's cell, and the scourge was applied over the clothing. It was the same when fraternities of the Tertiaries met for their devotions. But generally in every case it was a far cry from the bloody carnage of the heretical Flagellanti and their tolerated orthodox counterparts.

It is very true that more saintly or else overzealous individuals did whip their backs to blood in the privacy of their cells, and this was for long regarded as an outstanding sign of saintliness. As a result, the hagiographers vied with one another in multiplying such penances in the lives of the favorite saints they wrote about. But all this grim penitence would start breaking apart north of the Pyrenees when the Renaissance made its appearance with its return to classic pagan pleasures, to be ultimately challenged by the Reformation with what it called a return to the Bible.

11

The Cross and the Book

There were no Bibles in all of colonial New Mexico, except for a couple or so in the friars' library at their headquarters in the Mission of Santo Domingo. In fact, Spain had proscribed the reading of it by the populace throughout all her dominions, after seeing the divisions and confusion taking place in the principalities of northern Europe hard upon the open and effective proclamations of its text by Luther and Calvin as the sole source of faith.

It was a most natural defensive reaction on Spain's part. Not only had her several small kingdoms been united for the first time into one nation by Ferdinand and Isabella shortly before, but she had emerged from the Moorish wars as "Spain the Catholic," and her monarchs as "the Catholic Kings." It was as though the Spaniards considered the rest of Europe less Catholic than themselves, and for this reason worthy of being punished by these new scourges which they lumped together in the one term, *luteranismo.*

The oneness and very character of Spain had to be preserved intact. For Spain was not Europe, except geographically. Moreover, she felt the stern duty imposed by her self-assumed championship of traditional Christianity. Ferdinand and Isabella had considerable Nordic blood, as with most royal families, and the Flemish monarchs who succeeded them on the Spanish throne felt this duty all the more urgent, from their firsthand experience with nascent Protestantism in their own country.

However, these northern-born rulers had the poorest knowledge of an *anima hispanica*, the Spanish soul, which was their subjects' very being. Even without any influence from north of the Pyrenees, there had to be some Spanish *alumbrados* or "enlightened ones," as a few scattered dissidents were called; but the people as a whole would not have been much affected had their entire countryside been flooded with scriptural texts. For many centuries their realistic landscape had bred into them the unalterable conviction that everything the Scriptures contained had been fused together for them in the spiritual and material images of their crucified Nazarene and the queenly Virgin. Their long Crusade against the Moors on their very own soil had made this conviction all the more ingrained. This we shall pursue more fully when we examine the Spanish soul.

For theirs was not that Aryan romantic regard for the endless details of biblical lore. What they knew about them, chiefly from allusions made by their priests in homilies and sermons, was to them only a minor part of Christ's own autobiography, as it were, from Genesis to Apocalypse—and one in which his Mother played an essential role. Why bother, then, about endless "begats" and "saith the Lords"?

The colonists in New Mexico, of course, were no different. Moreover, few of them could read; as rustic stockmen on their own pastoral landscape beset by every peril, they also lacked the time as well as any taste for the printed page. In all the allusions they had made to Exodus and other Scriptures when entering their Promised Land, they had indeed identified themselves with the early pastoral Hebrews, not through any romantic self-transference, but with the person of their Semitic Nazarene cousin ever in mind as the single overall essence of the entire Bible story.

1. Nazareno and Conquistadora

In the 1714 Lady Chapel of adobe still preserved intact on the north flank of the present stone cathedral of St. Francis in Santa Fe, two objects immediately catch the eye. One is an almost life-size crucifix on the bare east wall; the other is a gold-leafed rococco altarpiece covering the entire apse wall. In its topmost niche a small regally dressed statue of the Virgin may be seen, and as the chapel's main attraction for additional historical reasons.

The Cristo on its plain black cross is typical of many such figures made in the ateliers of Mexico and other cities of New Spain during the seventeenth and early eighteenth centuries. The treatment is most realistic in characteristic Spanish fashion, from the real matted hair of the "Nazareno," and the glass eyes, to the bruises and streams of blood all over the torso and limbs.

The Virgin's carved figure of sixteenth-century manufacture cannot be seen for its dress and mantle of real brocade; only the tiny doll face shows under the wig and mantilla topped by a gold crown. It is called *La Conquistadora* for having been in New Mexico since the days of her very first *conquistadores*, and as such it merits this special shrine, which is the successor of the original one finished in 1629 and later destroyed in the Pueblo Revolt of 1680.

Both images of the Crucified and of the Virgin portray, in a broad sense, the spiritual and physical contents of every Catholic church and chapel since the era of Constantine. But more specifically in their extremely realistic style, they represent those of every church and chapel in Spain and all Spanish America. To the uninitiated, it all smacks of idolatry plain and simple. In the regard of Catholics in general, and more particularly those of the Hispanic tradition, it is no different from the visible and tangible Ark of the Covenant—containing the very tablets of the Law, yet paradoxically adorned with the forbidden images of Babylonian *kerub*—which served its high purpose as a seat and symbol of divine mercy.

*   *   *

Soon after the Cross came to be gloriously emblazoned in gold mosaics within the first Christian basilicas, following Constantine's act of amnesty, the giant figure of Christ also began appearing in the same situation and colorful medium, or else in frescoes, and always most majestic in his stern visage as the universal Savior. Almost at the same time there appeared the Virgin Mother with her little Infant Christ, always flanked by two cryptic Greek ciphers which read *Meter Theou*, or Mother of God.

For the early Church councils, in condemning heresies which questioned either the divinity or the humanity of Jesus, had accentuated his double nature of God-Man by declaring his earthly human Mother to be the *Theotokos* (God-Bearer) of his single divine and human personality. The touching human warmth of this latter depiction of Mother and Child naturally became more popular than the adult stern Christ by himself as the Judge of Doomsday, and from the church's apse it found its way by means of small *ikons* into the households of the faithful.

Gradually there also appeared the images of favorite saints accompanying those of the Christ or of the Mother and Child—at first the Apostles and John the Baptist as the Nazirite precursor of the Nazarene, then those of the local martyrs. For, since Christ's Second Coming had not materialized during the lifetime of the primitive Christians as they had expected with

Paul, the generations which followed now pleaded with all those departed "witnesses" of a promised blessed immortality to remember them before the throne of heaven. Not only had the cult of the saints been born out of this promise inherent in the Easter Cross, but the "sons of Japheth" saw no infraction of the first Hebraic commandment which forbade "graven" images but said nothing about "flat" pictures in fresco or mosaic.

There came one big protest, it is true, the one made by a Byzantine emperor called Leo the Isaurian, and who is known to history as Leo the Iconoclast, or Image-Breaker. No doubt, he had been influenced by the Muslims who now overran the lands just across the Dardanelles. The Council of Nicaea summarily condemned Leo and his followers, and the use of images by Christians was thereby sanctioned for all time. But it was the flat icons, as still used exclusively in the Eastern churches, which were in question, not the statues which by and by were to become the vogue in western Europe.

But even these pioneer western statues, when they first appeared in bas-relief or in the full round among the arches and columns of the brownstone romanesque and gothic churches, were merely a decorative relief amid the dark and colorless architecture, along with the hideous gargoyles spawned by the imagination of the demon-infested northlands. A further and more successful relief from the encircling gloom of the northern landscape were the stained-glass windows, which were really the true icons of the West.

Even after the Cross of light began giving way more and more to the material one, the image of the Crucified was merely painted on it, as with the famous St. Francis cross of San Damiano. When first carved in the round and affixed to the cross to form a "cruci*fix,*" it appeared high upon a lofty rood-beam above the chancel, or else among the images of saints upon an intricate chancel screen. The whole ensemble was more an integral part of the architectural motif than an object of veneration. The same may be said of the statues of the Virgin and all the saints.

Then came two most important epochs in the story of western Europe which, after all, is the story of the Cross. They are commonly known as the Renaissance and the Reformation. The importance of either one, because of their subsequent impacts on civil and religious life and thought, would require long chapters within other contexts, but here a much shorter summary of their influence on the cult of the Cross suffices.

First, the Renaissance, as a rebirth of classic Greek and Roman mythology with its literature and art, prompted the use of marble statuary in the churches then being built in neoclassical style. While meant originally as an integral decorative part of the new architecture, the images of Christ and the Madonna and the saints, now being carved in the highest perfection, began descending upon the very altars; and from there, further romantically tinted, they found their way into the household shrines of the ordinary folk.

All these statues, and also paintings, reflect the romantic Aryan view of mysteries which had taken place long ago in the altogether different Palestinian landscape. The best of them, from the dim lands of Flanders and Germany down to the sunnier ones of Italy, today form a major part of the world's art treasures and heritage. But in the landscape of Spain, stark realism had to produce the "Nazareno," whether carrying his cross or dying nailed upon it, in the bloody Isaian descriptions of the Suffering Servant. Likewise, the Madonna had to appear, for being the heavenly *Theotokos,* as a queenly Esther freshly bathed and combed, and arrayed in the richest fabrics, for the pleasure of her King and the pride of her devoted cousins.

Hence the display in the Conquistadora Chapel in Santa Fe. The New Mexican landscape carried forward this same Hispanic realism in its now very popular native *santos* when with the passage of time, and within its primitive isolation, the old Cristos from the motherland had become rare and only a single outstanding Virgin like La Conquistadora had survived.

But all these external trappings of the cult of the Cross, along with the penitential sentiments they represented, had suddenly been challenged in northern Europe in the years following the discovery of a New World. The same renascent movement which had inspired these graven arts in the round had also produced the printing press. Like a revived and strongly invigorated creature, the printed "Word" began questioning the validity of the sculpted and graphic "Image" in the area of man's way with the divine.

2. It Is Written

In published literature, whether factual or fictional, in which Muslims appear, they are often quoted as using a characteristic phrase: "It is written." They are obviously referring to their Koran as the ultimate fount of truth or credence. Muhammed himself, as we saw before, was the first founder of a major religion known to have composed a book detailing its origins and prescriptions. And his obsession with the written word, of course, had been sparked by the Hebrew Torah where he had come upon the story of his reputed father Abraham and his intimate relationship with the One Lord, Eloah. Not surprisingly, he was the first to refer to the Jews as the "People of the Book," a term used by his followers to this day.

The Jews' own profound reverence for every single word of their Torah and Writings was most natural. Even long before them throughout the Green Crescent from Babylon to Egypt, the art of writing had filled the uninitiated with extraordinary awe; it was a greater invention by far than that of the wheel or the metal tool and weapon, and all the more godly in its mysterious transference and preservation of man's very thought and speech. Consequently, divinity had to be the first writer. Anything profound that had been recorded on clay or papyrus from remotest times then had to be true. It was written.

But for the Jews in particular, their sacred writings were not merely the story of divinity and creation handed down to them, but their very own history most intimately linked with that same Divinity. For them, it was Moses himself who had written the entire Law under God's guidance. Hence Muhammed, deeming himself the promised Prophet-like-Moses, felt it his right and duty to write the complete Law of Islam himself.

Jews, Christians, and Muslims had no idea that their stories of the world's creation, of the first man and woman, of the extremely long-lived "patriarchs" before the Flood, and of the Deluge itself, were all adaptations of very much more ancient Akkadian or Sumerian myths which had come down to them in different traditions—and these had been edited and mixed together by priestly scribes only a handful of centuries before the Christian era. The Christians themselves, in fashioning their own gospels well after their Master was gone, had also edited and reedited their own varied traditions, richly dressing them with allusions which they "searched" out of the olden Hebraic Scriptures. But they did this borrowing from a Greek Bible which had been translated by "seventy scholars" for the Greek-speaking Jews of Alexandria; scraps from the Dead Sea Scrolls indicate that the Seventy had translated a version other than the one later adopted by Judaism as official.

As with the Jewish rabbinate in their recent painful sorting out of what prophets and histories were to be considered inspired, so the Church Fathers struggled with their own problems regarding what should be genuine and what apocryphal. The final book of Revelation, for instance, with all its millennial and other fantastic visions aping the ones in Daniel and Ezechiel, was not accepted universally for about five hundred years.

And yet, in the regard of those who were formulating the early Christian dogmas, every single word in Scripture had been directly revealed by God to each particular writer. Matthew and Mark and John, for example, had composed every single iota in the books bearing their names, just as Moses was believed to have written every word of Genesis and Exodus. Therefore, every little thing had to be true, for "it was written."

*   *   *

The Canaanite or Phoenician alphabet, the first significant and lasting improvement over the clumsy Babylonian cunei and Egyptian glyphs of old, endowed not only the sons of Shem in Palestine with their Hebrew letters but also the sons of Japheth with theirs all along the shores of Greece and Rome. Israel in time enriched the world with her Scriptures. Greece and Rome likewise fostered the world's greatest literature along with the profoundest philosophies. Then this latter treasure was scattered and lost for a long time when the barbarians of northern Europe overran the Roman-Byzantine Empire left by Constantine.

But gradually these Teutonic invaders, who had intermingled with their remote Aryan cousins in the south, began regarding the written word with an interest in some ways surpassing that of the Greeks and the Romans. As the monasteries spread northward, the newly christianized peoples were likewise drawn to the written page in which the monks had been preserving, by constant recopying, not only the Greek and Latin texts of the Scriptures but whatever classic lore and wisdom had survived the barbarian invasions.

It was something very strong in the Nordic nature, this love for reading and writing, which had lain dormant in their previous savage existence; perhaps it was a revival of still more ancient Druidic traits that had once created such wonders as Stonehenge. And the long northern winters which held them snowbound within the many towns of their newly civilized milieu encouraged it all the more.

In time many university towns like those of Oxford, Paris, Cologne, and Bologna became even more important than the flourishing commercial centers of a most vigorous new European people with such an innate passion for reading and discursive thinking. It went hand in hand with the one for physical work and material thrift. In the bosom of these universities and many other smaller monastic and secular schools, the remote ancestors of the Waldenses and Anabaptists—and of Luther, Calvin, Zwingli, and other reformers later on—had prepared the way for something that they never dreamed would come to pass.

Then, as if preordained, came the printing press with movable face-type, invented by one of their own in their winter landscape; for the long cold sieges also nurtured a talent for carving things from the hardwood of the great forests, and for producing gadgets which made the freezing northern life much easier to bear. Then, too, a spirit of nationalism had been developing; each ethnic section of a vast Latin Holy Roman Empire now hungered for a literature in its own particular language. And paramount for them was the Word of the Lord.

Not that the sun-filled dry landscape below the Pyrenees had remained idle or sterile in this regard. Spain had her own great universities like those of Salamanca and Alcalá, and her literature enjoyed its own preeminence, thanks to her peculiar Roman, Jewish, and Moorish heritage. It was through here that much of the classics of antiquity was passed on from the Levant to an awakening northern Europe. But the Castilian landscape's people as a whole, while having the same regard as their Hebraic and Arabic cousins for what was "written," lacked the Aryan European's passion for reading as much as they did the one for constant work and continuing thrift.

And so the northern Aryan protesters rallied around the Bible's every word as the one and only font of faith. Or rather, their leaders rallied around the concordance of each noun and verb for putting either creditable or fantastic creeds together. In self-defense the traditional Catholic establishment, while just as firm a believer in each word's divine inspiration, linked the text with "tradition" as well. In doing so it unwittingly went to the heart of the matter—never suspecting how much the olden as well as the more recent Scriptures were actually an ages-long compilation of human myths and recollections handed down through repeated editing.

But there is a more interesting phenomenon in this connection, for having to do with landscape and the people it nurtured. In their characteristically romantic view of what had taken place on the Palestinian landscape long ago, these self-chosen Aryan "People of the Book" identified themselves so much with the Israelites in Exodus as to shove them out of it in order to assume their place; in fact, they paradoxically began despising the very folk who had provided them with the story. It was an attitude which had to culminate someday in the pagan philosophy of superman and the ovens of Dachau.

Their Aryan Catholic counterparts, in continuing to express their faith in Scripture under the visible image of their Jewish Crucified One and their Jewish Virgin Queen, were not as brutally anti-Semitic, yet there were the ghettoes in the crowded cities because these aliens were forbidden to have lands of their own.

South of the Pyrenees on the Castilian landscape, things looked very much the same on the surface. But there was a profound difference which cannot be discerned unless one looks more closely at the *anima hispanica* upon its own Palestinian landscape, as we shall proceed to do in the next section.

All at once this thought makes one jump ahead of himself, because of a mental picture which comes up of the New Mexican landscape of not too long ago, in the latter part of the nineteenth century. Some Jewish immigrants from northern Europe appear on the quiet scene, peacefully enjoying after ages the pastoral life of their remotest Hebrew forebears as sheep and cattle ranchers. At the same time the native Hispanic hosts can be seen fêting their dear Conquistadora with lights around the feast of Purim. And in the solemn days and nights of Passover, the Penitentes go forth mourning their Nazirite

> with faces darker than blackness itself . . . unrecognizable
> through the streets, the skin shrunken against the bones. . . .

Part Three

ANIMA HISPANICA

Dulcinea derives her grand birthright from the House of Toboso in La Mancha, a bloodline which, though recent, suffices to give a noble start to most illustrious scions in ages to come. . . . I draw my pedigree from the Gachupines of Laredo, replied Vivaldo —hers is a Family I never heard of until now. Strange, said Don Quijote, that you never heard of it before.

—Cervantes, **Don Quijote**, Pt. 1, Bk. 2.

12

Semitic Spain

During a Lenten season of more than three decades ago, while I was driving north from Santa Fe with a priest who had come from Spain many years before, my good companion began commenting on the landscape on either side with what must have been deepest nostalgia. All along the way to Santa Cruz de la Cañada, which was our destination, he kept comparing each passing view of broken arid terrain and wind-carved ochre bluffs, of little *cañadas* running among them with their narrow fields and groves of cottonwoods now winter-tawned—and ever present beyond them to right and left, the spines of blue and green sierras etched against the spotless sky—with familiar scenes he fondly remembered back in his native Castile.

Once, I clearly remember still, he included the native local people with the scenery, especially the older generation. Just like the landscape, said he, they were *tipos castizos*, the same types he had known in the rustic countryside of his birth. At the time I didn't know what *castizo* meant, and was not ready to betray my ignorance by asking. Nor could he have told me in a few words, as I came to learn much later on.

Instead, I made some facetious remark about Penitentes still existing in Spain. It must have been the penitential season in conjunction with the landscape that brought it up, for we were now coming into so-called Penitente country. Without any change in his voice or mood, my mentor began telling me of flagellant societies he had known about in different rural localities back home. There were those who wore long tall-hooded gowns in Holy Week processions, bearing platforms on their shoulders heavy with tableaux of the Passion, and chief among those figures the bewigged Jesús Nazareno in a red robe bearing his cross.

He also told me of another place where a different class of penitential brothers, bare to the waist with black bags over their heads, carried short but heavy upper cross-beams pressed against their necks like yokes, their forearms hanging limply over either side of the beam; others among them went scourging along. And all were accompanied by their "brothers of light" in full dress and great black capes, bearing candles.

All this, too, he said, was *muy castizo,* and again I missed the point. He then went on to relate how as a little boy he had sometimes gone with his father to meetings of a Third Order fraternity to which he belonged. Following the routine business of small society meetings, his father and the other men recited set prayers and sang a hymn or two. Then they ended the session by falling on their knees and scourging their backs over their dress suits for a brief spell. It was a token flagellation as a humble sign of penance, my friend was careful to explain, not the outright self-torture of the overt penitential brotherhoods he had mentioned before. While called Orders of Penance, the Third Orders of the various mendicant friars were clearly distinct in aims and procedure from the groups directly referred to as *penitentes.*

I needed none of this last explanation, promptly recalling my years as a Franciscan novice not too long before, when my young mates and I made our mattresses bear the brunt of our prescribed acts of token penance. But what this now long-deceased clergyman had been doing as we rode along, and without knowing it, was stirring anew certain vague ideas about landscape and people—along with that of penitence—which soon began quickening new life in the roots of a lingering problem concerning our local penitential societies together with ancestral origins and customs.

It was the double enigma which had been sown on that unforgettable day long, long ago when a curious little lad barely escaped a whipping for being a naughty boy. Of course, it all would require a much more thorough acquaintance with countless other related matters, and many a season of long, long thoughts, before a certain mustard tree could begin flexing its leafy arms under the sunlight of a more fully understood *casticismo* which makes up the *anima hispanica,* the Spanish soul.

1. España Castiza

Like the Hebrew word *hesed* in its total association with Abraham's way with God, the Castilian term *castizo*—which implies all that is perennially Spanish—cannot be defined or explained by mere abstract theorizing.

Searching out its "chaste" Latin roots still leaves one with a bare word. Miguel de Unamuno tried to do so in a series of famous essays, but finally had to turn to the more tangible Castilian landscape and climate, his description of which was here made the heart of an earlier section. But even here he faltered in his philosophizing because of the elusive nature of his subject, and also because he was a Spaniard. As a *castizo* himself in his inmost being, he did not so much think out his idea as he saw it at a glance across the terrain and sky, what we might call pictorial intuition.

For much the same reason can this more ambitious mosaic or tapestry of Palestinian–Castilian–New Mexican landscapes and peoples be found at fault—precisely what was said in the beginning as something which strict science might frown upon but which art ought not gainsay.

Later on, when dwelling more particularly on the Spanish soul, Unamuno had to follow the same course by stating:

> . . . in this climate of extremes with no sweet-gentle features, of a landscape uniform in all its contrasts, the spirit is likewise sharp-edged and dry, poor in the philosophic sphere. . . . it generalizes upon facts as they are . . . seeing them sharp-edged as are the shapes upon its native countryside, and accepting them as they look in their own dress without reconstructing them. . . . as a result, it has sired a rugged popular realism and a dry rigid idealism which travel side by side in a partnership like the one of Don Quijote and Sancho, but never fusing.

For one thing, here one meets no sweet and soft romanticism as in the countries north of the Pyrenees with their leafy landscapes of misty transitions under diffused northern lights. Much less is there any deep rationalizing, that orderly intellectual search peculiar to the sons of Japheth which first sparkled on the mild picturesque hills and shores of Greece, and which finally sounded the very depths of thought and of the psyche itself in the dark cold valleys of the European northlands.

Here in the Castilian atmosphere, as in Genesis and Exodus, truth and *hesed* are not stated in logical propositions or dreamed up as romantic tales, but are seen sharp-edged in the stark figures marching across their naked native countryside. It is poetry, true, but pure poetry without the romantic frills. This can be seen foremost on the religious level, even long before the Spanish soul was fully formed.

The way of the Cross, from its original entry into the West as a sign of resurrectional triumph, until its eventual veiling under the blood-soaked sorrow of Calvary in the Middle Ages, is epochally the same in the Iberian peninsula as it is in the rest of Europe, yet with a difference. As in other places, there was that total and joyous acceptance of the Good News during the first era, when Spain furnished infant Christianity in Rome with the most famous of the western martyrs, St. Lawrence the Deacon. He was roasted on a gridiron according to legend, and, whether true or not in its details, only a legend about a Spanish martyr could have him casually saying to his tormentors: "I am done on this side, now turn me over on the other."

One cannot help but think of those apochryphal seven Jewish youths and their valiant mother in the second book of Maccabees whom Antiochus Epiphanes ordered to be tortured and killed, one after the other, as they steadfastly refused to break their Law by eating pork. Each lad had something similar to say with his dying breath. And, of course, there was Abraham with his direct literal responses to his *hesed,* particularly in that instance when he went about the business of sacrificing his boy Isaac.

*   *   *

In the eyes of the early convert folk of Iberia, the wondrous stories of promise and redemption, as related throughout the olden and more recent Holy Writings, had not taken place in a foreign land ages and continents away—in another world for their being so divinely miraculous—as it seemed to the other Christians of Europe in their inward discursive thinking and romantic fancies.

In Castile, a small huddle of stone and adobe houses, flat-roofed as they were then, and pressed against a bosomy slope of hill, was Bethlehem for the folk of that particular area; and the herders at dusk driving their flocks down to the same cozy slope's *majada,* or natural shelter, heard the angels singing the glad tidings as the darkening heavens suddenly burst out with stars. Another larger town was easily Nazareth, where the village wood-worker and his family lived over the same life patterns in that identical locale known to him who was called a carpenter and a Nazarene.

Over yonder stood Elijah's Carmel, and beyond it blue Mount Lebanon herself graced the far horizon. Over here rose that great mound of the vision seen by Peter and John and James—this last one the great Sant'Iago whose bones, having come home as it were, supposedly rested at Compostela—the very Mount Thabor, indeed, where these three Apostles had witnessed the transfiguration of their Master as he conversed with Moses and Elijah.

Here even the very sounds that Jehoshuah of Nazareth spoke forth from the Mount of the Beatitudes wafted all over the clean land, in the conversations of the many Jews who, ever since the destruction of Jerusalem, had sought refuge in this western Canaan as others of them had done in other parts of Europe. But here they were allowed to own land as brethren, tending their small gardens and vineyards while their large flocks roamed the pastureland around their settlements. This they did of their own choosing, not forced to live landless in urban ghettoes and thereby obliged to make a living exclusively through usury and trade.

Continually hearing these Hebraic and Aramaic voices, and likewise drawing from their more remote canaanitic heritage, the Celtiberians kept on changing the language of the older Roman legionnaires which now was being read to them from the Latin Vulgate—the Scriptures which their own countryman St. Damasus, as Pope in Rome, had commissioned St. Jerome to translate from the Hebrew and the Greek.

And there was the great and thrice-holy Jerusalem upon her holy mountain, to be seen in every larger city of an area crowned with its cathedral temple, and most particularly on that central giant mound in the country's very heart where stood the primatial see-city of Toletus—which would become the so *castizo* Toledo in her name's sound as much as in her physical aspect.

In each and every such city's garrison, it was not difficult to see Jesus being torn to crimson shreds by the Roman soldiers' whips, and then, his hair matted with blood and crowned with thorns, dragging his cross through the twisting narrow streets. Just outside the city gates, Golgotha was plain to see on the same hill's protruding shoulder, and there the Cristo on his cross expanding his bloodied rib-cage almost to bursting with the agony of his last cry of "Eli" to the Father.

Everything was so real because the land and atmosphere were authentic; and the people themselves, as an integral part of their own Palestinian landscape, "generalizing upon facts as they were, and accepting them in their own dress without reconstructing them." Old racial memories, hand in hand with landscape, still reached across Gibraltar to the North African coastline, and thence eastward past the Nile's green lowlands back to the lands of Genesis.

And so the Christian story in the West here emerges decidedly different in aspect and in its effect upon people from the one north of the Pyrenees. It is what eventually comes to make the *anima hispanica*. For this reason there were no Dark Ages in Spain. Whatever appears gloomy and forbidding in the darker and wetter countries of Europe, or is mistily romanticized in will-o-the-wisp tales, is here, in the sharp sunlight on stark terrain, what one might call sad and severe but never morbid or eerie. *Sad, dry, severe, real*—these are some of the many facets of the hard, clear, and sharp-edged diamond which reflects the word *castizo*.

Castizo are the air and the landscape which soon dry up the viruses of plague and do not allow blood to decay or wounds to fester, just as you seldom find mold on the stones of centuries-old cathedrals or rot in the wooden beams of the humblest hovel. And so the blood on the cross is a living crimson, not a dead maroon; the pains of the agonizing Christ upon it do not exhale death's dark terrors but tersely speak of a *hesed* consummated, a challenge met, the very moment of truth. It is no wonder that the more mundane *corrida de toros*, which in Spanish lands traditionally has offered an exhilarating pageant for sense and soul—and with its unwittingly shouted "Praise God!" in the thousands of *olés*—can be nothing but a messy slaughter elsewhere, or in the eyes of northern peoples.

In short, even if Spain did also happen to lose sight of the original Easter Cross, she kept on beholding it in its bloodier Good Friday manifestations more as a pillar of cloud by day, and one of fire by night, than as a gloomy spectacle lit only by an evanescent phosphorescent Grail. Let death itself pose its threat with drawn scythe or bent bow, or try to drum and fiddle at weddings as well as at wakes, it was met with the steady stare of the *matador*, whose name denotes a slayer, but the slayer of something which is far more fearsome than death itself.

2. Castles of Castile

The barbarian deluge which so drastically devastated the old christianized Roman-Byzantine Empire of Constantine, all along the horizontally curving Mediterranean shore, also spilled over the Pyrenean dam to flood the entire Iberian peninsula. Assorted northern warlords like the Goths, Vandals, and Suevi had ruled over its different sections before the close of the fifth century. But here the inundation was shallow. There was not that much of classic Greek and Roman antiquity to suffer destruction, and the invaders were relatively few in numbers and too thinly spread out to affect racial strains too much, much less beliefs and customs.

Of course, it was the superior Nordic zest for action which had sufficed to take over the land from a disunited and easy-going folk who for long had likewise allowed a few martial Romans to rule over them. The *castizo conquistador* was yet to be born. Like the Romans also, these new foreigners had occupied only the key centers, leaving the natives of the great plateau untouched upon their landscape. By its very nature it helped keep the alien at bay from the heart of things.

It was really the Visigoths, or Western Goths, already christianized in their own northlands if under the aegis of Arius, who did manage to implant a few of their northern features upon the land and its people. Like all the other previous conquerors, they exercised their power from the larger centers; but even here their Arian dilution of Christ's divinity evaporated before the Crucified's sharp image under the Castilian sunlight. What did take root of the more tangible Japhetic or "Aryan" genius was its feudal system of kingdoms, dukedoms, counties, and a litany of lesser badges of nobility which came to be symbolized by the solid hilltop castle.

Such Teutonic structures, as well as the churches resembling them in their turreted shapes, came to look in the native air like the wind-carved stone caps of the very bluffs on which they stand. These, and the many other crenelated citadels later built by the Moors, proclaim the one word, Castile, regally chaste and severe in her bright sun. Hence, the person who coined the phrase "there are no castles in Spain" was thinking purely of the English castle-manor, or the French chateau, both of which usually lie nestled among watery moats and green swards surrounded by dense woods.

Along with their austere battlements, long become one with the sharp-edged landscape, the original gothic notions of kingdoms, dukedoms, and especially the one of knighthood, are all likewise scraped of whatever northern lichen they had as regards divine royal rights and the fiefs of strictest loyalty required of peasant and townsman—all this so reminiscent of the servile lowland economy of those much more ancient agricultural fields and commercial centers built along the Nile and the Euphrates.

Unlike the peasants and townsfolk and urban dwellers of the lush lowlands or dense woodlands elsewhere, the pastoral swain in his bare Palestinian-Castilian uplands, congenitally deeming himself a potential patriarch with the passage of time, or else a tribal sheikh by some stroke of luck, changes all that in his own world. It is simply because in his heart of hearts he knows that the kings and dukes with their crowns and coronets are no better than he.

Also along with those trappings of feudalism, the Visigoth naturally left some of his genes which ultimately filtered down from the castle heights to the arid pastureland roundabout. They betray themselves in blond complexions and blue eyes, especially in the northern provinces, but this is something not altogether novel when one recalls the much more ancient Celts whose blondness tended towards the reddish. It is by no accident that *rubio*, the Castilian term for blondness, actually reflects Gaelic ruddiness more than Teutonic white. The word appears often in descriptions left of the pioneer colonists of New Mexico, where even to this day blondish or reddish complexions do not necessarily mean any latter-day injection of North European blood.

As for the northern passion for constant activity and the grim struggle for attainment, the one which for a time had enabled them to become masters of the land, whatever remained of what is now called the northern work ethic was finally dissipated in the dry air and eternity-fixed pastoral outlook of the great Castilian plateau.

To sum up, all indigestible Aryan or Japhetic matter which could not be thoroughly absorbed into the *castizo* soul was sloughed off completely. This was not to be the case, however, with regard to the next and much more thorough penetration of Spain from Morocco, the one which furnished the occasion for what is called the great Spanish Crusade. It caused the fabled biblical land of Tarshish, as the true western Canaan that she was in spirit as well as in landscape, to begin hosting a family reunion of longtime distant relatives which lasted for almost eight hundred years.

The party had some very sad endings for the guests, as so many big parties do. The hostess herself, upon emerging from it as the full-fledged Spanish soul, and still drunk from the experience, is in part to blame.

3. Three Cousins of the Hesed

The gentlemanly, and now universally familiar, game of *ajedrez* which the Moors first brought along with them into Spain—its Semite-jewel name now broken down to "chess" in English—happily provides a succinct and colorful picture of Spain's lengthy Crusade against Islam on her very own soil. As old a serious game of wits as man can remember, it had been picked up in the lands of fabled Eden by the Muslims of Arabia when they conquered Persia. Once brought to Spain, however, it must have been so much a part of the long Moorish occupation that the earliest known treatises on its intricacies were written by the Moors and Jews of Granada.

The Christians evidently gave the pieces themselves their ultimate form in castles, kings and queens, bishops and knights, and their squiring pawns.

What is most apropos with regard to a Crusade which lasted from 711 to 1492 is the fact that the struggle was less a long and bitter war, as is commonly supposed, then a sporting kind of jousting back and forth between individual Christian kings and Muslim caliphs, or just as often between their respective warrior champions. In the brief or longer pauses between moves and checkmates, time was found for a mutual camaraderie between the contestants, something which one would never have expected in any encounter between such bitter foes as the Muslims and Christians were elsewhere.

The main explanation is to be found in landscape and in a blood it had tempered for ages.

For some time back, the great squarish Iberian peninsula had been eyed as a land of milk and honey by the children of Allah in their hot North African deserts, much as had the children of Yahweh-El in torrid Sinai looked upon Palestine as their fertile land of promise. Finally, in active consort with the Jews living among them, the Moors took advantage of the Straits of Gibraltar as their Jordan of crossing. Wave after wave of seasoned warriors, many with their families in tow, kept sweeping across the historic narrows.

The unprepared natives of the western Canaan, so much accustomed to being overrun by previous conquerors for centuries, were much too quickly driven back to the small kingdoms of the Pyrenees and the northern coastlands of Galicia and Biscay. The Castilian did fight bravely, but the budding *conquistador* had yet to mature and test its mettle; hence, those small northern provinces would have been conquered also, save for the timely aid of the militant Franco-Teutonic Charlemagne as immortalized in the *Chanson de Roland*.

As for the landscape's people in the game of chess about to start, it is seldom realized that only the ruling classes and higher clergy had escaped the Moorish inundation by retreating northward. The ordinary faithful and their Jewish neighbors in the main portion of the peninsula were swallowed up by the new Islamic caliphates which kept supplanting the several little kingdoms, dukedoms, and bishoprics. But what must have been a surprise to the vanquished, neither a general massacre nor a total enslavement, expected of those whom they called infidels, came to pass. Not only were Christians as well as Jews allowed to keep their lands and property, but their churches and synagogues were left untouched.

To be sure, it was a wise policy for holding on more easily to a large territory while it was being taken over piecemeal. The conquerors themselves, enchanted by a new holy land so Semitic in nature and yet so rich and beautiful in comparison with what they had left behind, found the policy most convenient for establishing their gardened palaces of leisure along with their minareted mosques and other centers of Islamic culture.

Still, the underlying cause had to be a common if distant Semitic ancestry, which these *moros* felt somehow, besides having their traditional ferocity lulled by a land which to the desert Muslim was an earthly picture of the Prophet's Paradise to come. And yet one cannot help but own that these Saracens of Mauretania must have been a most enlightened enclave within Islam. Back home they had been harboring the Jews of the dispersion, much as the Jews' brethren had for long found a genuine home in Spain. Now in their newly found Paradise they could not fail to see how the Children of the Nazarene and the much older People of the Book treasured the *hesed* of Abraham as much as they.

Or, as the Near East peoples still say when referring to those whom they hold dear, in particular in the relationship between a bridegroom and his bride, they had found their "cousins." And the desert-burnt sons of Ishmael saw that the daughters of Iberia and of Israel were fair.

Just as the delicate ivory chessmen moved back and forth within the gardened harems of the caliphs, or in the Hispanic or Jewish commoners' taverns of Toledo and Córdoba and Granada, their armed counterparts began playing upon the landscape to and fro, north and south, all the way across the checkered board of kingdom and caliphate from Portugal on the west to Cataluña and Valencia on the eastern Mediterranean shore.

In these progressive and regressive moves and checkmates most especially, but also in the intervening periods of tactical reflection and mutual diversion, there matured those twin *castizo* elements which make up the Spanish soul: *hidalguía* and *catolicismo*. In the first one we find the *caballero, hidalgo,* and *conquistador;* in the other, the cross-bearing *penitente;*

and in all of them that rugged realism and rigid idealism traveling side by side within each individual like Don Quijote and Sancho Panza.

4. Men-on-Horseback

Far back in my youthful days a fine lady of Santa Fe, who was native born but of Scotch-Irish descent, published a popular book about the old Villa which she entitled *Caballeros.* The title, she wrote, was inspired by the then-frequent sight of native old men on the plaza who daily greeted one another with the chivalric term *caballero.* Faded though they appeared in their weather-worn features and garb, with perhaps just as worn-out memories of long hard lives spent in the restricted humble environment of past generations, these old fellows followed some age-old instinct which had them regarding one another's persons as proper gentry. The gesture was inborn, not something imposed by etiquette.

To detail the centuries-long Spanish Crusade here, in order to see how the *caballero* and *hidalgo* came about, is hardly necessary and much less convenient. The average schoolboy in Spain knows the names and dates of the most famous battles along with the deeds and persons of the most noteworthy champions of the Cross against the Crescent. Chief among these, as the rest of the world knows, was El Cid, whose Moorish soubriquet is much better known than his Castilian names. While ever loyal to his faith and his monarch, El Cid Campeador was not averse to campaigning on his own, or even forming friendships and alliances when it suited him with his *al-cayd* counterparts on the other side. Furthermore, the chronicles and ballads about him are starkly realistic with nothing of the sweetly romantic which permeates the northern songs and tales of knighthood.

It is very much the same with the story of other courtly warriors in this amicable but most serious game of chess as cities and castles were won or lost, but always won back for good, the Castilian chess pieces ever so slowly but steadily pushing southward across the landscape's board. As the contest progressed in the Christians' favor, even the ordinary pawns strove to become knights themselves, since not everyone can wear a king's crown. The "pawn," of course, was a *peón*, or foot soldier, and it is ironic that the word should someday come to mean an economic slave. But in either case the individual is still a crownless king.

The Castilian shepherd on foot inwardly knew that he was just as noble as any of the king's courtiers or the king himself—just as Abraham as a desert sheikh so casually comported himself as a peer of the King of Salem without actually coveting his diadem. Becoming a man on horseback sufficed for the nonce. Riding high off the ground on a prancing Arabian stallion, or at least upon an equally regal minded, skittish ass from the same deserts of Araby, the potential patriarch and sheikh (or *al-cayd*) in him began fulfilling what his blood had known and felt all along for ages.

Perhaps it is no accident that he subconsciously chose the horse-riding designation of *caballero* instead of adapting the Gothic term *knecht*—as the English language did in "knight"—since this word originally meant a "peasant servant." For the pastoral Castilian was by nature what he liked to call an *hidalgo*, literally a son of some substance which had nothing to do with wealth or knowledge, but was a part of the upland pasturelands that made him. This innate status now had to be recognized externally with this word also as he began to ride along on horseback.

All this makes one all the more certain that Cervantes did not make fun of Don Quijote on his skinny Rocinante, and of Sancho Panza on his donkey, for just trying to become acknowledged *caballeros*. They were merely being themselves as true *castizos*. He had the bookish old fellow go completely mad simply because Don Quijote had taken literally to heart those silly and maudlin northern romances of knighthood, like *Amadis de Gaul*, which had nothing in common with the stark realism and straight idealism of his own landscape and heritage. Nor was his naming of the deluded man "Don Quijote" after his lantern jaw, and his squire Sancho "Panza" because of his paunchiness, so satiric after all; for many a noble name in Spain actually has the same startlingly realistic origins.

There was that herder who showed his king a river ford which the royal forces could handily pass over, and which he had marked with a cow's skull. As a reward for the victory over Islam which followed as a result, the cowman and his descendants received the name "Cabeza de Vaca" with a shield to match. Another fellow took the town of Guevara by pure stealth, and in consequence received the name and title of "Ladrón de Guevara."

A dead cow and the title "thief" are by no means romantic, but they are *castizo*. In years to come these and other similar names would emblazon the annals of future conquests all the way from the Canaries to a great New World. The two surnames just mentioned came as far as New Mexico, besides others of similar origin.

If I also add for good measure that other widespread New Mexican surname, Chaves or Chávez, vanity as such is neither here nor there. Its distinctive shield of five keys denoting the name's meaning was won in the twelfth century when two warrior brothers, Garcí and Ruí López, wrested a castle town of this name from the Moors—and the "Ruy López" strategy in chess happens to come to mind at the moment as a happy coincidence. This in turn prompts another item most illustrative of all that is being said.

It consists in a typical gesture, several years back, by the late Doña María Flora de Chaves, Duchess of Noblejas. Having read my books on Spanish Colonial New Mexico, she began a correspondence in which she kept addressing me as her *pariente,* her blood relative, convinced from the birthplace of my name-ancestor and other circumstances that I belonged to her noble branch of the family which can be traced to King Ferdinand the Saint, who first united the Kingdoms of León and Castile. At first I had replied in good humor that in a poor commoner like myself, after three centuries of admixture with mostly lowly folk, any such pedigree should have long since been dissipated. But she continued her correspondence and further surprised me when, finding herself in New York, she flew all the way to Santa Fe with her sister. They came to visit their "cousin" and see the land of New Mexico for themselves, and were delighted to find their native Castile in the landscape; as for our mutual blood kinship, it must remain a nice thought at best.

Yet, what English, German, French, or any other titled folk of Europe would have done the same? As a romantic bit of idle curiosity perhaps, and if the American subject happened to be wealthy or else prominent in national or world affairs. In this case it was simply the Spanish soul's conviction that no bumpkin with Castilian blood is really a commoner, and that all Castilian titled gentry share the same pastoral origin with him. Even if the noble family of Dulcinea del Toboso did not exist, as Vivaldo implied, Don Quijote had to answer, "Strange that you never heard of it before."

*   *   *

The evolution of the Castilian man-on-horseback, specifically as a full-fledged *conquistador,* even if in times to come his descendants should ride herd over sheep and cattle only, was intimately allied with the service and furtherance of the Cross throughout the Moorish Crusade—and afterward with regard to the heathen in a new world yet to be discovered, as we shall see anon. But in the meantime, much more valuable contacts were going on. As the martial game of chess progressed, a close interchange of kindred cultures kept on apace, the Castilian profiting the most from his guests.

In this context the Moors brought on the western world's revival of the lost classics of Greece and Rome through Arabic texts, and these spurred further developments in knowledge (*al-gebra,* for example), along with a prolific literature in prose and poetry by Jewish and Christian teachers as well.

Among the Castilians, the idiom was not only softened further, as its now well-adapted clear Latin vocals took their turn in sanding off some rough Semitic edges; at the same time it was further enriched with the very type of *mashal* aphorisms which both Palestine and Arabia had long ago contributed to the Hebrew books of Wisdom. Cervantes did not invent all those pithy sayings that kept tumbling from the mouths of Sancho Panza and other rustic characters; he merely scooped them up in handfuls from the common language's mother lode.

Also, Moorish names for places and rivers, and hundreds of terms for familiar objects were remodeled, as was *ajedrez,* within the natural cadences of the Castilian language. Upon the landscape itself, the romanesque and gothic architecture of former conquerors, already become sharp and severe in ultimate harmony with landscape and people, now began integrating into itself that flat but gracious touch in bas-relief of arabesques, tapestries, and colorful tile-work which so distinctly beautified façades, towers, and interiors without violating their chastely dry sternness.

And as the vocal sounds of the ancient lands of Genesis floated all over the land in the cadences of Arabic, Hebrew, and a further semitized Castilian Romance, so did the just as ancient music with its accompanying dances. Whether as manifested today in the distinctively lively strains in minor key and the rhythmic throbs of the *paso doble,* or in the drawn-out tremulous lament of the *cante jondo,* its ancient melodic base was none other than that sad quaking cry of joy or sorrow from the heart's depths which accompanied the psalms of the Canaanites to Elyon and Baal, and of the Israelites to Yahweh-El, the very same tonalities which David played and sang before Saul and before the Ark, or which the Beloved strummed to his Shepherdess throughout the Song of Songs.

It lilted in the lullabies which Jesus heard his mother crooning in their little home in Nazareth, and shuddered in the Psalm "Eli, Eli" which he tried to chant while agonizing upon the cross. It had flowed from the parched throat of Muhammed to console him during his Hegira, and for centuries thereafter it fluttered down in the muezzin's call to prayer from the top of La Giralda, or else mingled with the strains of lutes among the fountains of the Alhambra. For that matter, it had been heard like the voice of the turtle all over the Castilian landscape ever since the first migrants from the Atlas Mountain region had come upon their land of promise.

All this has to be tempered, however, with another quality of this singing, to avoid falling into the romantic pit. Spaniards ably express it with the word *gangoso,* an onomatopoeic for what is definitely adenoidal. Along with the soft but clear sixteenth-century language of Castile, this nasal sound from the heart's deepest caverns would someday echo over a similar landscape a whole world farther away from Spain than Spain is from the lands of Genesis—in impassioned *seguidillas* at wedding fiestas in New Mexico's early pastoral settlements, or in heartrending Holy Week *alabanzas* in the mission churches recalling the Descent from the Cross and the Holy Sepulcher. And when these were becoming atrophied, the language as well as the music, after two centuries of grim isolation at the far edge of a new world's wilderness, a resurgence of the ancient lament in the *alabados* of stark penitential figures against their own Palestinian-Castilian landscape would keep on telling the bleak hills and mesas of New Mexico about the sorrows of their Nazarene.

13

Conquistador and Penitente

One morning in Sevilla exactly twenty years ago, while dressing in my little upper room of a modest but pretty *pensión* just off the Plaza de la Magdalena, I stepped over to the window and looked down the narrow patio's geranium-festooned well upon the *dueña* of the hostelry and two clergymen in their black cassocks. They were seated at a table having their continental breakfast. What had brought me to the window was a question she had put to the priests, and the answer one of them gave. She had asked what Protestants believed in, and he had said, "They don't approve of the Crucifix, and they don't believe in Mary as the Mother of God."

All she said was, "Válgame Dios, qué barbaridá!" And this closed the topic.

From snatches of their conversation reaching me as I finished dressing, I gathered that my fellow guests had attended an international Eucharistic Congress in Barcelona and were on their way back to their mission in South America. There, I suppose, they were well acquainted with Protestants. But I could not get over marveling with some amusement at the way the one padre had solved the simple lady's problem. Although his reply was negatively indirect, he had not lied to her, nor had he put down the separated brethren in any way. Perfectly aware of his countrywoman's limitations, he had passed up all theological niceties and simply stated what her Spanish soul could readily grasp.

Her reaction was just as final. After all, she must have thought, where else did true Christianity lie if not in the agonizing image of the Crucified Christ along with that august Lady whose virginal womb had provided the cross with its victim? Such a barbaric and un-Spanish omission by Protestantism was not worth considering further.

1. Castile Revisited

My own presence in Spain, by the way, was one of many rewards reaped from serving my own dear country. As an army chaplain in World War II, I had made beach landings with our infantry on Guam and the Philippines; recalled to active service during the Korean conflict, I convinced the topmost authorities of my being no longer fully capable, physically, of enduring once again the hardships peculiar to the Pacific's Far East, and they assigned me to our occupation troops in Germany instead. Here I hoarded my leave time in order to make a motor tour through Spain that summer.

Unlike the ordinary tourist, however, I skipped the pleasant storied coastlines, and even many a city and castle of prime historical interest which I regretted missing, solely because I needed all the time I had to scour the entire central Castilian plateau and see for myself the very landscape and several of its small villages where so many of my forebears had been born and reared.

Toledo in its very heart was one focal point, from which my car braved the hazards of primitive roads to find ancestral homes throughout the rolling plains and hills of La Mancha. But before starting out I prayed and reminisced within the parochial chapel of Toledo's primatial gothic cathedral where the ancient and queenly vestured statue of Nuestra Señora del Sagrario is enshrined; a tiny replica of it had played a very significant role in Santa Fe before and during the Pueblo Indian Revolt of 1680. Seated before the original statue, I also spoke to her of the Toledan families in 1598 who had brought her likeness in miniature as a reminder of home, of my earliest known ancestor among them who was the first to die when entering a new land a world away, of his Debborah-like daughter who had scared off enemy invaders at San Juan that first year, and of her husband and brothers who had stormed the heights of Ácoma.

This was not being romantic, as it may seem. Ruggedly realistic and at the same time rigidly idealistic, yes. For time and space, like a camera lens zooming in upon a scene, had shrunk together into this one pinpoint of existence, making Joshua's arrested sun no greater a miracle. Had this been Jerusalem, I would have done the same, telling the venerable stones the story of one particular ancestor and the Inquisition, and about certain earnest if misguided men back home who took Calvary and the Via Dolorosa much too literally.

Of course, the rural Castilian landscape I had already seen while driving between cities had everything to do with this my being so *castizo*. Its influence was all the more intense as I drove away from Toledo in search of hidden towns on La Mancha's plains with their semiarid hills and bluffs which had me back in the countryside of my birth. From here I meandered slowly westward into Extremadura, homeland of the great Conquistador Cortés, and of the not-so-great Pizarro and Alvarado, and of those many obscure self-styled lesser ones who had first settled my own land so similar to their birthplace.

Wherever I looked, my eyes recognized snatches of landscape that one can pick out on every side while driving all the way from Socorro up to Taos. To assure myself that this was no self-deception, I took photographs; when I showed these later to people back home, all invariably tried to place the scenes somewhere in the Rio Grande watershed of central and northern New Mexico. As for the villages visited, first in La Mancha and now in Extremadura, they naturally did not look like their New Mexican counterparts for their being whitewashed and roofed with red tile, but their interiors were the same along with the folk who dwelt in them. To detail every such impression and many other historical associations would throw this section out of joint; but the two following adventures at Guadalupe and Valverde de Llerena have to be told.

From the city of Trujillo—Pizarro's hometown and site of El Marroquil, the ancestral *finca* of the Duchess of Noblejas—I found my way to the top of a mountain where stands the shrine of Nuestra Señora de Guadalupe. It is the oldest of its kind in Spain. Its name is derived from two Arabic words meaning "hidden river," referring to a small stream which, like so many in New Mexico, occasionally loses itself underneath its sandy bed. The great monastic pile itself, a breathtaking jewel of combined gothic, baroque, and *mudéjar*, is not visited as often now by Spaniards (and scarcely ever by outsiders) as are the shrines of El Pilar in Zaragoza and Monserrat in Cataluña. But as the first Lady of Spain in her day, the Guadalupe Virgin still wears on festive occasions those precious mantles embroidered with the first gold and pearls which Cortés had sent as personal love tokens from the Indies.

No less had she been the beloved Queen of my own forbears who had nothing else but nostalgic thoughts to send back to her from their poor New Mexico, their miserable kingdom. This is precisely why I came seeking her isolated throne in their stead after more than three centuries, as I told the friars in charge. They were amused when I half-playfully embraced the little image in her *camarín,* calling her "sweetheart" when I kissed the cheeks of age-blackened stone, and one of the older padres put his hand on my shoulder and said, "Now, that is what I call *castizo.*" When I told him and the other kindly men about the image and cult of New Mexico's La Conquistadora in Santa Fe, how she had replaced the Extremaduran Guadalupe from the start by taking part in all the vicissitudes of my people, they were very much impressed because it was most *castizo* also.

* * *

I finally tore myself away to drive all the way south to Sevilla as the next focal point for my tour of discovery. The great city was the birthplace of only one Andalusian Montoya forefather in the Oñate colony, but the banks of the Quadalquivir, in no way resembling our "big river" for having so much water, had for weeks and months harbored many another ancestral individual or a whole family from north of the Sierra Morena while they awaited their call to the port of embarkation.

On the day of that amusing incident at the *pensión,* after touring the clean-as-new gothic cathedral with its famous Altar of the Kings and the tomb of Columbus, I witnessed Sevilla's famous Corpus Christi procession. My one regret was that it was not Holy Week, so that I could have seen the city's more famous penitential processions. The next day found me backtracking northward over the Sierra Morena out of Andalucía onto the southern Extremaduran plateau and its several out-of-the-way villages whose names had kept ringing in my ears since the moment I first read them in the settler lists of my homeland.

And so the highest adventure by far began that afternoon when I rode into Valverde de Llerena. It was a hamlet not far from the isolated small city of Llerena which in the distant past had been a crossroads of commerce as well as the original headquarters of the equestrian Order of Santiago. My Chávez forefather boasted of this very fact when he signed up for the expedition into New Mexico in 1600. As soon as my modest American car came to a stop in Valverde's tiny plaza, some townspeople came out of shops and dwellings to inspect what must have looked to them like a millionaire's limousine.

When I gave them my name, and told them why I had come, several villagers began introducing themselves as my namesakes. It turned out that Valverde de Llerena, the birthplace of my name-ancestor by at least half a dozen lines, still had many families with the surname more than three centuries after Don Pedro Gómez Durán y Chávez had left home to seek his fortune across the ocean sea. But to the good folk crowding about me it could not have been more than a generation ago, the way they accepted me as a relative.

The village priest then joined our chatting group. On learning who I was, he reminded me that it was the feast day of San Antonio de Padua, the widely popular disciple of St. Francis who had been born in Portugal not too far west of Valverde. That morning there had been a mass and procession, he said, and if I would deign to do the honors, we could have another procession that very evening with myself as the honored celebrant. The others present seconded his proposal by acclamation, and after dark the entire village gathered again to conduct San Antonio by candlelight through the town.

In my flowing Spanish cape I must have seemed to them like some visiting prelate from the Indies; but I myself, while fully realizing where I was, felt no different from the many times I had presided over similar festive processions in different New Mexican towns. Back in the church, as the acolytes or *monecillos*—a word used only in Extremadura and New Mexico—were lighting the altar candles for the service of Benediction, the pastor announced to the faithful that I would speak "four words" to them, which is the Spanish equivalent for a sermon as short or as long as one cares to make it. Since by now I had already found out that these good people's Castilian was like my own, I felt no embarrassment or hesitation as I told them of all my *extremeño* forebears and of a new homeland they had found across the world so very much like their own birthplace. In fact, I had never been so eloquent in the tongue of my fathers.

All during this trip, that conversation with an old Spanish priest many more years before, while en route between Santa Fe and Santa Cruz de la Cañada, had come to me as I was gradually learning what he had meant by the word "castizo." Years later, on first coming upon the Essays of Miguel de Unamuno, I was well prepared to understand and appreciate his profound pictorial intuitions about the *anima hispanica* along with her *hidalguía* and *catolicismo* as seen marching hand in hand across the Castilian landscape.

2. España Católica

Current in Christian worship long before the gospels were written were the primitive liturgies of baptism and the eucharistic service. They were the orthodox confessions of faith before the new Scriptures of the Cross were finally put together, from these very rites and from those other varied traditions spun out from the threads of Old Testament allusions. In the liturgy of baptism, the catechumens and those in attendance recited what they regarded as a creed composed by the Twelve Apostles themselves, and which ended with "I believe in the Holy Spirit, the holy Catholic Church, the Communion of Saints," and so forth.

Here Greek *katholikos* was the key word with regard to a new faith which welcomed all the tribes of earth with open arms, and which Paul had characterized as the fulfillment of Abraham's *hesed*. In short, "Catholic," or thoroughly universal, was Christianity's earliest official designation for herself, the term "Christian" being a satiric pagan epithet originally.

"Catholic" has continued in official use to this day in the traditional churches of East and West, although the Eastern ones came to emphasize the word "Orthodox" following unfortunate schisms brought on by ethnic and political squabbles down the centuries. But in Spain, as the Islamic Crusade's game of chess progressed ever more and more in her favor, the venerable official title, all the while it was taking on the *castizo* shape and sound of the landscape, was likewise being absorbed into the Spanish soul's own sentiments of *hidalguía* and *conquista*.

As the kings of each small realm and their emerging *caballeros* kept on steadily replacing the crescent with the cross on Moorish castle and mosque, *conquistador* and *católico* blended together in a very peculiar partnership. A third ingredient, *penitencia*, would soon be coming to the surface.

By the time Ferdinand and Isabella had united all of the Iberian kingdoms and dukedoms into one Christian Hispanic nation in 1492, and were directing the conquest of the very last Moorish stronghold in Granada from an encampment which they named "Santa Fe" with pardonable arrogance, these monarchs themselves were already being designated as "the Catholic ones"—as if no other Christian king or emperor since Constantine had ever deserved bearing the name. On this occasion, too, as Isabella the Catholic, the same queen underwrote the discovery of a New World, and subsequently set the pace for its conquest for the Cross.

*   *   *

That the Cross covered the entire mainsail of Columbus' flagship, or that its name was "Santa María," was nothing unusual, of course. Hundreds of galleons were to ply the great ocean sea bearing the same emblem and the various Hispanic devotional titles of the Virgin Mary, such as "Concepción," "Asunción," "Santa María Montemayor," "Santa María de Hondiz," and many others of this kind. It was part of the general heritage of Eastern and Western Christianity ever since the first appearance on church walls and apses, following Constantine's amnesty, of the great mosaic and al fresco images of the Cross itself, then of Christ as universal Redeemer and of the Virgin and Child as the *Meter Theou,* and all with their coterie of worshipping saints. But these elements, as with others already treated, had undergone a particular development upon the Iberian landscape.

The earliest religious paintings in Spain are evident renderings of the old Byzantine *ikons,* but already a softer and chaster simplifying of lines and tones can be seen—and, curiously, very much resembling those on New Mexican *retablos* more than a millennium later, as if the untaught *santeros* of Chimayó, while copying from angular block-prints, had breathed back to life that same ancient limning and coloring through some atavistic miracle.

As to sculpture, there were those earliest romanesque and gothic churches built by the north European invaders, with their many stone statues which had served purely as ornament on chancel screens and exterior arched entrances. It is entirely possible that the conquering Moors, who were even more conscious than the Jews about the biblical prohibition of images, had done away with most of them, although time itself had to take its toll. Whatever happened in this regard, as the Castilians steadily took back their country from the Muslims and began erecting new churches and monasteries all over the peninsula, the people began unearthing some of these stone statues that had been lost for centuries. But now these old Nordic creations looked all the more drab and coldly unreal. Hence, images of the Virgin and Child, in particular, began to be dressed in rich fabrics by the folk of each area, also receiving crowns and scepters to have them resemble the queenly consorts of their conquering kings during the Crusade against Islam. Kingdoms and cities vied with one another in enshrining and lauding their particular celestial Queens as their symbols of triumphant liberation, and quaint (though unromantic) legends grew around the original discovery of each one.

Such were the origins of famed Virgins like those of Guadalupe in Extremadura, of the Sagrario in Toledo, of the Pillar at Zaragoza, and scores of others throughout the land. After all, since the *Theotokos* and *Meter Theou* of Byzantine iconology was the true Mother of the eternal kingly Redeemer as her Conciliar titles implied, and since she had been the victress over the serpent in Genesis and the dragon in Revelation as the Church Fathers had taught, why should she not also be the Lady Conqueror, *La Conquistadora*, of the great Spanish Crusade against Islam?

The main significance of this typical outlook is that, to the Castilian, the Virgin Mary was not the sweetly delicate Madonna of the Italians as romanticized by their greatest painters, nor the tenderly dear Notre Dame of the French from the melifluous hymns of St. Bernard of Clairvaux. Much less could she ever be the mushy "Blessed Mother" of English-speaking countries under the influence of an Irish complex called "momism." The Virgin of the Spanish soul and landscape was none other than that regal Esther of the lands of Genesis who, by means of her personal God-endowed grace, had successfully intervened for her very own blood cousins; and the candles lit in her honor were more like the lights of Purim. It is this same regard for the Virgin as a *castizo* Queen and Conquistadora that would thread social and martial events together for three hundred years in a New Mexico yet to be.

The Cross itself, of course, held the preeminence during the entire Crusade in Spain, as it had also done among the northern Europeans in their Crusades upon Palestinian soil. It floated on standards and penons, and emblazoned the breasts and shields of the warriors. It took fanciful heraldic shapes to distinguish the knightly Orders of Santiago, Alcántara, and Calatrava, as it had for those of Jerusalem, Malta, and the Knights Templar and Hospitaller elsewhere.

But for the fast-maturing Spanish soul this was not enough. If the glories of the Virgin Queen had come alive for her in those newly vestured old images, so much more must the Cross—not the one of Constantine but the *Vera Cruz* of his mother Helena—express its own reality through the lifelike figure of the Suffering Christ upon it. While it displayed the battle wounds which had won a great victory over death and sin, it should also recall its triumph on Spanish soil over the infidel.

The major religious and national feasts were those of the Cross. One recalled the Invention of the Cross, or its discovery by Helena, on the third day of May. The other was the Exaltation of the Cross, observed on the fourteenth of September; both were observed in all countries, but in Spain they were patronal feasts of the civil and military arm. The latter one commemorated another old Byzantine legend, which told how Helena's precious find had been stolen by a pagan Persian king and then was restored to Jerusalem in the year 629 by Heraclius, the Christian king of the East. In the following year, Heraclius was conquered by the Muslims.

Spain's own triumph over Islam had now righted the wrong, and memories of it would echo anew two hundred years later in the annals of the Reconquest of New Mexico and its Villa of Santa Fe.

In her climate of extremes with no sweet-gentle features, generalizing upon facts as seen sharp-edged upon her native landscape, the *anima hispanica* had at long last fully attained that rugged popular realism and dry rigid idealism which assured her land's and her people's preeminence as the one Catholic nation of the Cross. She now deemed herself the one and only Chosen Israel and keeper of the *hesed,* not by any romantic transference, but because her own Palestinian landscape and ancient Semitic feeling demanded it.

"La Santa Fe" was therefore the Castilian Faith primarily, and from here it was but a short step to the *auto de fe.*

3. End of the Wedding Feast

Immediately there looms up before one's eyes, with all the ugliness painted by the outside world, that awesome specter of the Spanish Inquisition. During their centuries-long Crusade, as the Spaniards had kept on recovering each of their kingdoms, Muslims and Jews had remained undisturbed in the same way that Jews and Christians had done previously when the Moors took over the land. After the fall of Granada, however, this venerable conviviality among the Cousins of the Hesed suddenly ended. The party was over. Many of these non-Christian cousins had held important positions in commerce and government—a Jew was even the chancellor of the exchequer at the time—and one can presume that envious resentment on the part of some Spaniards was somehow to blame.

But the all-pervading reason was that inbred notion of *catolicismo* now so intimately blended with that of *conquistador.* Fraught with her ages-old and more recently renewed Semite heritage upon her own Palestinian soil, and drunk with her Christian *hidalguismo* acquired during the past centuries of triumphant checkmates, Spain had become the latter-day Israel of Exodus in her own eyes. His Holiness in Rome might be Aaron, as if by generous concession, but his Spanish Majesty was Moses.

Just as the Chosen People in Scripture had ignored all ties of blood when they first expelled the Canaanites without any qualms whatsoever, the new Israel must now do likewise. The remaining Moors and Jews, no matter if by now they were as much natives of the land as any of the Spaniards themselves, had to accept Christian baptism or else leave their western Palestine forever. Many of them chose baptism and broke with their dearest traditions, but a goodly number did it with reservations. And who can blame them, when ties of homeland are strong whereas faith cannot be forced? One thinks of Shakespeare's Shylock mocking the Venetian *goyim* with undisguised sarcasm: "to smell pork, to eat of the habitation which your prophet the Nazarite conjured the devil into. . . ." Here the reference was to that gospel story where Jesus drove the evil spirits of the possessed into a herd of swine.

It was to ferret out these *moriscos* and *marranos* that the Inquisition reared its ugly head and mighty arm. This is how the anti-Spanish Black Legend of the northern lands would put it. True, there were long imprisonments, cruel tortures, and burnings at the stake. Yet these procedures were not confined to Spain or the Spaniards. The more gruesome ropes and racks of northern Europe, the damp and rat-infested dungeons, the more sluggish burnings, and finally the distinctively English beheadings followed by the grisly quartering and display of human parts in public places, were just as frequent and even more widespread in the northlands—and without benefit of a dry landscape and climate to do away with the blood and the stench.

Like the *corrida* of the bullring, a stake-burning on a Spanish plaza could even be colorfully dramatic, however inexcusable in itself, when compared with the more prosaic human slaughter in the foggy marketplaces of the northern countries. Moreover, the majority of Inquisition victims were fellow Spaniards who were often vaguely and wrongly suspected of *luteranismo,* which was a still more heinous crime. This was the general term used, with all apologies to Martin Luther, for the entire Protestant movement in what Spaniards considered the "less Catholic" countries north of the Pyrenees. The Castilian champion of the Faith over the infidel must now carry on the same war against the Aryan heretic who, in romanticizing the scriptural text, suppressed the image of the Crucified Nazarene and denied the Virgin her queenship.

The *anima hispanica,* now so much the more given to exaggerating the concrete symbols of faith as she saw them in her Crucified Suffering Servant of Isaiah and in her heavenly Esther, as against the text-bound new peoples of the Book, was now well set for further conquests in a newly discovered world across the great ocean sea.

*   *   *

Because of certain poignant associations with what later took place in New Mexico, the term *marrano,* as first applied to baptized Jews in Spain, here calls for a pensive aside in passing. It has a doubly Semite derivation: from Arabic *maharrana,* meaning "forbidden food" (pork, for one), and from Hebrew-Aramaic *maran-atha,* referring to someone who is under a curse. The word was used in connection with one ancestral captain in Santa Fe, Francisco Gómez by name, the husband of Ana Robledo who was a daughter of that Debborah who had scared away the Indian foe at San Juan. He was accused by his political enemies of being a *marrano* who practiced Judaism in secret, and there is a long Inquisition process telling the whole story.

Long having lost all memories of this episode, and also of the origin of the word itself, Hispanic New Mexicans have to this day used *marrano* almost exclusively for "hog" and the flesh thereof, as in *carne de marrano,* and in a reverent culinary sense only. They also employ the Latin-derived *puerco,* the more common term for "pork" in Spain and the rest of Latin America, not as a noun but always as an adjective for what is physically dirty, as several local muddy streams called "Rio Puerco" attest. Another word, *cochino,* of ancient Celtic derivation from the province of Galicia, is likewise used more often as an adjective for what is morally filthy.

But *marrano,* the forbidden food of many a remote cousin or even a forebear, whether Jewish or Muslim, has never meant physical or moral dirt. And it has continued as a blessing instead of a curse in *carne adobada* and other combinations of pork with the New World Canaan's incomparable manna called *chile.*

To conclude this aside, this "chile" as prepared in New Mexico is also *castizo.* Whether used red or green, it is enjoyed for its own flavor, not romanticized beyond the truth with tomato sauces and hotter spices like the *chili* of Mexico and Texas.

*   *   *

With all that has been said, the Inquisition still remains an ugly and unfortunate phase in Spanish history, for persecutor and victim alike. But it must be emphasized again that the Spanish soul did not execute or exile her Moorish and Jewish cousins because she hated them—or for the Jews being "Christ-killers" as other so-called Christian nations have done ever since —but because at the time her landscape and her basic blood made her deem herself God's exclusive Israelitic remnant, as it were.

Any latter-day Hispanic Jew-baiter or Arab-hater is one who has been infected with alien ideas, just as were the authors of those false old tales about Hispanic Jews secretly crucifying little Spanish boys; these canards were the spawn of certain Gallican-minded clerics who thought they could aggrandize Spain's *catolicismo* with such falsehoods, as they likewise tried to do by inventing spurious lives of native saints for every Spanish town and sainted bishops for every Spanish diocese.

Today the average Spaniard, especially the northerner who happens to be Gaelic ruddy or Visigothic fair, might protest that he has any Moorish or Jewish blood in his veins. But deep underneath, a tender feeling from a much older Semite kinship willy-nilly haunts him with its silent thrill. As a case in point, it is most significant that Francisco Franco, a modern El Cid to some and a fascist knave to others, might not have been able to start his successful counterrevolution without the aid of his devoted Moorish troops from North Africa. And few know that he actually saved more than sixty thousand north European Jews from slaughter at the hands of those neogothic Aryans, the Nazis, by granting them Spanish citizenship so that they could find safe passage through Spain's Palestinian landscape to freedom.

There is a strong element of the penitential in these gestures, but at the same time it does look as though blood is thicker, and landscape quicker, than occasional mad moments in human history.

4. Brothers of Light and of Blood

The external trappings of titled nobility and armed conquest could not keep a third *castizo* element entirely submerged for long. It came into full flower both at home and abroad as the discovery of a great new world was giving full play to the other two during the sixteenth century.

Santa Teresa de Ávila wrote that when her mentor, San Pedro de Alcántara, passed away, he appeared to her bathed in glory and saying: "Oh, blessed penitence which brought me this reward." Or words to this effect. And far across the ocean, when Captain Pedro de Alvarado lay dying and groaning from mortal battle wounds, an aide asked him what hurt him so much, and he answered, "My soul." In these extreme cases of two Castilian Pedros, one a holy Franciscan ascetic of Extremadura and the other a brave but rapacious Extremeño *conquistador* in the New World, the sixteenth-century Spanish soul was expressing through saint and sinner a third element, *penitencia,* which had come into prominence within the intense consciousness of her peculiar *catolicismo.*

Basically, it was that older universal notion of personal penitence which had spread throughout Europe in the Middle Ages when the material cross of Helena, emphasizing Christ's actual sufferings, came to overshadow the Cross Triumphant of the Easter light. Some medieval penitential features from the northern countries, like those of the heretical and orthodox Flagellanti, could not help spilling over the Pyrenees onto the Iberian peninsula, but with relatively minor effect at the time.

The Spaniards were too busy fashioning their own brand of Catholicity during their martial chess games with the Moors. The Cross had to win the contest first. But when the great Crusade was over, with Spain become one nation on her own particular landscape, and her soul arriving at full maturity in its distinctive climate, the innate personal devotion to the Cross of Suffering and everything it implied quickly came to the fore.

That same rugged realism and rigid idealism which impelled her to expel the Moors and Jews for not accepting their brand of *hesed,* as embodied in her image of the Nazarene, now began generalizing further upon the facts of Christ's Passion as they appeared in the gospels, seeing them sharp-edged as they appeared upon their own Palestinian landscape without reconstructing them. Besides, that new religious revolt of Luther and others in the northern countries which, in romanticizing those very same gospel texts, claimed that only an internal act of faith was necessary for salvation, and that all palpable good works and penances were in vain, made this preoccupation with corporal penitence all the more imperative. No less an incentive was furnished by the Italian Renaissance, in what was supposed to be the heart of Christendom, with its blatant return to the pagan ideas of pleasure once rampant in Greece and Rome before Constantine.

Instead of creating a general spirit of laxity in religion, as prosperous times had done everywhere among other peoples, Spain's triumph over Islam and her national unification—and soon the discovery of a New World which began pouring Aztec and Inca gold into the coffers of church and state—curiously worked in the opposite direction. Not that the Spaniards became saints all of a sudden. As in all human society, Cain still murdered Abel, and Judah occasionally went out to solicit Tamar at the crossroads—or upon her balcony in the approved style of Don Juan Tenorio. Achab now and then appropriated the poor man's vineyard (or more commonly his livestock), and there were Davids having troubles with a Uriah because of some irresistible Bathsheba.

But with the *castizo* sinner as much as with his saintly counterpart, guilt was not swept under the carpet of Christ's own sacrifice. Corporal penance, specifically and solely as a gesture of loving empathy with the Suffering Christ, was the all-healing antidote, the saint applying it toward God's mercy upon sinful mankind and toward his own eternal glory—as with San Pedro de Alcántara—and the sinner in reparation for his crimes. When death unexpectedly caught up with the latter, as in the case of Pedro de Alvarado, his soul was sore indeed.

This exaggerated penitential spirit began permeating the monasteries and nunneries which in many instances had become lax in their discipline, chiefly from too large a number of recruits who took the vows whether they had a true calling or not. For by now the *anima hispanica* had also created a sort of levitical *hidalguía* within the monastic sphere, placing the various religious garbs on the highest of pedestals in her militant theocratic system. Those youths who did not put on the breastplate and morion of the *conquistador* rushed to don the cowls and habits of white and black and gray and brown of the different monastic regiments of the Cross.

The laxity which resulted made the Spanish soul react in typical *castizo* fashion with a two-edged sword. On the one side, it was a dry and sharp sarcasm which the language has kept in so many *mashal* refrains connected with the word "friar," as in the one cited long before: *Entre criados, putas, y frailes. . . .* On the sword's other edge, it was a keen penitential effort at reform through the agency of such mystical giants as the Carmelites Santa Teresa de Ávila and San Juan de la Cruz, the Franciscans Cardinal Cisneros and San Pedro de Alcántara, besides many others of the Dominican Order and other Spain-born religious congregations of the period.

If greater emphasis is being laid here on the Franciscans, it is because of the peculiarly extreme penitential reforms that were initiated among them, and the equally significant role they subsequently played in the spiritual conquest of the New World. The first took place simply because the rugged and rigidly idealistic Spanish soul could not grasp the sweet Italian romanticism of St. Francis of Assisi; hence it is Spanish art which began depicting the merry poor man of God with the severest of faces and with a grim skull in his hand, a mistake from which the lovable saint has not fully recovered. His Lady Poverty, while not exactly transformed by her Spanish admirers into a forbidding hag, lost most of her poetic beauty in the strictly penitential rags with which they dressed her.

The most penitential of these Franciscans were the friars of San Gabriel in Extremadura, from whom San Pedro de Alcántara sprang, and who furnished the New World with her first group of missionaries now admiringly call "The Twelve Apostles of the Indies." From them also came the Franciscans of New Mexico some seventy years later.

All this had the strongest impact upon a naturally receptive layfolk, among grandees as much as among the common people, all of whom vied with one another in sharing the merits of such holy personages, both by assisting them in their penitential and missionary enterprises and by joining their "Third Order." As "Tertiaries" they observed frequent periods of fasting and abstinence, and it was not unusual for any one of them to be wearing a hairshirt underneath shiny silk or tattered wool during Lent. Aware of the bloody scourging that some of their saintliest heroes practiced in their cells, some followed their example in their own privacy, or else they observed a token disciplination over their clothing at fraternity meetings. But here it was a short step to public penitential processions in times of plague or serious drought, and to the formation of male groups who came to be openly classified as *penitentes.*

The Spanish soul, as we shall see still further, had conceived and carried to full term a third element inherent in her landscape and in her ancient heritage from the lands of Genesis.

*   *   *

Those many picturesque penitents disguised in full robes of different colors with tall pointed hoods, which the tourist goes to see in the famous

Holy Week processions of Sevilla, are but a remnant of the scores of flagellant societies which once covered the entire Iberian peninsula in the sixteenth century—and before public flagellation was proscribed by church and royal ordinances.

Similar but smaller groups may also be seen in other Spanish cities and towns, each individual avidly anxious to perform his private penance by bearing on his shoulders those weighty litters on which heavy images portray gospel events, particularly Christ's Passion and Death. Today, if some of these men practice bloody flagellation in secret, it is their own affair; but there is also evidence to show that, up until not too long ago, genuine "brothers of blood" could still be found in the isolated countryside.

Two classic examples in Spanish literature amply suffice to depict what went on in this regard. Cervantes provides one in *Don Quijote de la Mancha* at the start of the seventeenth century—exactly at the time New Mexico was first colonized. A more detailed one is given by Jesuit Padre Isla in the eighteenth century through his much more satiric work, *Fray Gerundio de Campazas*. Both are fictional instances, to be sure, but they furnish a much truer picture of the times than any pedantic thesis could.

One night, while traversing a desolate hilly countryside, Don Quijote and Sancho came upon a penitential procession for rain which the townspeople had arranged with the clergy and the local penitential fraternity. It consisted of *penitentes ensabanados* (flagellants robed and hooded in white as if with bedsheets). Among them were the armed officials of their *santa hermandad* (holy brotherhood), and priests of the village carrying lighted tapers while they chanted the rogation litanies for rain. Prominent on the shoulders of a quartet, there also rode a black-draped statue of the queenly Virgin in her veiled palanquin. In character, Don Quijote mistook the penitents for evil masked knights who were kidnapping some noble lady; rushing into the attack, he was knocked senseless to the ground by one of the men, while the rest prepared themselves for a formal defense —the flagellants waving their whips as they tore off their hoods, the officers with their crossbows at the ready, and the clergy wielding their hefty waxen tapers like ball players at bat. But this proved unnecessary, since the battered mad knight had to be carried away.

The incident told by Padre Isla about another class of penitents has many more details. Fray Gerundio, a silly young Carmelite friar given to the most outlandish metaphors and puns in his sermons, was invited to give a *plática de disciplinantes* (homily for flagellants) to a *Cofradía de la Cruz*

(Confraternity of the Cross) which had vowed to hold a procession for rain. For this occasion, Fray Gerundio concocted a hilarious sermon by mixing farfetched references to pagan mythology with ideas suggested by the words *rogativa* (liturgical spring prayer for rain), *cofradía, cruz, penitentes;* but especially *pelotillas* (scourges tipped with metal balls), *ramales* (whips made of strands of rope), and "the Penitentes of Light, who satisfy themselves with illuminating the Penitentes of Blood, so that these may burn and braise themselves with their whipping, either among the thickets of leafy boughs [pun on scourges, *ramales,* made of rope-strands] or among the bushes [pun on pains] from the metal-tipped scourges."

Isla's division of this pentitential brotherhood into brethren of light and of blood evidently refers directly to one particular organization which was founded in 1533 by a pious nobleman of Sevilla, Don Fadríque de Ribera. During a pilgrimage to Jerusalem, he had been much edified by the Christian natives and pilgrims from other lands who carried heavy crosses on Fridays along the Via Dolorosa, or legendary route of Christ's journey to Calvary. On his return he founded his own penitential society, calling it *La Hermandad de Nuestro Padre Jesús,* "The Brotherhood of our Father Jesus," in which the use of the word "Father" with Jesus is not quite consonant with traditional Christian dogma. It is as if the Trinity had been broken down to identify the Son with the Father—Yehoshuah with Yahweh!

Moreover, besides its Brothers of Light and of Blood, it had a third group called *Nazarenos,* "Nazarenes" with a Nazarite connotation because of their appearance and function. The first group, wearing their ordinary clothes and typical Castilian black capes, carried big lighted candles. The second, bare to the waist and with black bags over their heads, whipped their naked backs to blood. The third, with loose long hair and robed like the cross-bearing statues of Christ as the Nazarene, carried the heavy *maderos* or timber crosses.

At their head a *muñidor,* or beadle, went blaring a horn or else piping on a flute some eerie tune from the mournful *cante jondo.*

Here a most interesting and apposite connection can be found with Spain's most famous statue of Jesús Nazareno bearing his cross. It is "El Cristo del Gran Poder" in Sevilla, which has replicas in other Spanish cities, and was obviously so called for its purported "great power" in dispensing miracles. Just as the very title and organization of Don Fadríque's foundation now bring to mind the much later Penitentes of New Mexico with their identical name and functions, I myself recall the many times that individuals from Penitente circles used to request masses to be offered in thanksgiving to what they designated as "El Gran Poder." However, they had Almighty God's infinite Power in mind, having forgotten down the years that the term referred originally to that one particular image of the Nazarene in Sevilla.

From all that has been said from the start, it is so very evident that this is all a part of the stark Castilian landscape. As for its Palestinian heritage, neither is it difficult to hark back to the children of Canaan whipping or mutilating themselves in sincere mourning for their beloved hero-god Baal, and to the primitive Hebrews who had to be prevented from doing the same by repeated admonitions and threats from their leaders in the name of Yahweh. In the same way, to certain followers of Muhammed in times of stress and sorrow.

But it is most certainly not the vicious fanaticism displayed by the Aryan-Japhetic Flagellanti and other such groups in the rest of Medieval Europe who, in their blind way of protesting religious and moral laxity in high places, damned to hell all those who did not follow in their steps. The *anima hispanica,* profoundly moved by seeing her Semitic Jehoshuah flogged and killed upon her own Palestinian landscape, only wanted to show her Nazarene how much she loved him. It is perfectly expressed in that most beautiful of her poems, which ends:

> It is your love that moves me: if there were
> no heaven, I would love with love to spare;
> were there no hell, my love would still be there!

14

A New World Babel

One June day in the year 1524, twelve barefoot Franciscan friars in their ragged gray habits were being escorted by some soldiers and Indian guides from the port of Vera Cruz to the Aztec capital of Mexico. On the way thither, after having left the tropical lowlands far behind, they were met by none other than the great *conquistador,* Don Hernando Cortés. He was accompanied by his mounted staff and other captains at the head of their armed companies. With them also came scores of Aztec and Tlascaltec chieftains on foot, leading their own brightly feathered troops and a great motley mob of plebeian natives.

As soon as these two most dissimilar groups met, Cortés dismounted and knelt down on the hard ground to kiss the hands of each one of the twelve beggarly figures; his staff followed suit, and then as many of the other officers and men who could manage to do so. A cavernous hush fell over the Indian multitudes, and then a shout of astonishment left their thousands of throats like a whistling whirlwind.

For the past five years, ever since the fall of their mighty empire, these vanquished natives had witnessed the Spanish soul's qualities of *hidalguía* and *conquista* at their bravest and at their worst. Now, to their utmost surprise which sounded even joyful, they were suddenly meeting her third element of stark *penitencia* in a most dramatic fashion. They had just seen the godlike Cortés himself, who had brought down their divine emperor and most valiant princes to their knees, and who brooked no insubordination from the toughest of his own men, making the humblest obeisance to what he obviously deemed much higher than swords and shining armor, something ever so much nobler than the richest raiment and lordliest plumes.

Motolinia! This was the most frequent word piercing the air. It was the

Indians' expression for "poor" which in their minds had something to do with godliness. It was as though all this was a token from high heaven which somehow would begin making up for all their gold stolen away, for all the humiliations and sufferings undergone since the hapless day when the Castilians first came into their land.

1. Search for a New Tarshish

The vast and totally unexplored newfoundland now coming into Spain's grasp was proving more fantastic than she herself had once been as the mythical land of Tarshish to the ancients of the Near and Middle East, or as the Pillars of Hercules to the Greeks of old. But what had led in part to its discovery was itself a myth in many ways more incredible and of much more recent vintage.

Some romantic raconteur in medieval Gaul or Gaulish Portugal had dreamed up a fantasy about a goodly number of Portuguese Christians who, led by seven bishops, had fled westward in ships in the year 714 to escape the Muslim invasion of the Iberian peninsula. Out on the uncharted western ocean they had come upon a big enchanted island where seven great wealthy cities had been flourishing ever since. Many a voyager had tried to find this Utopian island, called Antillia, but only one of them had caught a glimpse of it, in the year 1414, before it vanished like the Holy Grail into its misty enchantment. So the legend ran.

The cabalistic number seven stands out plainly in the number of bishops and cities, and also within the two dates, as having been suggested by the scriptural Sabbath and the Church's seven sacraments; yet these and other exotic elements did not deter Flemish, German, and Italian cartographers from placing Antillia as a proven fact upon their maps of a circular flat world. Being that Marco Polo and others had long ago found the really fabulous realms of Cathay and India in the extreme Far East, and that now some men in learned circles had suspected that the earth might be round like an egg, Antillia then appeared on at least one later map—one which Columbus studied—as a western stepping-stone between Europe and far eastern Asia.

As luck would have it, Columbus and his mariners came upon an inhabited island at the moment they might have turned back to avoid being swept over the cataract of a world which was not spherical after all. The map-makers in Europe naturally had to designate it and other nearby islands as the "Antilles." However, these islands' dark-visaged and wholly uncivilized natives could not by any stretch of the imagination be descended from those Caucasoid Christians who had fled the Moors so long ago. And so Columbus and his men, convinced that they had bypassed Antillia and reached some outlying island off the coast of India, misnamed these strange new peoples "Indians" for all time.

Still, while Antillia's name was left behind, attached to these western "Indies," her inner mythical core of Seven Cities did not remain static, but went on ahead for almost another century as an ever-receding mirage beckoning Spanish adventurer and missionary alike. It was in the mind during the subsequent conquest by Cortés of the fabulous Aztec city of Mexico, and spurred further voyages and land trips of exploration northward, by himself and by others, which ultimately led to the naming, then the discovery, and finally the settlement of a "new Mexico" out on the upper edge of this as yet terra incognita.

Despite their rugged realism, or perhaps as a temporary measure of relief from it, the Castilians had fallen into the same spell which addled poor Don Quijote's brain from taking Gallican romances much too seriously. That realism had to reassert itself. Now, five years after his glorious conquest of Mexico, the cruelties perpetrated upon the native Indians gravely hurt the soul of Don Hernando Cortés. Fully aware that this bad taste unfortunately left by Castilian arms and bravado would not be washed away under the pompous Spanish hierarchy, he strongly advised his monarch to send him those poor and humble friars whom he had long admired in his native Extremadura. *Penitencia,* Castile's most solemn ingredient of her *catolicismo,* now so sadly missing here, would both complement and perfect the elements of *hidalguía* and *conquista* that he himself had brought along, and thereby draw these new peoples to the bosom of the Cross. It was not so much a dramatic or diplomatic ruse which made the proud conqueror stage the welcome that he gave the twelve little Franciscans of San Gabriel, but the Spanish soul at her sincerest best.

*   *   *

For Fray Martín de Valencia and his eleven lowly companions, their arrival continued to be an unbelievably fantastic adventure. Both the landscape and the people were altogether different from what they had known in their own arid western Spain. While so vigorous and handsome in their own way, the natives looked like no European people they had known. Their attire made the contrast so much the greater. The sharp angular designs in red and green upon the white kilts of the warriors, and the same colors glinting from those unbelievably large plumes which made up the great circular headgear of the chieftains, had never been seen on the brightest rainbows of Castile's crystal sky.

The scenery was just as different. The lower vegetation was as sharply angular as the designs on the kilts or within the arc of the feathered headdresses. Some plants looked like snakes, or the carapaces of turtoises, and many of them bristled savagely with the sharpest of needles; others were bunches of thin Toledan blades bursting out from rocks that were as black as cinders from a cyclop's furnace; still larger ones were menacing giant broadswords that were edged with canine teeth.

And along the far horizon there appeared deep blue mountains, like the Sierra de Gata back home, yet also extremely angular and repetitious like the vegetation, as if just fashioned by the Creator when the world was new. Insofar as enchantment was concerned, the newcomers could well have reached Antillia, except for the people. This enchanted feeling reached its height when the great valley of Mexico and its city hove into view in the far distance. Amid emerald sweeps of planted fields there shone a vast lake, and from its middle rose tall pyramids from a low white line on the waters announcing fabulous Tenochtitlan. Not too long ago it had been the proud capital of the just as fabulous Moctezumas.

These simple men, like the *conquistador* himself and his more sophisticated captains, had nothing with which to compare the city's skyline. From verbal descriptions sent back to Europe, painters and engravers would soon be making the lake-city a Venice of Romanic domes and colonnades, or else a Gothic castle-walled town in Flanders. But, had the Hebrews of Exodus or the Jews of the Captivity been with these humble envoys of God, they would have recognized the visage of a templed capital of the Pharoahs along the Nile, or the hanging gardens of Babylon on the Euphrates—save that, on coming closer to the surrounding plantations, they would have noticed that the swards of growing maize were altogether different from that much older world's familiar fields of wheat and barley.

And after climbing up the towering steps of this new land's main *ziggurat*, they would have come upon the temple of Moloch.

2. Moloch and the Twelve Apostles

By the time these twelve apostolic-minded Franciscans arrived in Tenochtitlan, however, Moloch himself was no more. Shortly after his initial taking of the city, Cortés himself had overthrown and pulverized the giant horrendous image of Huitzilopochtli, the Aztec War God, on whose altar thousands of human beings had been cut open alive in sacrifice, and their palpitating hearts placed in homage at his feet. The public human sacrifices also were no more, but much that was connected with them would make Father Valencia and most of his companions begin yearning for the more civilized people of the Seven Cities of Antillia. All these ugly facts they soon learned from the soldiery and from an extraordinary brother of theirs who had preceded them the year before.

Fray Pedro de Gante, a Franciscan lay brother from Ghent in Flanders, had come to Mexico with two other Flemish friars, both of whom perished in a shipwreck shortly after the twelve Spanish ones arrived. A man of genteel antecedents, and well versed in the arts and sciences of his day, Brother Gante had been instructing the children of the Aztec nobility in Christian doctrine while he taught them the European arts of writing, painting, and music. At the same time he had been learning from his pupils his own "theology," as he told the twelve, meaning the Nahua language of the natives and what lay behind their thinking and their customs.

From him, and from what Cortés and his men had gathered from grim experience, Father Valencia and his eleven companions soon had a comprehensive picture of what had been and of what lay ahead of them. As we ourselves know more fully now from the subsequent findings of archaeology and history, this section of Middle America had reached an astoundingly high degree of civilization under the Toltecs, Mayas, and other similar nations, many centuries before its discovery by Europeans. What is most amazing, their engineering and architectural achievements, their use of hieroglyphic writing, and most especially their precise computations of time, all parallel those of Egypt and the Middle East to a most remarkable degree.

More significantly, these Middle American cultures were strictly based upon an agricultural economy, more so since their peoples completely lacked such major domestic animals as horses, donkeys, cattle and sheep. Just as in the fertile Nile and Euphrates countries ages before, their temple cities owed everything to a similar beehive or anthill bustle of peasant farming by the lower classes and subordinated tribes. And like those of Babylonia and Ugarit and Egypt, these great civilizations had died.

It was upon these foundations that the Aztecs had since built and further developed their own empire which finally fell to the Spaniards. According to their traditions, they had migrated in slow stages from a far land in the mysterious north. Some groups had tarried along the way in a region of seven caves—a detail which would soon begin reenforcing the Europeans' myth of Antillia's Seven Cities. And upon the great lake of Tenochtitlan, by whose shores a brown eagle was seen perched upon a cactus while devouring a snake, they had established their home which in time became their great golden capital.

It was also called *Mexitli*, and this name the first Spaniards selected as more easy to manage, rendering it into "Mexico" for posterity. Cortés had soon stripped it of its golden treasure but, for the waves of adventurers who came after him, "Mexico" became a symbol and synonym for riches and gold. Then a new myth was born from parent myths and man's desire. Since the Aztecs had come from the mysterious north, they must have brought along their gold from there. The seven caves they spoke of were either a lapse of ancestral memory or a clever deception, and so the mystic number clearly pointed to seven cities, and now seven cities full of gold.

Therefore, that northern land of so much mystery and promise had to be another, a new Mexico. And so the name of New Mexico was born. It would take a while before the land destined to receive it was discovered, and empty of any Seven Cities of gold at that. For in the meantime the task of building New Spain into a new civil and religious empire, on the one where Moctezuma and Moloch had just reigned, had to come first.

*   *   *

Just as the Indians were so thoroughly charmed by the extreme poverty and penitence of the "Twelve Apostles," the latter were completely taken at first by the penitential response among so many of their charges. Because these natives had been so strongly attached to the graven images of their idolatry, these fathers wisely refrained from setting up the customary images of saints now so common in Europe. For they could easily take them as substitutes for their gods.

But the Cross, the bare Cross of salvation, this was a safe symbol. Carved out of monoliths by the gifted Indians themselves, it was set up in public squares, and the Indians vied with their teachers in rendering it the profoundest homage. And when they saw Father Valencia and other friars scourging themselves in season, many of them brought their own disciplines and followed their example. For it must be noted here that some of the twelve were overly addicted to this practice.

Fray Pedro de Gante, in his phlegmatic and more practical Nordic nature, and in his romantic devotion to his own charges, must have shrugged his cowled shoulders in quiet toleration, as he continued his own calmer methods of doctrinal instruction and his classes of writing, music, and the graphic arts.

For it turned out, at least in one known case, that the Indians who had set up a great stone cross had also enclosed some of their household gods inside its pedestal. While the simple men of God venerated their beloved symbol of faith, their charges worshipped their own *lares penates* hidden underneath it. As for their being so much attracted to flagellation, the friars soon learned that they had been addicted to the strangest forms of self-torture in connection with the sacrifices of Huitzilopochtli and their scores of other major deities. The commonest form was that of slitting the earlobes, nostrils, lips, or the loose skin of other parts of the body including the penis, and then passing razor-edged slivers of reeds back and forth through the bleeding openings.

This was only a minor feature of their sanguinary worship, as they learned from Cortés and those of his men who had witnessed human sacrifices before the New World Moloch with their own eyes. After the living victim's heart was cut out and offered to the War God, the body was flung down the steep steps of the temple's pyramid for people waiting below to partake of it in a cannibalistic rite of communion. Sometimes the bodies of the more valiant foes captured in battle were skinned from head to foot, and warriors then danced wearing the still pliable human hides. Racks of picked skulls had lined the places of worship like stands of vigil candles in Christian churches.

The sacrificial priests themselves were the filthiest creatures imaginable, since they never washed away the blood encrusted all over their black gowns. Their long hair was just as filthy and unkempt. Curiously, one of the twelve compared it with the matted hair of the Penitente *nazarenos* back home in Spain.

Medieval Christian Europe had enjoyed her macabre Dance of Death as a reminder of Everyman's fate, but this necrophilism was beyond imagining. She had held in reverence, and unfortunately trafficked in, the long-dried relics of the saints, but this ghoulish preoccupation with skeletal death for its own sake was altogether the opposite of Spain's regard for death as the supreme moment of truth. Even the ancient Egyptians, in their solicitous embalming and entombing of the dead, had followed nobler motives in their hungry search for immortality.

In spite of the sincere love which the twelve had developed for these people as a whole, and the sufferings they underwent for them at the hands of the Spanish enemies of Cortés, Father Valencia and some of his friars began harking back to the myth of Antillia, where people "more capable" of grasping Hispanic Christianity might be found. Their hopes were abetted by the scuttlebutt of the soldiery, who now firmly believed that the original home of the Aztecs had been not one Mexitli but seven such cities of untold wealth in the hands of a more civilized people. For the friars it meant great populations of more capable folks on which to build a new Church of the Spirit.

Some of the Twelve Apostles of the Indies were still alive when, in 1539, Fray Marcos de Niza first saw the fabled seven cities of New Mexico from afar, and called them "Cíbola" because the wild Indians of the Sonoran desert said so. In the following year, Coronado found only villages of mud in Cíbola, and then crossed the great bison plains of North America in search of the golden cities in a nonexistent place called "Quivira," again on the word of some local Indians. Others looked for them in the Sonoran wilderness itself, now using the term "New Mexico" more and more. And from here, in 1581, those three little friars mentioned in the beginning picked it up to christen the land with it and with their blood.

*   *   *

In the meantime, the poor natives of Mexico and of all the surrounding continental section between two oceans went on suffering indignities from Spanish officialdom and the military after Cortés had lost favor at the Royal Court. In their misery they naturally went back to the traditions of their forebears, or sought some solace in the hidden shrines of their ancient gods. Many of them had indeed become the sincerest of Christians, thanks to the genuine charity of the Twelve and of Brother Gante, not to mention others of similar caliber who had joined them. There was also Fray Juan de Zumárraga, the first bishop of Mexico, who suffered the worst indignities because of his humble devotion to the most downtrodden of his Indians.

At this period the *anima hispanica* herself was most confused, and the good bishop bore all the consequences upon his aged shoulders. Not only was Spain's proud *catolicismo* being stained by the backsliding taking place among Indian converts, but so much the more by her *hidalguía* gone rampant under the inebriation of the *Conquista*. Bastard *mestizos* were all over the place, the sour fruit of armed invasions everywhere and in every age. Religiously as well as economically, they posed a graver problem than the poorest of the pure-blooded plebeian natives. Worst of all there were the avaricious newcomers pouring in from Spain—merchants and farmers and miners from the coastal provinces—whose sole aim was to pile up fortunes at the expense of the common run of Indians. In the face of all this injustice, the bishop won many a battle for them.

It is no wonder, then, that Fray Juan de Zumárraga became the focus of a beautiful legend which sprouted within the hearts of all the people concerned, to burst out into a bouquet of roses and a song of hope exactly a century after he was dead.

3. The Song of Guadalupe

Not far beyond the northern shore of the great lake on which Tenochtitlan had been founded there stood a hill called Tepeyac. It was reached from the city by means of a long causeway. From ancient times the Aztecs and other Indians had been coming here to worship Tonantzin, the mother of the gods. The pioneer Franciscan missionaries were sure that they still came in droves to visit their "mother of the gods" while the Christians were honoring the Virgin Mary as the "Mother of God" at a chapel built there under the advocacy of Spain's Lady of Guadalupe.

The story has to be told here in its entirety because without it one cannot begin to know the Mexican soul.

The first small chapel had been erected in 1556, or shortly before, following the arrival of Bishop Zumárraga's successor, the Dominican Fray Alonso de Montúfar. A *ganadero* (sheep or cattle owner or herder) claimed that he had been miraculously cured at the spot by Spain's Virgin of Guadalupe when she appeared to him. This furnished the excuse for building the chapel. Then a most attractive picture of the Virgin Mary, painted on a canvas of maguey fiber by an Indian named Marcos, one of Brother Gante's art pupils, was installed over the altar as its main ornament.

We do not know who the *ganadero* was, but he must have been from

Extremadura to recognize her patronal Virgin of Guadalupe in what he saw or imagined. And it is most certain that the original devotees were all Spaniards, particularly those of the higher classes which included the Viceroy himself and the titled members of his court. The titular feast being observed, moreover, was that of Mary's Nativity on the eighth of September, which covered all Marian feasts not specified by name in the Roman calendar. Archbishop Montúfar himself took the shrine under his wing, and there is also record at this time of a handsome income accruing from the many offerings left there.

No doubt, the uniqueness of the painting by Marcos was the chief attraction for the Castilians, most of whom were Extremeños. The concept, or visual theme of it, was a large lozenge shape formed by the Virgin's crowned figure within an opening among clouds. She was surrounded by the sun's rays while standing upon a silver crescent; the lower hems of her gown were upheld by a fetching little winged cherub. This tunic of the Lady was done in traditional pinkish red, brocaded like damask with outlines of leaves and flowers in gold. Her equally traditional blue mantle teemed with stars.

The entire artistic concept with all its details was undeniably Gothic, however, not Spanish or Indian. Marcos either got it from a block print in some prayerbook—most Spanish books were printed in Flanders—or more likely he copied it from a Flemish print which he had gotten from his old instructor, Fray Pedro de Gante. For it also closely resembled a Flemish carved statue in the monks' choir at the shrine of Our Lady of Guadalupe in Extremadura.

To be sure, the new painting did not represent that ancient romanic little statue whose discovery had inspired the building of the original Guadalupe shrine in Spain centuries before. Practically smothered in her Spanish Queen's bejeweled mantles, that image stood barely visible in her dark lofty niche atop the very high altar—the very statue which I myself hugged and kissed from her *camarín,* or royal chamber, which is directly behind her niche. But the Flemish wood-carving in the choir on the ground floor, what with its nearness to the beholder and all its bright coloring and gold leaf, had become more familiar to the public at large. This is the one which the Spaniards of Mexico now recognized in Marcos' painting. Nor did it matter that painter Marcos had added an original touch by surrounding the entire lozenge of figure and clouds with a garland of big roses.

Through each succeeding decade in that first century, occasional secular references are made to the existence of the shrine and to the Spaniards' recourse to the place as a font of miracles. From here, also, each new viceroy made his grand entrance into the city of Mexico over the long causeway. The earliest references, along with old Indian pictographs, specifically state that the Virgin of Guadalupe appeared in 1555 or 1556—that is, to the *ganadero* who was cured. No miraculous origin is ascribed to Marcos' painting.

During all this time, for obvious reasons, the missionaries of the different orders, especially the Franciscans, withheld their approval of this shrine of Tepeyac. In fact, on one occasion their own major superior, when the shrine and the painting were new in 1556, publicly rebuked the archbishop for making so much of it. For Father Bustamante and his brethren strongly felt that the Indians, while the Spaniards went there to honor the *Theotokos* of Christian devotion, would keep recurring in greater masses to worship *Tonantzin,* or mother of their pagan gods.

But there is a different account which was first published in the following century, concerning a miraculous origin of the painting itself in connection with good Fray Juan de Zumárraga. This particular legend cannot be lightly dismissed, because it helped weave the most diverse elements of the vast motley population of New Spain into one distinctive nation, the Mexican nation.

*   *   *

It was the year 1648. As said before, exactly one century had gone by since the death of Bishop Zumárraga. It was also, curiously enough, exactly half a century since the birth of my people at La Toma on the banks of the Rio Grande in a still-mysterious land far north of Mexico and Tepeyac.

The same vast Sinaitic wilderness still separated the little colony of New Mexico and its single tiny town of Santa Fe from the big populated centers of southern New Spain, which by now had attained the proportions of empire. Those of my pioneer forebears of 1598 and 1600 who were still alive, along with their adult sons and daughters and their children, had only a vague idea of that teeming world which had grown around such bustling cities as Vera Cruz, Mexico, Puebla, Guadalajara, and myriads of large towns between them.

All of this my people dismissed as *tierra afuera,* the world beyond. They were perfectly content with their simple Extremaduran pastoral and patriarchal life in their spacious Castilian landscape that was their very own, not the Old World estates of the feudal gentry or of a growing aristocracy in New Spain. Practically unbothered by officialdom and other such burdens of civilization, they could care less about the fortunes of that outer world to the south where the Crown's viceroy and his court held sway.

It was altogether different in southern New Spain. While constant commercial and cultural intercourse with Europe had built New Spain's cities and towns with their many palaces, churches, schools, and marts which rivaled those of Spain herself, it had also given the ever-growing common population a very distinctive character through a more specific kind of intercourse. For over a century now, Spaniards from every maritime province, and of every profession in the arts as well as commerce, had been arriving with every ship. Many brought their families along, but others—like those soldiers of Cortés who found the Aztec women not unlike the pretty *morenas* back home—took the daughters of the former Aztec chieftains to wife.

Among the much more numerous lower classes, there had been that production of bastard as well as legitimate *mestizos* who, through further intermarriage among themselves or with the Indians, and sometimes with Spaniards, now composed a large segment which was fast catching up with the Indian natives. There was some African admixture also, from slaves introduced in the previous century. This general *mestizo* class stood between the European Spaniard and the American-born Spaniard (Creole) on one side, and the various Indian nations on the other. Generally, the two kinds of Spaniards were of the educated and more affluent class. But, contrary to common belief, a great number of both Indians and *mestizos* had not only been bettering themselves economically but had reached high attainments in learning and all the other arts.

By now, as in other similar situations in human history, subtle tensions had been building up which were to end in revolution generations later. Even the Creoles felt themselves discriminated against, even if more subtly so, and all that was needed was a unifying factor.

Then it happened in 1648, when a Creole priest published a booklet in Spanish telling how the Virgin Mary had appeared on Tepeyac to a peasant Indian named Juan Diego in early December of 1531. The Virgin had ordered him to tell Bishop Zumárraga that she wanted a chapel built for her on Tepeyac. After the bishop requested a sign from her, she placed some roses in the folds of Juan Diego's mantle of maguey fiber, and when Juan

Diego released the flowers before the bishop, there on the mantle was the heaven-wrought painting of Our Lady of Guadalupe. Consequently the shrine's feast was now set for the twelfth of December, the day when the miracle took place. Then the shrine's chaplain, Lasso de la Vega, published what he claimed to be the original story in Nahuatl, the Aztec language.

This account is a poem in 170 uneven stanzas. Its simple charm, entirely different in form and flavor from the verbose Spanish versions in prose, shines forth even in literal English translation, as in these passages:

> Ten years after the city of Mexico was conquered,
> when the arrow, the shield that had been stilled,
> when it was already peaceful among the dwellers
>
> it came to pass that a humble vassal,
> a poor young man named Juan Diego,
> it is said he was a native of Cuauhtitlan. . . .

And when Juan Diego entered the bishop's house, clutching the mantle filled with roses by the Virgin's own hands, the prelate's menials tried to see what he carried. Here the poet must have been thinking of the garland of roses which Marcos had painted around the original figure:

> And when they saw they were various Castilian flowers
> and that not their season at this time,
> they marveled indeed greatly over them . . .
> and indeed three times they brought about
> an attempt to seize them,
> they could no longer see the flowers,
> only like paintings, or embroideries, or
> something sewn.

The composition is more like those doctrinal plays whereby the missionaries entertained and instructed both Spaniards and Indians on major feast days. And yet it is not Spanish *castizo* in nature, but sweetly romantic in the extreme—not so much the romanticism of the north European countries as the flowery speech and thought of the native peoples of the Americas.

This touching drama was immediately taken for history. Another myth was born. That it so happened is most understandable, for now the native majority of New Spain's inhabitants had found a rallying point sent directly from heaven. The Spanish Creoles discovered themselves represented in the name of Guadalupe, in the Castilian roses, and in kindly Bishop Zumárraga. In the language of the poem itself, in the native canvas, and especially in the lowly person of Juan Diego, the Christian Indians beheld their traditional Tonantzin reappearing to them in the lovely person of Mary. In the now sallow color of the Lady's face—and, by wishful projection, in the lineaments of its features—the *mestizos* began discerning the faces and complexions of their own daughters.

Nor was this unquestioning credulity due merely to an exaggerated Spanish Catholic belief in miracles, or to the basic idolatrous superstition of the Indians. Similar fantasies of delight have always clothed the universal yearning for the divine in man's spirit so much bound to earth, particularly in times of stress. And no better comparisons can be found than in those two most charming books of Judith and Esther in Hebraic lore.

In the first account, a beautiful but virtuous Jewish widow employs all her charms to put the besieging Assyrian foes to rout; in the second, a just as lovely Jewish girl in the harem of Persian King Xerxes turns the tables on Israel's foes through the use of her feminine graces. Whether one or the other book is not included in the Hebrew or some Christian canons, is neither here nor there; what counts is that these beautiful tales had served their purpose in bringing courage and comfort to so many good folks in trying periods of their history.

For the Mexican, too, the fact that the roses of Marcos had disappeared from the painting without leaving a trace by the seventeenth century, and that the Virgin's painted crown was no longer there by the nineteenth—or that the material of Juan Diego's mantle was found to be maguey fiber at one period and palm-weave at another—is all part of the miracle. That such a pious man as Bishop Zumárraga did not mention the greatest event of his life even in his last will and testament, or that the feast of Guadalupe was not celebrated on December twelfth until after 1648, is something which only an unbeliever *and* a traitor would dare to bring up.

The situation is no different, only much more recent, from those of other great religious poems since Genesis which have been taken word for word as literal truth through ages past.

4. The Eagle and Serpent

When I was a boy, I heard a man from the eastern states ask my father what difference there was between Spanish and Mexican. With his typical grin, my father said: "It's the difference between a horse and a jackass, but don't ask me which is which."

At the time I had come to know only three Mexican families; their respective heads were very intelligent fathers whom I admired because they spoke such elegant Spanish while they could make almost anything with their hands. The only Spaniard I had ever seen so far was our assistant pastor from Spain, a rather aloof fellow whom I immediately excluded from any comparison with beasts for his being officially a man of God.

Since my mother always insisted that we were Spanish and not Mexican, I compared those three Mexican fathers with the men of our people, and concluded that they were the horses and my own countrymen were the burros. Had I mentioned this marvel of juvenile logic to my mother, she might have brought the old razor-strop to my legs this time. As for telling my father, I already felt that he didn't give a damn "which was which," so long as they were nice fellows.

Across the street from us lived an English-named physician and his wife who liked me to play with their one little son, some two years younger than I. He had all kinds of expensive erector sets with which I enjoyed making odd objects for the tot's delight. While he was busy entertaining himself with my creations, I took advantage of his father's bookshelves loaded with encyclopedias, scores of issues of the National Geographic magazine, and many illustrated medical tomes. Anyway, despite anyone's natural curiosity about male and female anatomy, it was the photographs in the other books of landscapes, structures, and peoples in all parts of the world which fascinated me the most.

I now clearly recall, through a chain of hindsights going far back, that even at that early age I had begun to notice how much the scenery of Palestine and Spain resembled the one of my own homeland. The shapes and the clay hues of the poor folks' dwellings made me think of ours in New Mexico. In the faces of the countryfolk I discerned the features of local people whom I knew, including some of my own relatives who would not have been always flattered by it.

An equally strong fascination was with archaeology, in my trying to imagine how people of ages long dead had lived among those mammoth piles of prehistoric Asia and America as depicted in the National Geographic. When comparing the ruins left by the Babylonians and Egyptians with similar ones left by the Mayas and the Aztecs, I got a persistent feeling of *heaviness* with regard to the latter. The temples and tombs along the Nile were by no means graceful Greek Parthenons, but they seemed light alongside the ground-pressing tonnage of those in Yucatan and Mexico; the carved friezes of Assyrian and Babylonian kings on the hunt, while massive and stiff, seemed airy when compared with those ponderous angular frets of giant serpents weighting down a Mexican landscape which itself seemed oppressive to me with its tropical vegetation.

As time went on, it all helped to explain, at least to me, why the beautiful colonial churches all over Mexico, whether built along the lines of simple Spanish Baroque, or in the rambling confusions of Chirruguera, likewise have a heavy air about their general mass and sculptural details. Even the long rows of the ordinary people's low dwellings, while conventionally Mediterranean, have a disproportionate distance between grilled windows and the roof-line above which gives them the look of jails.

*   *   *

Here was the *anima hispanica,* no doubt, but vastly if subtly transformed. Even the dear Virgin of Guadalupe herself betrayed the heavy hand of Marcos in the flat delineation of the entire portrait, in the gold Flemish traceries of brocade that ignored the folds of the Lady's tunic, in the angular forms of the blue mantle's hems defying reality, and in the stiff sunrays echoing the ponderous Aztec calendar stone. Even the tiny cherub beneath, cut short under the armpits because Marcos mistook European perspective, also had wings tinted with the red and green of the Aztecs. These inspired the colors of the Mexican flag when Padre Hidalgo gave out the first cry of liberty in 1810, when he also placed the Mexican image of Guadalupe on its middle white center-field. It was an abortive revolt against Spanish royal domination, but by that time the so-called Mexican *raza* had been kneaded from Creole, Mestizo, and Indian cornflour, and baked to a good crisp in the hearth of Guadalupe, to insure the necessary vigor for future attempts. When independence did finally come in 1821, the sacred image had been replaced with the eagle and serpent of Mexitli's legendary founding.

In the hearts of the population, however, the sacred image of their Guadalupe blossomed more than ever as the darling symbol of nationality as well as religious devotion. In consort with the new democratic ideal it wrote into the first constitution a most significant statute which has been observed ever since in spite of subsequent revolutions with their own sets of laws. That statute in the 1822 Plan of Iguala prescribed that, in future, none of the people would be classified, whether in daily speech or in any civil and church documents, according to racial origin or admixture. Henceforth, all would be "Mexican citizens" pure and simple. The Enlightenment might have put down the law on paper, but the Lady of Guadalupe had been engraving it for generations upon the fleshly tablets of the people's hearts.

Then, one might ask, how much of the *anima hispanica* remains in Mexico? Very much of it: in the language, in the religion, in certain social customs; also, within the music and all the other arts in which the average Mexican is so proficient, not to mention the faces of the more Caucasoid of the inhabitants. But in all of them one cannot help but feel that same heaviness which can be discerned in the land's pre-Columbian and colonial architecture—and still most evident in modern structures expressing the native spirit. It is there in the Castilian language which, along with long-adapted Indian terms, is spoken with a slow precision and certain pleasing tonal inflections which nonetheless echo a weighty sadness. The existence of universities and schools from the beginning also insure, outside of regional words and expressions, a correct and up-to-date use of the language. The words indeed are the soul of Iberia, but the voice is the lament of Moctezuma.

The religion is Spain's own realistic vision of the Crucified with a total love for the Virgin in other roles than the dominant one of Guadalupe. It all includes Spain's penitential devotion to her Nazarene, which became so intense since the arrival of the twelve Franciscan apostles that public processions of blood were even too much for the Spanish colonial authorities. Despite strong attempts at suppression ever since colonial times, pockets of Penitente brotherhoods persist in many out-of-the-way places; Mexican persons who know have told me about actual nailed crucifixions among them. And one can see the stark casual penitence of Castile turned heavily Aztec in the earnest men and women grinding the paving stones with their knees as they slowly pace their way across street and plaza to a favorite shrine, particularly the one at Tepeyac.

The Mexican is especially fond of the days commemorating the dead, not so much in confronting the moment of universal truth as with the Spaniard, or like the north European of any faith romantically envisioning the departed in better pastures, but eerily recalling that dark communion at the base of the sacrificial pyramid, as when adults and children casually eat skulls and skeletons confected from chocolate and sugar at the graves of their departed ones.

One could go on detailing similar impressions in every phase of the national life, and most especially in the very faces of a most diverse people which has produced some of the handsomest swains and most seductively beautiful women in the world, as even our own country's motion pictures have borne witness to ever since they started. But even these faces convey a heavy sadness, especially when in repose.

All in all, one can see what has been said in the familiar costume of the *charro,* or Mexican dandy. The cut of trousers and jacket with their silver adornments is stiff and sombre; the massive sombrero alone further emphasizes the "heavy" Mexican soul. While still Hispanic in many essentials, its wearer is no longer *castizo.* He is himself, ethnically and nationally. Going back to my father's quip, we might ponder the difference between Don Quijote's severe nag along Sancho Panza's skittish donkey —and Pancho Villa's heavy-saddled bronco accompanied by Cantínflas' forlorn burro.

15

The Lost Tribe

Passing reference was made at the close of Part One to Jeremiah 35, in which this prophet excitedly praised a small Hebrew clan of Rechabites for having kept the primitive shepherd life of the Jews' early ancestors on their pastoral uplands—"not building houses to live in, owning neither vineyard nor field to sow, living in tents." This was his poetic way of saying that urban living and drinking, together with the earthbound occupations of agriculture, somehow stifled the voice of Yahweh and the *hesed* of his servant Abraham.

For by this time the Jews in general had committed themselves to urban dwelling and commerce, along with whatever vineyards and wheat-fields their arid land allowed. Stockraising was no longer Israel's one way of life. As an open crossroads of culture and trade between the great commercial kingdoms of the pagans, Palestine in her own royal economy had joined the inexorable stream of what is called human progress. Because the Rechabites did not, they disappeared from the scene as an entity. They became a "lost tribe."

It can readily be seen why a parallel was drawn with those pastoral families of the Oñate colony which chose to stay alone in New Mexico when the Colonizer himself and all his professional adventurers went back to New Spain. Not having found any rich cities or gold deposits, nor any quick sea or land access to the trade centers of India and Cathay, the fortune hunters saw no reason for staying in the land. But for these traditional raisers of livestock from the high Castilian plateau, these wide unclaimed spaces so much resembling their own places of origin were indeed the Promised Land.

They would build houses according to their rustic tradition out of the native soil, yet not in big urban clusters but spread far apart among their pasturelands. Since there were no artisans among them, and the Indian pueblos had gotten along marvelously well with flat roofs and earth colors which were one with the mesas and the plains, there was no need to bother with tiled gables and whitewashed walls. They would plant little gardens and orchards near their homes, but only as a supplement to the staples derived from their flocks and herds.

For this was the only way of life that they knew and loved, and it was what the land called for. They did not care if they were completely isolated from the mainstream of Hispanic civilization in Spain across the sea; they had found their own Spain. As for whatever contact should come with New Spain beyond the great Sinaitic wilderness to the south, the least the better. In short, it was a blessing to live away from kings and viceroys and landed lords as independent patriarchs on their own upland landscape. At last Don Quijote had led Sancho Panza to his very own dukedom around the time that their fictional history was being written.

And, like the Rechabites of old, these people would become a lost tribe in the Hispanic family. Moreover, and sad to say, once settled in their new land all to themselves, they began losing that sense of biblical self-identification with all the scriptural allusions which are so vividly brought out in the expedition's itinerary and in Villagrá's poem. For their isolation was also religious; most of the people who lived away from the Villa of Santa Fe seldom heard a sermon from the padre residing at an often much too distant Indian mission.

But the one thing that they did preserve with their rustic *castizo* consciousness upon their newfound Palestinian-Castilian landscape was the feeling and flavor of Abraham's *hesed,* even if they had never heard the word.

1. The Times of Fray Alonso

The Christmas season of the year 1625 was a signal one for the little Villa of Santa Fe, now barely fifteen years old, and for the rest of the sparsely settled Kingdom of far-flung Indian pueblo missions and the small Spanish homesteads scattered between them. The mission supply caravan of every three years had just arrived from the city of Mexico twelve hundred miles away across the wilderness. It was a long train of two-wheeled carts bearing the King's bounty for the missionaries and their

Indian neophytes, and news from the outside world. It was also the occasion for the triennial turnover in civil and mission government.

This particular trip marked the arrival of Fray Alonso Benavides with a new Lord Governor. For us it means the arrival of a man who wrote the first comprehensive Memorial on the entire kingdom, one which unfortunately has been misread as were the epic stanzas of Villagrá. Father Benavides also brought along an attractive little statute of the Virgin which, as La Conquistadora, would come to reflect a chief feature of the *anima hispanica* in New Mexico down three centuries to our day.

*   *   *

As mentioned repeatedly, the Kingdom consisted of one tiny adobe capital surrounded by endless open country on which many Indian pueblos and a few Spanish homesteads were scattered all about. North of the capital the region was called Rio Arriba, meaning upstream, and its opposite Rio Abajo, two major designations still in common use today. Those permanent homesteads adjacent to the spacious pasturelands on either side of the great valley were called *estancias* in the first century, then *haciendas* in the next, although they were far less imposing than those luxurious establishments in the rest of Spanish America which the words conjure up. As the herds and flocks kept increasing, some owners established smaller places for their herdsmen and families which were called *ranchos*, from the term then being used for military encampments during an expedition.

In the Villa of Santa Fe itself there lived the current Lord Governor and Captain-General with his staff and family in the adobe *casas reales*, or royal compound. At the *convento* or friary adjoining the parish church of Our Lady of the Assumption dwelt two or three friars. The rest of the adobe houses around the treeless *plaza de armas* were the residences of the more prominent stockmen who were obliged to live in the Villa during their tenures as major officials of the militia or as regents of the Kingdom.

Across the capital's pretty mountain stream, in a *barrio* or ward called Analco—"across the water," in their language—lived Mexican (Tlascaltec) Indians whom the first settlers had brought along as voluntary servants. They had their own chapel of San Miguel. They were occasionally joined by diverse *mestizos* and *mulatos* who arrived with the mission caravans as officers' manservants and then stayed after their masters returned home. Some of these resided as herdsmen in outlying *ranchos*, as for instance at Atlixco, "across the river" from present Albuquerque. These folk of Analco and similar castes did not return to New Mexico after the Pueblo Revolt of 1680.

And, of course, there were the widespread native Indian pueblos with their Franciscan missions, all divided into provinces according to their respective languages. In the Rio Arriba were the Tewa and North Tiwa, and directly south and southeast of Santa Fe the Towa of Pecos and the Tano of the Galisteo basin. In the Rio Abajo were the Keres along the river, and others further west at Ácoma, the south Tiwa down to Isleta, and the western Towa in the Jémez mountains. Southeast in the Salinas area lay the pueblos of Piro, Tompiro, and Humana, and much further to the west those of the Zuñi and the Hopi. All these more than forty pueblos formed a roughly uneven cross embracing a sweep of mountains, plains, and deserts larger than Palestine or Spain, or any other European country for that matter.

Here it is plain to see that the Kingdom of New Mexico actually consisted in the main of Indian pueblos with their mission establishments. The few Spaniards in Santa Fe and the rest at their outlying pastoral homesteads were a small minority. In fact, the pueblo missions, as the Kingdom's original reason for being, were the King's pets, not the Spanish settlers.

In this one respect the settlers did not care, so long as they were their own masters with free use of the boundless pasturelands. But for them this *castizo* satisfaction was not quite complete without those other elements of *hidalguía* and of *catolicismo*. The necessary civil setup of the Kingdom as part of all the Spanish realms, and in conjunction with the royally supported missions, helped to fulfill this double need. To start with, the heads of families had officially received the much too general and undefined status of *hidalgo* if they remained in the land; but it meant absolutely nothing here without any other countrymen of lower status with which to compare it.

Furthermore, each Lord Governor sent by the Viceroy every three years had little or no respect for their tenuous *hidalguía,* and this was one reason why the settlers resented most of them. For these surly Vivaldos from the castle gentry of the old country were telling the Quijotes of the new land that they had never heard of Dulcinea's noble family. To make up for this lack of stature, those leaders who had come with the Oñate colonial expedition began distinguishing themselves by reveling in the fact that they were the *conquistadores* of the country. When their stock and few crops were raided by the wild Indians, they were happy to emphasize the status through armed excursions against the "barbarians" or "infidels" of the plains while holding captaincies over Pueblo Indian auxiliary troops when fighting their common enemy. Other avenues were found by holding such civil offices as regents, high sheriffs, and *alcaldes* of the Kingdom.

As for their outward exercise of *catolicismo,* there was nothing better at hand toward this end than one's being designated an *encomendero* over one large or several small Indian pueblos. In the past century, the *encomienda* system farther south in New Spain had been an unfortunate experiment whereby Spaniards, to whom groups of Mexican and other such Indian villages had been "commended" for their economic betterment and religious indoctrination, had misused the office for their own advancement at the expense of the natives. But here in New Mexico it was different, except in very rare and quickly corrected instances, both because the Franciscans had a more direct influence with the Crown and because the local *encomenderos* were themselves unspoiled by those previous bad examples in New Spain.

They sincerely desired the conversion of the Indians as their Hispanic as well as their Christian duty, and worked toward this end. Whenever they failed, it was because of personal clashes with successive governors and some unsavory officials these brought along, or when they blindly took sides in controversies between them and certain missionaries. Thereby feeling their muscle of unfettered *hidalguía* in their own rustic dukedoms far away from kings and castles, they found that taking sides on each and every issue filled their need for political intrigue. In this one respect Hispanic *casticismo,* even under primitive circumstances such as these, had never had it so good until our modern American elective processes gave it more play.

Into this political and religious mélange, so far away at the fringes of empire that it seemed another world, came Fray Alonso Benavides with definite plans of his own. A native of the Canaries, he had entered the Order in the city of Mexico as a mature man, having served the Inquisition there as sheriff. Wiser in the ways of the world than his convent-reared brethren, he not only had a flair for organization but a fine expertise in politics along with a tendency for self-promotion within the system of a closely allied church and state. In the parlance of our day he was a promoter.

With little trouble he soon had the civil authorities cooperating in the mission enterprise, which he likewise began expanding. At his mere suggestion, both the government and the settlers quickly built a new permanent church in Santa Fe, and in it he enthroned that little statue of the Assumption which he had brought. It bears repeating to say that the settlers soon adopted this Esther-type figure as their own land's Lady of the Conquest, a natural continuation of that custom which had begun with the Lady of Guadalupe in Extremadura as the victress over the Moors, and which was carried on in the city of Mexico with the Lady of Remedies as a symbol of its conquest by Cortés.

Here it must be noted that among the several pueblo missions of New Mexico which were given titles of the Virgin Mary, not a one had been named after the Mexican Guadalupe. Not only was the Franciscan silence still in force regarding the legend of Juan Diego and his mantle, but the 1648 story of the roses was still to be propagated. New Mexico's heavenly Esther was still the Lady of Remedies on the royal banner, and she would soon be joined and surpassed by the Benavides statue of La Conquistadora.

As commissary of the Inquisition, Fray Alonso encountered no major problems for exercising this office, no heretics or latent Judaizers to prosecute, only rumors of piddling witchcraft among the Spaniards, and one single case of bigamy. Because this one concerns a direct ancestor of mine with some poignant overtones, it bears telling. Some years before, young Diego de Vera, a Canary Islander, had come to Santa Fe and married into the prominent Baca family. Alarmed by the mere presence of his country-man as Inquisitor, Vera sheepishly owned up to the fact that he had a wife back home in Tenerife. Not only was he separated from his new wife and their two little girls, but he was shipped back to the first one as his only punishment.

This small incident was buried for centuries in the acts of the Inquisition, but not the plans which Father Benavides had for the Kingdom. He could not help but envision the Kingdom as a full ecclesiastical entity, a bishopric no less, and with himself as the first bishop. To this end he composed a report after his return to New Spain in 1630. In this his Memorial he not only recorded the actual facts about places and peoples, but he elaborated them with exaggerated statistics along with some fantastic fables and asides. In other words he padded his report.

Of particular interest here are certain observations which Benavides made concerning penitential practices among the Spanish settlers. While he was visiting the Piro pueblos in the Salinas district, he wrote, an Indian sorcerer remarked to him that the Spaniards were fools because they practiced flagellation. Then Benavides proceeded to say that this medicine-

man "must have seen some Holy Week disciplinary procession in some
Christian [Spanish] settlement, and thus said: You Spaniards are so crazy
that all of you go scourging yourselves through the streets together shedding
blood. . . ."

From the way this incident is worded, and from the tenor of the
author's way of reporting, it is obvious that Benavides was transferring an
experience of his in some city or large town far south in New Spain. Or he
made up the story, basing it on general Spanish experience around the
valley of Mexico. The case is very much the same as that Holy Week scene
of flagellation in the desert which Villagrá inserted in his poem, with the
sole purpose of enhancing the piety of Oñate in the eyes of the Crown.
Benavides, too, wanted to impress his Majesty with the Hispanic piety of
the local Spanish population as fully deserving of an episcopal see.

For in those times, Indian missions alone did not call for such a high
distinction; yet, to show that the local Indian natives were also good
prospects for the true *penitencia* of the Spanish soul, he added two instances
of heathen asceticism. The Indian women, he wrote, in order to reduce their
plumpness and so please their men, went outside the village to perform acts
of fasting and scourging; when an Indian male was elected to office, his
fellows tied him to a stake and flogged him to test his endurance. These
sound more like stories that Benavides had heard about the Indians of the
plains than any customs among the Pueblos. At any rate, they were simply
aboriginal rites of purification, or tests of endurance, not acts of penitence in
the Christian sense of the word.

The friars themselves, living alone in the missions and away from all
community observances of asceticism, considered their isolation and perils
as sufficient penance. Benavides brings out this fact by emphasizing the
flagellation practiced by only one missionary, Fray Asencio Zárate, who
thereby won the respect of the notoriously fierce Indians of Picurís.

Much less could have the colonists done any public scourging when
one considers the unsettled conditions of the times. If it did happen on
some occasion during the earliest years, it was not because there was a
society of Penitentes among them. Without the year-round rituals as they
were being observed in the well-staffed churches of the populous towns in
faraway Spain and New Spain, they could not help but keep on losing the
customs associated with them as the years went by. This is why even private
token flagellation had to disappear, if in fact it was ever practiced at all.

On the secular side of their *casticismo*, the only trace left of any sense of *hidalguía* would be a dim memory of forebears having been the *conquistadores* of this very landscape, along with a tendency of calling one another *caballeros* in their mature years. Centuries would go by before they learned that, during the colony's first years, a genius named Cervantes had published a famous classic describing their rustic relatives back home as well as their own selves in the rustic characters of *Don Quijote.* And that, while the Castilian language further evolved in Spain and elsewhere in Spanish America, their children would someday be found still speaking the language that Cervantes used.

Coached by its archaisms, and instinctively seeing from amidst their herds and flocks the same panoramas that Abraham knew, the same clear skies through cloudless days and star-filled nights of their Palestinian-Castilian landscape, they continued feeling his *hesed* nonetheless. Superstition went with it, of course, as had happened with their primitive counterparts in other ages across the world.

2. Witchcraft and Rebellion

For many years now, whenever I have given a talk on any phase of New Mexico history, some person of non-Spanish or of north European descent has invariably stood up with raised hand and asked to be told about the Penitentes. The next most common question asked by the same type of person has been about witchcraft in New Mexico.

Penitentes and witches, blood and magic. To me, this strange deep preoccupation with the gory and the arcane is not Hispanic but definitely Nordic, what was long before commented upon as a northern Druidic fondness for stories about Frankensteins, vampires, poltergeists, and such things.

Now, it is true that spilled blood is most familiar to the Spanish soul, what with her proneness toward sanguinary penitential acts as we have seen, and as regards the *corrida de toros.* But her approach to both these features is different. Religious flagellation is an act of loving empathy with what once happened upon a cross, not any particular interest in the bleeding itself. While the Spaniard enjoys seeing both the pageantry of the bullring and the grace with which the *torero* dispatches a bull at the moment of truth, the Nordic thrills at the sight of blood being spilled and then goes home decrying the cruelty of it all.

It is also true that the Spanish soul has always meddled with witchcraft, not because it is a peculiar trait but because the phenomenon itself is universal; the manifestations of black and white magic are the oldest and most widespread liturgies among all peoples on every continent and island of the world. Even with all their monotheistic awareness of Yahweh, Abraham in Genesis and Moses in Exodus observed magical rites which were innocently passed on as phases of acceptable orthodox tradition; despite already fixed divine prohibitions, Saul had to consult the witch of Endor.

But only in the gloomy landscape of northern Europe has there been a dark gothic literature of long standing. In the Palestinian type of landscape, the magic is that much less spooky one of the Arabian Nights.

Here in New Mexico, evidences of witchcraft appear from the very beginning of colonization. While some of the roots are Spanish, going back to ancient Semitic, Hamitic, and even Gaelic sources, others are Indianic from the Aztec and Tlascaltec environs of southern New Spain and from the local Rio Grande pueblos, and not without touches of Africa introduced by the first slaves brought to New Spain. All the practices are so similar, for being universal, that it is impossible to keep them apart.

Some scattered incidents hinted at in the extant documents have to do mostly with love-philters; usually the alleged victims are Spaniards, while the perpetrators are folk like the Tlascaltec people mentioned as having come with the first settlers. Later on there are mixed Aztec and Mulato individuals, like those of Analco in Santa Fe, who are suspected or accused of such arcane practices. Even the friars are as much conscious of their dire effects as were their contemporary Puritan dominies in New England.

But it is the famous Pueblo Indian Revolt of 1680 in which Hispanic, Indian, and African dealings with sorcery come most dramatically to the fore. Here it is a most happy coincidence. Since the subject of witchcraft is of such abiding interest to the outsider, it can be brought in as we proceed with the fortunes of the Spanish people of New Mexico during the most trying period of their early history.

In August of 1680, the united pueblos at last managed to drive out the Spanish colonists, after having killed over a score of missionaries and several of the settlers in one single day.

*   *   *

The dreams that Fray Alonso Benavides had for the Kingdom, and for himself, never materialized. While his exaggerated statistics and made-up comments did nothing for the land, he somehow did obtain an appointment for himself as auxiliary bishop to the archbishop of Goa in India; but he perished at sea unconsecrated and unsung. The sufficient number of missionaries which he had projected, for the many schools which he had recorded as already existing, never came. In fact, the friars became fewer as the years went on, due to the fact that their province in the city of Mexico was spreading itself too thin with additional missions elsewhere. In the meantime, the few who were in New Mexico continued quarreling with the successive royal governors and their henchmen over the latter's maltreatment of the Indians.

The nub of contention was witchcraft, as most of the friars regarded it. In the Indians' ritual tapping of the mysterious Power in Nature through dances, fetishes, and incantations, most of the friars saw nothing but pure idolatry and black magic, as Christian missionaries have always done elsewhere before or since. Here they lumped all these practices under the term *catzinas,* after those supernal beings who had aided the people's ancestors when they emerged from their own Sheol underworld of Shipapu. Since the chants and other traditions were rehearsed inside the underground *estufas* (now called *kivas*), they regarded such secret chambers as the temples of the devil.

A very few friars did not, and the Spaniards later considered them as saints for having lived in good harmony with everyone. But the rest were always in trouble, not only with the medicine men whom they called *hechiceros* (warlocks), but with those Spanish civil officials, mostly outsiders, who would not honor their demands to destroy the *kivas* and put a stop to the *catzina* dances. For these officials, always being thwarted by the friars from abusing the Indians, got even by encouraging the Indians to disobey the friars.

It was a vicious circle and, as usual, the ordinary settlers were caught between the quarreling factions. Otherwise, they and the pueblo folk got on splendidly by respecting one another's life-patterns. Moreover, the religion of the Spaniards fitted in with their traditional beliefs. *Tata Dios* was a good "fatherly" personification of the Great Power, and the Virgin Mary of the *Yaya* or Earth-Mother who watched over them from the gates of their own Paradise of Shipapu; the helpful Catholic *santos* were so much like their own *catzinas,* and their venerated images served the same purpose as the fetishes which they dearly treasured.

The hidden tensions which kept ever growing in the pueblos existed among the village leaders, specifically the headmen of clans and curing societies, those who had the "know-how" of the Ancient Ones. It was most natural for them to resent the rivalry of the milder friars and their beneficent ministrations on the one hand, but much more so the successes of the more fanatical ones in having their *kivas* destroyed by the Spanish officials. Moreover, the church-state squabbles they saw among the Spaniards served to encourage them in their resolve to expel the intruders from their land, and several attempts at rebellion were made between the years 1610 and 1670.

But, simply because of language divisions and age-old feuds among the different groups of pueblos, and certain animosities within individual pueblos, all such attempts were frustrated by the Spanish authorities, and the poor instigators were shamefully hanged. Those captains of the colonial militia who took part in these suppressions naturally gloried in their feats of *conquista, hidalguía,* and *catolicismo,* which made them feel that they were deserving scions of ancestors who had won fame during the Moorish Crusade in Spain. This did not help matters at all.

Finally, unity of purpose did come to the pueblos, both as to tactics and motivation; but it had to come from outside their own circle of inexperienced leaders. Among the original Oñate colonists there came a strapping black mulatto as a manservant to one of the soldiers. He married one of the Tlascaltec female servants whom others had brought along, and from this union was born Domingo Naranjo. From his father, Domingo must have learned some of the arcane lore of African ancestors, from his mother the ancient one of Indian Tlascala, and from both parents all the injustices which the Europeans had wrought upon their respective peoples.

Hence Domingo Naranjo was a man of darkest anger. Physically he was a giant of a man, with the blackness of what must have been a strong paternal line, and with the big piercing yellow eyes of his triple admixture. Conversant in the tongue and the customs of the Spaniards, the gifted man also came to learn some of the language and lore of the different pueblos, to end up as an awe-inspiring shaman in the northernmost pueblo of Taos.

In the religion of all the divergent pueblos there was a commonly known supernal being called Pohe-yemo, the one who was in charge of the sun. To Naranjo he was much like the war god of the Aztecs and, for all we know, like some African deity of the same sort. From within the inner *kiva* of Taos, he gradually made it known to the medicine men of the entire

Kingdom that he was the earthly representative or alter ego of Pohe-yemo, who wanted the Christian religion destroyed and the paleface intruders killed or expelled. Wisely keeping himself hidden in this mysterious background of his own design, Naranjo formulated plans for an effective rebellion.

It so happened that an excitable friar at the Tewa pueblo of San Ildefonso felt so strongly that the Indians had bewitched him and some relatives of his, that he prevailed on the Spanish governor to initiate a pogrom against the medicine men of all the Tewa pueblos. As a result of their imprisonment and the execution of some, the Tewa leaders vowed complete revenge, and chief among them was one man named Popé, from the pueblo of San Juan. From his secret lair in Taos, Naranjo knew that Popé and other such angry leaders were all that he needed to carry out the will of Pohe-yemo.

*   *   *

In the meantime, the Spanish colonists were preoccupied in this same connection with a mysterious happening closer to their own religious beliefs and Hispanic traditions. There lived a little girl in Santa Fe, of the prominent Robledo-Romero clan, who had been crippled since childhood by some illness. Suddenly she found herself cured, as she herself told about her experience, by a little statue of Nuestra Señora del Sagrario which she had by her bed. It was a tiny replica of the famed Virgin of Toledo—the one which I purposely visited in that city's cathedral. Moreover, the girl said that the Virgin had prophesied that the Kingdom would soon be destroyed by the Indians, chiefly because the settlers themselves had often proven themselves irreverent towards the missionaries.

The impression made by the combined cure and prophecy was such that those colonists who had written complaints against the friars and filed them in the governor's office for the day the next supply caravan returned to the city of Mexico, promptly had them destroyed. That many of the colonial leaders had often vexed the friars for the past seventy odd years was due primarily to those constant quarrels between successive governors and the mission padres. As said before, the Indian *catzinas* and *kivas* were the bone of contention, and as a direct result of the alleged prophecy, the colonists prevailed on the new governor to proceed on an overall destruction of *kivas* and other shrines of the Ancient Ones, in the suppression of *catzina* ceremonials and the punishment of the "witches" who were behind them all. Ironically, it was a most effective means of making the prophecy come true, just what the Spaniards were trying to avoid. The anger of the Indians brought to such a high pitch played wonderfully into the hands of Black Naranjo, and most able Popé with other willing hands carried out his long-devised plot with dispatch.

On the tenth day of August, while the Spaniards were distracted in celebrating the feast of San Lorenzo, the first Spanish martyr—that famed Lawrence the Deacon telling his tormentors to turn him over on the gridiron—twenty-one Franciscans died at their respective missions along with any colonists found in the vicinity.

The Villa of Santa Fe itself underwent a terrible siege of two weeks. Its inhabitants and those of neighboring *estancias* and *ranchos,* corralled within the courtyards of the spacious *casas reales,* saw the church of Father Benavides set afire and the Indians dancing around its blaze. At the edge of its glare they also saw a black masked giant hanging an Indian who had once been a friend of the cured girl's Romero family. Evidently the giant was none other than Naranjo, but the Spanish folk were sure that it was Satan himself executing their rebel friend for betraying some sign of repentance.

Since the larger statue of La Conquistadora, the one brought by Benavides, had been taken from the church before the siege began, the women and the children and the aged now prayed before her for deliverance while all the men able to bear arms kept the enemy at bay. They were sure the prayers were answered when the defenders managed to put the Indian warriors to rout temporarily, and this allowed enough time for the Lord Governor and his people to flee three hundred miles southward to the newest mission of the Kingdom at Guadalupe del Paso.

Black Naranjo had not only won his private war against the hated European Christians by means of well-planned tactics, but through his impersonation of the mythical Pohe-yemo he had put to good use the arcane beliefs of the Pueblo Indians in conjunction with the Spaniards' deep credence in witches and devils. Incidentally, the tiny Toledo Virgin which had foretold the debacle was smashed by an Indian's stone mallet, and two years later a voluble friar, one who had not even experienced the revolt personally, took this shattered little image and its story to the valley of Mexico. There it was expertly restored and then enthroned in a church, to receive a great popular veneration which lasted almost down to our times as Nuestra Señora de la Macana, Our Lady of the Indian War-Club. This shows how much the Pueblo Revolt of 1680, what with the martyrdom of so many missionaries in one day, brought the isolated and almost forgotten land of New Mexico back into the consciousness of the motherland and her other more developed colonies in the New World.

But again, as with the Memorial of Father Benavides some fifty years before, it was an impact productive only of passing wonder and high oratory in Spain across the sea and in New Spain beyond the southern wilderness. Over there, for the nonce, the land of New Mexico was once more Holy Land; and its people, practically a lost tribe in the Castilian family, were for a brief space acceptable as scions of the Spanish soul's *hidalguía,* if only out of the noble house of Dulcinea del Toboso.

Then, practically forgotten once more as a very minute outpost of empire, they had to endure a twelve-year exile away from their natal landscape, until a brief new resurgence in interest flared up again back home in the Castilian landscape. It caused a new conquest and settlement to be tried under a now much celebrated Castilian gentleman from Madrid whose name was Don Diego de Vargas.

16

Return from Babylon

Some years ago, during the annual Fiesta of Santa Fe which commemorates the reconquest and resettlement of New Mexico by Don Diego de Vargas in 1693, I was confronted with a startling realization. Each year a young man is chosen to play the part of the great *Reconquistador*. Usually he presents a reasonable facsimile in a broad theatrical way; costumed in what passes for the panoply of the period, he and his staff of Castilian captains preside over all the religious and civil ceremonials of the capital's now famous celebration.

In this one year, while I was idly picking out faces that I knew from among the *castizo*-featured helmeted captains, I noticed that the face of this particular year's "Don Diego de Vargas" was not Hispanic at all. Immediately his Spanish plumed morion of gilded tin began to look more like an Aztec headdress with the stolid mask of Moctezuma or Cuauhtemoc framed beneath it. Or it also could have been the profile of some Great Plains chieftain under his feathered Sioux bonnet.

This in itself is not what startled me, since Amerindian genes interlock complicatedly through many a New Mexican family strain, and throughout all of Spanish America for that matter. Nor is it anything to be ashamed of. What dismayed me was the fact that the various Hispanic social groups of Santa Fe, the people who do the selecting for the pageant, could no longer distinguish between what is the Spanish look and what is pure Indian physiognomy. For in this instance the theatrical effect was ridiculous, like dressing a Hottentot to represent a Viking.

It made me realize the subtle changes brought about by time and circumstance, while at the same time the continuing influence of our Castilian landscape was still there, I knew, as validly *castizo* as ever. Amid the flowing banners of Spain's royal red and gold, the emotions deeply felt were those of La Toma when Oñate first took possession in 1598. Amid the pennants stiff with Crosses and Virgins, and most prominent of all the statue of La Conquistadora, there burned the same feelings which witnessed the repossession of the land by Vargas in 1692–93. *Conquista* and *catolicismo. Hidalguía* and *penitencia.*

Only the exterior vision was clouded in one or the other feature, and this happens when people have lost sight of their remote origins, not to mention the subsequent development of their life and culture upon a specific landscape. To me, the further cultivation of this book's theme became all the more urgent, before that tradition became further roiled by Mexican influences from south of the border—and before an overwhelming American technology of our times erased it completely along with the very landscape which had preserved and nurtured it until now.

1. By the Waters

The loss of the Kingdom in 1680 was much like the Babylonian Captivity, when the folk of Israel and Judah had to leave their upland shepherd landscape so painfully gained by their own forefathers. The main difference here was that these latter-day pastoral people, instead of being led away captives, were being forced out by the original inhabitants. But neither the escaped refugees of Santa Fe nor those of the downriver settlements who had fled ahead of them, believing that the people of the capital had perished, thought of any such comparisons. Yet their feelings must have been the same during their painful hegira southward to lower levels, as their beloved Palestinian-Castilian hills and plains receded behind their backs, and their Lebanons and Sierras Morenas finally sank below the northern curve of horizon. After crossing the Negeb desert of the perilous Jornada del Muerto, they came once more upon their lengthy muddy Jordan. While it served as a continuing tie with their lost home, it made the loss all the more poignant.

Now prominent along the river's green banks, bare Mount Robledo recalled the first death in the Oñate colony, especially to his granddaughter Ana Robledo, now eighty years old and long widowed of her Hebraic Gómez husband. For this Hannah grandmother of mine, as brave herself as her Debborah mother had been, this was the final straw after the siege of Santa Fe and the long Jornada, because she died a few miles further downstream; and thereafter they called her lonely grave "the place of Doña Ana," which comes down as the name of a town and county to this day.

Finally the caravans of oxcarts laden with the meagerest of salvaged household possessions, and with the sick and the aged and the smallest of the children, all flanked protectingly by the footsore adult men and women driving just as hoofsore livestock ahead of them, arrived at the outer gates of the lost Kingdom. Soon after fording this storied Paso del Norte they reached the southernmost mission of Guadalupe del Paso. But after a brief rest there, the Lord Governor had them proceed further downstream to the place of La Toma.

For his lordship had no intention of letting his subjects intermingle with the inhabitants of Guadalupe del Paso. They had to be kept intact for the regaining and resettlement of the Kingdom. The present settlement of La Toma was to be a Santa Fe in temporary exile, even though named San Lorenzo for the saint on whose feast so many friars had attained martyrdom; however, its chapel did carry over the Marian title of Santa Fe's parish church under the popular name of La Conquistadora.

Here also the Kingdom's standard was set up, the very one which had presided at the birth of its people at La Toma eighty-two years before. As we know, it carried the embroidered image of Nuestra Señora de los Remedios, patroness of the Spaniards in Mexico. Whether done consciously or not, this fact of keeping the northern people separate under their own banner symbolized a subtle distinction being made between the Kingdom's colonists and the new adherents of the Indianic Virgin of Tepeyac at the Guadalupe mission. Symbolically, they were still on the side of Vivaldo's Gachupines of Laredo, if only as scions of the house of Dulcinea del Toboso.

Along the same bank of the river, farming villages were founded for all the northern Piro Indians, and some of the Tiwa who were brought down the following year, and these three towns receive the name of their respective home pueblos: Socorro, Senecú, and Ysleta. For these New Mexican Indians, like the Spaniards, were supposed to return to the Kingdom some day soon. This did not happen, as things turned out twelve years later. Nor did the so-called Mexican Indians of Analco come back to Santa Fe. But ours is the story of the Hispanic folk who did.

What kept succeeding governors from retaking the Kingdom, some futile attempts having been made at the start, was the lack of sufficient weapons which the Crown failed to furnish, together with the extreme

poverty and low spirits of the people in a region little suited for
stockraising. Often they must have wept by the waters of Babylon during
those dozen years, while keeping themselves alive with what little farming
could be done along narrow lowland patches by the river. Giving up all
hopes of ever returning to their homeland, a good portion of the clans
forsook the colony and went south into New Spain in search of new if less
ideal country for grazing, and this was a further blow.

Then came Don Diego de Vargas. A scion of Madrid's noblest families,
he had gathered some most fanciful notions about the Kingdom of New
Mexico from the old epic verses of Captain Villagrá and from the elegiac
collection on Oñate's son published by Francisco Murcia de la Llana. Upon
reading the reports on the Indian Revolt of 1680 and the glorious
martyrdom of so many missionaries—not to mention the tiny miraculous
image of the Toledan Virgin now enshrined in a suburb of Mexico—he
already imagined himself not so much a new conquering Cortés as a pious
Ezra destined to restore the Symbol of Faith and a brave Chosen People to
their Promised Land. Due to his close connections with the Crown, he had
no trouble securing royal aid and recruiting a hundred choice "gentlemen
soldiers" throughout Spain. In the New World, the viceroy himself was
most willing to assemble for him two large groups of new colonists from the
valley of Mexico and the mining country around Zacatecas.

To Don Diego, it was like a rebirth of the medieval campaign of King
Fernando the Saint against the Moors of Sevilla when he entrusted his
successes to the Virgin. "Valme, Señora," my vaunted royal ancestor is
supposed to have said—"Lady, be my strength"—and thereafter a shrine was
built to his little statue of her as "Nuestra Señora del Valme." In the same
way the glories of *conquista, hidalguía,* and *catolicismo* would redound once
more upon the House of the most aristocratic Vargas. And if the reconquest
were to be accomplished with the least shedding of blood, as the sainted
king had done in his martial game of chess with the Moors, and more with a
grand show of Castilian bravado and piety as in the memorable sallies of El
Cid than the slaughter that had taken place in Mexico and Peru under
Cortés and Pizarro, so much the greater would be the triumph of the Cross
over the infidel.

All this, and what actually happened as related in the annals of the
reconquest of New Mexico, explain the subsequent preeminence of Don
Diego de Vargas in the memory of the local people, to the exclusion of all
other important events and personages before and afterwards. This recon-

quest and resettlement also ushered in a new century of marked changes in the blood patterns of many of the inhabitants even when their pastoral way of living, as preserved by their landscape, remained the same sixteenth-century rustic one of Extremadura and La Mancha.

2. A New Conquest, New People

Today the Vargas martial accounts, while altogether factual, read like the myth-colored conquest of Palestine when the sun stood still and the walls of Jericho came tumbling down. Here at least, the walls of Santa Fe and the Indian pueblos were still up, while Jericho was already a mound ruin in Joshua's time. In the fall of 1692, Don Diego led his well-ordered small army of old colonists and new recruits from Spain back to the lost Kingdom. At every rebellious pueblo he grandiosely parleyed with its chieftains like another Cid, pointing to the Cross borne high by a friar, and to the Lady of Remedies on the old banner raised aloft by the standard-bearer, as the symbols and assurances of everlasting brotherhood between Spaniard and native Indian. To the amazement of his men, the strategy worked like a miracle when pueblo after pueblo made willing obeisance to "both Majesties," as the Spaniards then referred to God and King.

No doubt, the visionary Governor and Captain-General did realize that the various pueblos had fallen apart among themselves, returning to ancient tribal animosities since that brief show of unity effected by the black representative of Pohe-yemo and his man Popé twelve years before. In this situation, any resistance by them would have proved futile and disastrous. Nevertheless, he wrote a glowing report of his "peaceable conquest" to the viceroy, as if his own Castilian charisma in unison with the Cross and the Virgin had worked the wonder.

All this stands out more particularly in his solemn act of repossession in Santa Fe. This he purposely staged on the feast of the Holy Cross, which was the fourteenth of September. The Tano Indians of the Galisteo basin had converted the Villa into a strong fortress of adobe, something like those walled towns of the Sahara which one sees in *National Geographic* pictures or in old movies about the French Foreign Legion. Yet the occupants graciously allowed the Spaniards to enter the plaza where a large timber cross was blessed amid the chanting of Te Deums, followed by pious addresses by Don Diego and the father superior of the Franciscans.

Here I must mention that Don Fernando de Chávez II played the coveted part of *Alférez Real,* or royal standard-bearer, as he had done in the entire campaign. Other direct forebears of the Baca, Romero, Montoya, and other original clans escorted him on their prancing Arabians. Then there were those new officers and soldiers from Spain, like Ignacio de Roybal of Compostela and Jacinto Peláez and Juan Fernández de la Pedrera of Asturias, all of whom married into the old Robledo family from Toledo to inject new blood into our older ancestral mainstream. For it must bear repeating that all of us old New Mexican descendants of theirs are truly cousins, cousins of the loins as much as the *hesed* that was theirs.

In the fall of the following year, Don Diego de Vargas returned to Santa Fe with his troops escorting back what was left of the old Oñate families. Having learned the story of La Conquistadora, how the pretty little statue brought by Benavides in 1625 had for so long been the prized patronal image of the destroyed parish church as the avowed "Queen of the Kingdom of New Mexico and its Villa of Santa Fe," he himself had just vowed in a letter to the viceroy that his first act of reconquest would be the restoration of her throne. This, of course, was on the supposition that his entry would be as peaceful as the one of the year before. But the Tano inhabitants of the Villa soon decided otherwise.

The time was late December, when the temperature dropped suddenly, as it likes to do today, and a mighty curtain of thick snow and sleet swept down from the great sierra. The Tano Indians barricaded the town's entrances and began taunting the governor and his people from the flat rooftops. By evening long lines of warriors from the northern Tewa and Tiwa pueblos began appearing menacingly on the crests of the juniper-studded foothills. At the base of one of them, where the Rosario chapel now stands, the desperate colonial families began praying fervently before their Conquistadora as the storm worsened. The friars and the heads of families begged Don Diego to launch an immediate attack, and the only recourse left to him was a surprise assault well before dawn when the Indians least expected it. It was a bloody affair but, by dint of desperation and superior European tactics, the capital was taken by morning and all the Indians put to rout.

A colorful ceremony of repossession, exactly like the one of the previous year and with the same people playing the same roles, then took place on the cold white plaza. However, it marked a victory paid for with considerable Indian blood, and Don Diego could no longer boast of a peaceful reconquest. But the rites of possession of 1692 and 1693 were so much alike that the people have telescoped them into mistakenly celebrating the Vargas Reconquest as a bloodless one under the aegis of La Conquistadora. Another way in which myths are born.

Nonetheless, strictly factual are the Conquistadora processions which have taken place every single year from that time until our day. And now, when the fall Fiesta of Santa Fe comes around each year, the real original statue of 1625 joins the current make-believe "Don Diego de Vargas" with his staff. They all recall a pair of events of long ago which, fused together, have erased from the collective memory other more intimate and lasting results of the Vargas Reconquest and the final return from Babylon. The most important among these are the two new colonies which were sent up by the Viceroy.

*   *   *

That very cold winter which hung on after the retaking of Santa Fe kept the new colony from the valley of Mexico at Guadalupe del Paso until the spring of 1694. Officially these families were referred to as Españoles-Mexicanos, not that they were part Spanish and part Mexican as the uninformed like to write, but that they were true Spanish folks who had been residing in the city of Mexico and its suburbs for some time. Some were recent arrivals from Spain, while others were second generation Creoles but no less pure Spaniards.

Their surnames were Castilian, and a goodly number of them must have been traditional stockraisers from the central Castilian plateau, for they fitted right into the local pastoral pattern; in fact, they must have volunteered for this reason, because a life of exclusive farming, mining, and commerce in southern New Spain was not to their liking. It is with these families that Governor Vargas founded a new villa at La Cañada north of Santa Fe in 1695–96. With the militant Cross of Spanish arms foremost in his mind, he called it La Villa Nueva de la Santa Cruz de la Cañada, just as he had named the capital's new garrison El Presidio de la Santa Cruz.

About a year later the other colony from Zacatecas arrived. Again most of the names are Castilian, and likewise all of the families accommodated themselves to the landscape's pastoral ways. Most of them were pure Spaniards, but marriage records show that this or that individual or family were *mestizos* who through subsequent intermarriage were integrated into the overall Castilian family with its Extremeño-Manchego speech and pastoral life patterns. It is here that a little of the native blood of America, most likely Tlascaltec, trickled into the New Mexican lifestream as it had done when three or so of Oñate's soldiers married Tlascaltec maidservants a century before.

While many of the people in these two new colonies were of the same pastoral tradition, there were enough among them who knew how to use the land more extensively for farming. Not that those of the preceding century had neglected this phase of life altogether. Like the shepherd folk of antiquity they had taken advantage of whatever skimpy bottomlands there were for crops that tempered the fat of beef or mutton. Each family had tended its vegetable garden with some fruit trees, and small fields of wheat or maize or beans ever since the first ditches were dug at San Gabriel. Vineyards almost never did well because of the short summer season of those times, and the cold winters which froze the Rio Grande solid from bank to bank.

But now a much enlarged population created a bigger demand for agricultural produce as it further increased, and larger stretches along the Rio Grande and near any smaller stream or spring became irrigable through bigger and better planned *acequias*. Also, these new tillers of the soil began taking advantage of the Castilian plateau's method of the *temporal*, or dry-farming, for their larger fields of maize and *frijol*.

But as in the preceding century, landscape itself was the final arbiter. As a strictly pastoral one it continued the stockraising tradition and economy that existed before the Pueblo Rebellion. Even those few people who happened to be farmers or traders by tradition were forced by landscape and circumstance to depend directly or indirectly on this economy to survive. That some prospered as generations went on while many others did not depended on good or ill fortune, or on the usual give-and-take that has existed among pastoral brethren since long before the days of Esau and Jacob.

Then, again, it was the Palestinian-Castilian landscape itself which, for all its beauty and close propensities with divine *hesed*, could turn very cruel in periods of prolonged drought, and with no rich Nile valley anywhere to seek relief during famine. In the same scriptural setting, there were the natives of the land—not the Pueblo Canaanites any more, but the surrounding tribes of roving Edomites—who still resented the conquering intruder or else coveted his mounts and the fruits of his labor.

It is at this point that the Spanish soul's *penitencia* begins to come more to the fore, and it persists all throughout the following eighteenth century when the two other elements of *hidalguía* and *conquista* begin receding into the background. From 1700 to 1800, roughly, the foundations are also laid whereby in future distant generations some youth with the features of an Aztec or a Sioux can be selected to play the rôle of that most *castizo* of Castilian *castizos,* Don Diego de Vargas.

3. The Times of Father Domínguez

The year 1776 is a precious touchstone in the history of our American nation, what with all the pictures it conjures up of the Liberty Bell, the Declaration of Independence, the Stars and Stripes, and all the great heroes and events associated with the person of George Washington. Through the happiest of coincidences, it also provides a talisman for evoking and presenting the story of eighteenth-century New Mexico at a glance. It happened that in this very same year, a Franciscan inspector of the missions, Fray Francisco Atanasio Domínguez, wrote a lengthy report which is to his century what the memorial of Fray Alonso Benavides was to the preceding one. But while the Benavides document shines with a promoter's dreams and the simple credulity of his times, this one by Domínguez is soberly factual and much more detailed—and sadly severe in the impressions it leaves.

Father Domínguez actually provides a comprehensive view of the entire century for anyone cognizant with all the period's documentation prior to his time and on through the remainder of the century. Since his avowed purpose was a thorough account of all the Indian missions and Spanish churches with their respective friaries and ministers, the report is a treasure trove of information regarding the shape and size of buildings and all the paraphernalia contained in them. But in describing their relative locations as well as the different folk connected with each one, he also paints a broad but vivid picture of the landscape and the people's way of life as they were affected by it, and especially by other influences such as the fierce enemy tribes menacing them on all sides.

Here the halcyon notions of Hispanic *hidalguía* no longer hold sway, as so colorfully suggested in the preceding century by Villagrá's epic poem and the Oñate chronicles, then by the Benavides memorial, and finally by the Vargas journals. Even the Otermín accounts of the intervening tragic debacle of 1680 had caught the same glow in bridging the acts of conquest and reconquest. They are the stuff of legend. Hence the foregoing century's myth, as we have developed it against its necessary background of race, religion, and landscape, has up until now taken that much more time and space to tell.

Without any such props, harsh reality stands out more clearly, and penitential hardship as the element closest to it takes the stage. Thanks to Father Domíguez, the tale of this second century can be told in a trice. It is still a very primitive story, entirely unlike the one of the prospering English colonies along the Atlantic coast far across a continent. In fact, the people of New Mexico at this time know very little or nothing, and care less, about the great developments taking place in New England in 1776.

*   *   *

The penitential aspect is greatly due to the land's isolation and the vagaries of climate, but the chief scourge is in the hands of the enemy Indians. Long before the Spaniards came, the nomadic native hunters of the plains had been in the habit of raiding the Pueblo Indian agriculturists at harvesttime. The advent of the Europeans with new kinds of crops, not to mention their varied livestock—and especially the horse which immediately caught the hunter's eyes—soon made such raids a year-round occurrence. But those very first Spanish settlers had been able to cope with them either by fending them off or by making retaliatory forays into their own plains country. At the same time these sallies gave them the opportunity to exercise their *hidalgo* feeling for armed conquest.

As this new century progressed, however, the colonial militia with its Pueblo auxiliary troops had to contend with an enemy which sometimes proved more than a match for them. For the wild tribes all around them had been increasing steadily through new migrations from the north. Also, resentful Indian peoples which the English had driven westward from the deciduous forests east of the Mississippi kept filling the spacious plains. From stray Spanish *mesteños* (mustangs) and from other horses they had stolen, all these tribes had been breeding their own mounts which they rode like the prairie wind who was their brother. Far more adept by long hunting tradition with the spear and with the bow and arrow, they were hard to match with Spanish muskets that deteriorated in time and were seldom, if ever, replaced. The colonial militia itself had to have recourse to the bow and arrow, and to scrub-oak lances with fire-hardened points, while often the enemy had newer firearms which the French along the Mississippi traded them for cured pelts and hides.

Obviously, a lack of adequate assistance from Spain and New Spain was chiefly to blame for this state of affairs. Once the glorious accounts sent in by Don Diego de Vargas were celebrated and then forgotten, especially after he died during a campaign against fierce Apaches who were holding up the resettlement of the Rio Abajo, the New Mexican colony gradually sank back into near oblivion. Jeremiah's Rechabites were on their own once more, and under much greater danger of being wiped out by all sorts of marauding Edomites.

All through the eighteenth century, not only large numbers of livestock kept disappearing from the pasturelands, but also some of the men and boys who tended them were either found dead or were missing. Sometimes small bands of Apaches, Comanches, or Navajos, sneaking up to the small tilled fields along the riverbanks, made off with young Spanish women and children. And yet, what one reads between the lines of such tragic accounts is a sad echo from the early biblical pages. Either it was the Will of God—blessed be his Holy Name—or it was a punishment for the sins of the parents, to be borne as a penance. Thus many a couple bewailed the death of a shepherd-son Abel, and many a Rachel mourned her children who were no longer there.

This brings to mind the grief expressed by Don Fernando de Chávez after the needless tragic death in 1705 of his eldest son Bernardo at his estancia of Bernalillo. Whenever the women and girls went to the river to do the laundering, an armed man went along with them to protect them against any sneaking Apaches. This time it was a young Gallegos cousin of the family who stood guard. Bernardo, already married and the father of three small children, should have had better sense than to play the prank that he did. Now, as he sneaked up and let out an Indian whoop to scare the girls, his Gallegos cousin spun around and shot him dead. Later, when Don Fernando apprised Governor Cuervo about his eldest son's death, he wrote: "I give thanks to God that his divine Majesty has rewarded me with the burden of losing a son such as the one I have lost. . . ."

All this matter of constant peril can also be read between the lines throughout the descriptive accounts of Father Domínguez in 1776. The land is beautiful, he says, even if he does not compare it with Palestine or Castile, since he had never been out of his native valley of Mexico before. He names and briefly sketches all the new towns and villages which had sprung up since the Vargas reconquest along the big river's valley, from Taos down to Tomé and Belén, and some others away from the valley on the flanks of the great sierra.

But at the same time he observes why the inhabitants had not spread further out in all directions. New mountain settlements like Truchas and Trampas, for example, have to be constantly on the watch for the Comanches; others at the valley of Taos and in Ojo Caliente were either decimated or completely wiped out by the Utes. To the west and south, the Navajos and Apaches are keeping the increase of people from seeking new pasturelands.

On the pleasanter side, Father Domínguez, while generally overlooking the pastoral nature and economy of the landscape, simply because of his own urban and agricultural background, focuses his attention on the little orchards and fields which the villagers cultivate by some stream, listing all their fruits and crops while admiring what the people can do with such a meager and poor soil.

Also, one can feel how much the author misses the arches and carvings of the stone architecture of New Spain, both in the churches and the people's dwellings, as he niggardly dispenses a word of praise for an occasional happy combination of humble adobe and corbeled beams of rough timber. Accustomed to the urbane manners of his much more civilized native land, he looks patronizingly upon the native folk here as a strangely rustic species of Spaniards. (He frequently makes mention of a distinct people called *genízaros,* and these we shall dwell upon soon for their being an important feature of the century.)

Finally, being altogether used to the more modern Castilian spoken in his native city of Mexico and all of New Spain, even by the unlettered, Domínguez often refers to the local *españoles* as speaking a Castilian "according to their own fashion," never realizing that he is hearing the older language of Extremadura and La Mancha as he could have read it in Cervantes. For there are no schools to speak of, he also points out, and the overall picture he gives is one of general poverty and of a dearth of culture as he sees it.

He also mentions individuals of means, or *ricos,* especially merchants out of Guadalupe del Paso originally, who like to defraud the missionaries. The poorer folk are remiss in their tithes, and will get out of paying a stipend on the occasion of a baptism or a wedding. If a friar puts up an extra adobe room, or happens to have more *ristras* of *chile* or onions in his pantry than they have, they accuse him of opulence. This has nothing to do with their faith or their spirit of penitence, we might add; they are just being *castizo* as in instances commonly found in Spanish literature.

To an informed reader like myself, there is a particular wistful note whenever New Mexico is no longer referred to as a Kingdom, only as an ordinary province. The Crown had awakened to the fact that the region no longer had a golden future; the great land masses of India and China were now located where the Creator had put them in the first place. In fact, the northern provinces of New Spain, once the great *despoblado* or uninhabited wilderness, are much more developed by now, due to the discovery of rich mines of every kind. Now New Mexico is only the outermost and least important of all these Internal Provinces, as they are officially called. Their Commandant General has his headquarters somewhere far south in Sonora, and so the small mud town of Santa Fe is only a minor provincial capital now, and her governor only one of several provincial ones; he is no longer the royal Governor and Captain-General of a Kingdom.

However, one ray of hope runs through the Domínguez report. A more or less regular trade route has been developed between Santa Fe and the other Internal Provinces, with counting houses at Chihuahua and in the halfway town of Guadalupe del Paso by the gates of the Kingdom that was. Merchants from these two places ply the route with Chihuahua silver for their mutual exchange, and with manufactured articles for more common barter in the north.

One or the other such trader has established himself permanently in the land, while some local natives have come to learn the tricks of commerce. The livestock of the region and their products, particularly their wool and hides along with the cured skins of deer, elk, and bison, are bringing in some silver bullion and currency, and heretofore absent goods and utensils.

But it will take a long time for all these new benefits to filter down to the common people, especially those away from the capital. For them the land is still the ancient upland Canaan. The old *patrones,* who heretofore had been richer than their countrymen only for having larger land grants and greater flocks and herds, are now becoming more like true *ricos* in the tradition of the more affluent parts of Spanish America, even though their homes remain the same undisguised adobe. Nevertheless their wealth is earned with great risk and at great expense because of an ever-growing Apache menace all along the trade route.

In this connection, Domínguez also mentions the importation of wine, from excellent vineyards at Guadalupe del Paso. Up until now the only wine known had consisted of very small amounts sent to the missionaries, for them to hoard and use sparingly for sacramental purposes. The winters of those times were too cold for the cultivation of grapes, except for rare racemes in some scattered sheltered spots, and so it comes as a surprise to learn that the early New Mexicans were willy-nilly as well as unwittingly the truest of Nazirites in this regard. But even now, only the *ricos* can afford the luxury of an imported wineskin. The wine tavern, so much a part of life in Europe, is therefore unknown. Some might say that it is a blessing for the inhabitants as a whole, but it is also a form of penance when a poor fellow happens to see a rich *patrón* or a padre enjoying an occasional cup.

As for the people's religious faith, the Spanish folk are thoroughly commended at least indirectly, when Domínguez describes their flourishing church confraternities together with the accessories of their chapels. There are the fraternities of the Franciscan Third Order at Santa Fe, Santa Cruz, and Albuquerque, and an extra one of Carmelite associates in Santa Cruz. Also there are the universal sodality of La Conquistadora and an elite one of Our Lady of Light in the capital, and associations of the Holy Sacrament or the Poor Souls in all the larger towns.

All the churches and chapels abound with painted or carven images, particularly those of the queenly Virgin under her many titles, and of the Suffering Christ in the various aspects of his bloody Passion: first the Crucifix, then the Ecce Homo or Sangre de Cristo, and the Jesús Nazareno bearing his cross, and the Holy Sepulcher. Sometimes one such single *Cristo*, because his limbs are hinged and he can be dressed or denuded to represent any aspect of the Passion, supplies for them all. These and many oil paintings of saints are faded and peeling away, having come from New Spain at the beginning of the century. To replace them, and also to supply *santos* for the newer churches and chapels, amateur artists among the friars have been painting new ones on bison hide or elk skin. They have also been carving new *bultos* out of cottonwood. Needless to say, Father Domínguez does not like them.

But there are no Penitentes as yet, nor any sign of moradas. Their existence would not have escaped the eye of an observer like Domínguez, especially since, had they actually existed, the Penitentes would not have been a secret society. Secrecy was forced upon them by the circumstances of our times. Evidently the members of the Third Order did not even practice token flagellation; for our most observing author writes with wonder as well as admiringly about a practice recently started in Abiquiú. On the Fridays of Lent, young Father Fernández, a native of Asturias in northern Spain, leads some volunteer members of his congregation in taking the discipline. None of the other churches have it; none of the other friars observe the practice. In fact, the friars in the other missions, whether disheartened by their loneliness or by internecine quarrels, do not exhibit much personal piety in the regard of Father Domínguez.

Obviously, what young and new Father Fernández is doing is an innovation as well as an exception throughout the entire region. It is very much like what a contemporary of his, Father Junípero Serra, was doing in southern New Spain before he came to California. He belonged to a new wave of Franciscans from Mallorca who had founded their "missionary colleges" in the cities of Mexico and Querétaro. In Mexico and other centers Father Serra and others of his brethren scourged themselves in the pulpit. Some of their audiences followed their example, but this does not mean that these padres started brotherhoods of Penitentes either there or afterwards in California.

In short, the *anima hispanica* in New Mexico had needed no specific acts of bloody penitence like flagellation to express her commiseration with her Suffering Christ. The burial books alone, in tersely recording the recurrent deaths of individuals and groups massacred by the infidel, or as victims of frequent epidemics of smallpox and other short-lived but mortal plagues, amply demonstrate how that entire century had provided direr means of penance, and to spare. These and other scourges, like periods of prolonged drought, and the occasional abduction of their children, their Palestinian-Castilian landscape promptly converted to *hesed* in their hearts.

For there were no other sights or sounds to turn them away from all the Calvaries and Thabors and Bethlehems which their senses fed into the brain, and which then kept draining into the living essence of the person.

4. The Genízaros

But now to an ethnic feature mentioned just before in passing. In this very context of a century-long penitence, specifically in its relation to the Plains Indian scourge, a significant change gradually took place in the character of the population at large. What in other climes and among other

Europeans would be called a "white man's burden" came as a result of a practice carried on by the Spanish settlers with regard to Indian captives all through the century. Begun with the most pious of motives, this practice in the long run did prove to be a social and economic burden from which Hispanic New Mexico never fully recovered.

The problem is that of the so-called *genízaros*, one which has been little understood by the local folk, not to mention the newcomer.

During their traditional intertribal wars, the Indians of the plains were accustomed to capture one another's young women and children to be used as slaves. Many of these they sold to the New Mexican settlers during trading *ferias* which were held in periods of truce, when local articles like pottery and cutlery were traded for cured hides of bison, elk, and antelope. As the Spaniards themselves put it, they "ransomed" these so-called infidels in order to rear them as Christians. Of course, there also had to be an underlying motive of acquiring free servants for their households and herders for their livestock. They were not considered slaves, however.

Having received a Christian upbringing with their baptismal names and their adopters' surnames—along with Spanish ways and the Spanish language—they were on their own around marriage time. But, since there was little outside the pastoral economy, many of them continued in more or less necessary peonage, as it also happened, for that matter, among the less fortunate Hispanic folk in true biblical tradition.

When they intermarried among themselves, these assorted young men and women—designated in church and civil records as Apaches, Utes, Comanches, Kiowas, Pawnees, and some members of lesser known tribes—they produced a type of hispanicized and christianized people which were neither Pueblo Indians nor infidels, having lost the tribal language and traditions of their respective mixed parents. Nor could they be classified as *españoles*, even if one or the other was the offspring of a *patrón* or some other passionate swain of the family and a handmaid, all in the hoary tradition of Abraham and the other Hebrew patriarchs.

In accord with the worldwide belief of the times, that two different elements or organic species could produce an entirely new one, these nameless people were called *genízaros*, a new creation among humanfolk.

By Domínguez' time, the *genízaros* already made up almost a third of the population. Settlements had been founded for them at Abiquiú in the north and at Tomé and Los Jarales in the south, and at Santa Fe in between they occupied the *barrio* of Analco, originally the home of the preceding century's Mexican Indians and other castes who had not returned from Guadalupe del Paso with the Vargas reconquest. But still many others lived scattered among the several other Spanish towns and outspread *ranchos,* employed as household help and livestock herders.

In time, a number of them married into the pueblos, giving rise to the later belief among the Pueblo Indians that "Mexicans" had joined their respective communities. Others intermarried within the lower economic stratum of Hispanic society, while the rest continued intermingling among themselves within the general ambience of the Spanish-speaking population.

Here and there one finds an *español* of the upper stratum marrying a *genízara,* no doubt because he found her more physically attractive than the Spanish women, much as had the soldiers of Cortés preferred Aztec beauties to the Spanish brides which the Crown was sending. The same thing had happened in Spain during the Moorish Crusade, from whence the word *morena* usually designates a dark beauty. The kings of Israel and Judah, and much later the caliphs of Arabia, liked to stock their harems with a great variety of concubines from all the nations around them.

In this connection, it must be emphasized that there was no intermarriage of the Spaniards with the Pueblo Indians, as the outsider has always taken for granted. If a Spanish woman did happen to marry a Pueblo man, she joined her husband's way of life. For the two peoples lived strictly apart within their own different cultures, and the Pueblo leaders allowed no social mixing that could lead to a Pueblo girl leaving her kinfolk; the white man's diseases, like smallpox, had so decimated the Pueblos that they hoarded their sources of generation.

The results of the gradual integration of the Edomite *genízaro* proselytes into the atmosphere of the *anima hispanica* appear strongly in the following century—in periods of civil unrest, in the phenomenon of the Penitentes, and ultimately in the spectacle of a descendant of theirs playing the hidalgic role of Don Diego de Vargas.

Nevertheless, there still remained that dominant part of the population, as much among the poor *castizo* stockmen as among their *rico* cousins, which kept very much alive the birthright and the blood line of Dulcinea del Toboso.

Part Four

SANGRE DE CRISTO

Ver a Jesús encarnado
es cosa muy eminente,
vá de espinas coronado,
Nazareno Penitente.

Ay, Jesús de Nazareno,
que es cosa muy eminente,
yo te ofrezco este alabado,
Nazareno Penitente.

Seeing Jesus crimson-gowned
is a thing so evident,
going forth nettle-crowned
as Nazarene and Penitent.

Oh, Jesus as a Nazirite
so manifestly in my sight,
I offer you this my lament,
Oh, Nazarene and Penitent.

—Hymn of the Brotherhood

17

Secular Interlude

The distinctively beautiful sierra which begins as Santa Fe's natural backdrop, and then billows gracefully northward along the Truchas and Taos country into the vaster Rocky Mountain massif in Colorado, bears the arresting name of *Sangre de Cristo*—"Blood of Christ." For years now, ever since the publication of Willa Cather's *Death Comes for the Archbishop,* lesser craftsmen have kept on piecing the mystic name with the rose-carnelian alpenglow of the rounded peaks whenever these absorb the reds of a vivid sunset.

Surely, they say, some pious friar or poetic captain of three hundred years ago must have shouted out the name for the first time in a moment of inspired exaltation.

The truth is that this great range bore the more common and prosaic general designation of Sierra Madre, "Mother Range," until the beginnings of the last century. In daily parlance, sections of it had been called after the nearest locality, such as La Sierra de Santa Fe, La Sierra de Truchas, La Sierra de Taos. By the year 1818 there was a military post on the Ute frontier north of Taos called Sangre de Cristo, and the section of mountain nearby was mentioned as La Sierra de la Sangre de Cristo in the same breath. It took some time before the name spread southward to cover the entire range.

Hence, this alone would not make the name attributable to the first brotherhood of Penitentes, which was introduced into the region at Santa Cruz around this time. Figures of the "Ecce Homo" in the several churches and chapels had borne the title of "Sangre de Cristo" long before this. Whatever its inspiration, this ritual designation for the entire sierra came at a latter time when Oñate's captains of 1598 and 1600, and those of Vargas in 1692 and 1693, were only a dim memory, and a few sluggish Franciscans lingering on the scene a faded blue shadow of their former selves. Yet for this reason it is all the more intriguing.

For me, since my early childhood, "Sangre de Cristo" has had a very special connotation. Whenever my good father had to punish me for some mischief, he would remark loud enough for my mother to hear: "One of these days I'm going to turn this *bribón* over to the Sangre de Cristo!" My mother inevitably became furious for the moment as she scolded her helpmate for saying such a thing, while he grinned with some inner satisfaction. At first I thought she was objecting to her darling firstborn being called a *bribón*, what among us meant the lowest form of rascal. But then, on calling to mind many a chapel *bulto* of Jesus as the "Ecce Homo," I thought that she was trying to prevent a future paternal whipping so severe as to leave me looking like the blood-streaked Christ after his flogging by the Roman soldiers. Moreover, I learned in time what this conjugal feuding was all about.

There were Penitentes in the prairie town of my birth, and their windowless *morada* stood next to my paternal grandfather's little ranch just outside the village. Whenever the flagellant brethren ritually inducted someone into the brotherhood, they said they were receiving him "into the Blood of Christ." By using this expression my father was having his fun; it was all part of a running game of sharp teasing between my parents, like that ripost of my mother's on a later occasion, and in another town, when she said that the menfolk on her side were too high a type of Catholics to be Penitentes, while none on my father's were good enough Christians to deserve being one of them.

Today both the name and very sight of the Sangre de Cristo range do stir up lyrical emotions within me. But at the same time they recall the more realistic grim processions of a flagellant brethren who first appeared on its foothills around the time the name itself was being applied to our beautiful mother range. Furthermore, they bring up visions of a Lebanon overlooking a much older landscape of ancient ritual sacrifices, nazirites, and a Nazarene bearing his cross; then, of a Sierra Nevada and a Sierra Morena which witnessed the birth of the Spanish soul's sense of *hidalguía* and *conquista* during her Moorish wars, followed by that of *penitencia* in her austerest of saints and in the cults of brothers of light and of blood and of *nazarenos*.

All in all, they conjure up the whole panorama of one's pastoral forebears unfolding against the range's most scenic backdrop, and spreading all over the entire Palestinian-Castilian landscape below—all the way from the mythicized days of Oñate and Vargas through a penance-fraught eighteenth century, and then through most radical religious and civic innovations in the nineteenth, down to our day.

1. The Old Order Changes

The nineteenth century's first decade or so, which saw old civic and church patterns turned topsy-turvy in western Europe, also brought distinctive changes in faraway New Mexico which on the surface appear unrelated. Napoleon's spreading empire had met with effective resistance in Spain, but this very contact with the French introduced ideas which resulted in a constitutional monarchy presided over by a parliament called the Cortes. Previously, the American and French revolutions had also caused stirrings of social unrest in Spain's New World colonies; now the new century's developments encouraged the valiant but unsuccessful revolt of Padre Hidalgo in southern New Spain under his banner of Guadalupe in 1810. And far to the east across the North American continent the young American nation of 1776 was testing her growing vigor and sense of destiny following the War of 1812.

Any such political facts were fed from viceregal headquarters in the city of Mexico to those of the Internal Provinces' commandant in Sonora or Chihuahua, and from here copies reached Santa Fe for the perusal of the governor and his officials. These men, by and large, were not natives but outsiders from New Spain. Merchants plying the trade route between Chihuahua and Santa Fe also conveyed rumors of the sort; likewise, occasional French traders from the Mississippi who in the past century had been finding their way to New Mexico.

But there was no reason to get excited over these reports. The region lay too far away to be affected by what was happening in another world, as it were. If the news ever filtered down to the common folk in their isolated villages and ranchos, it meant little or nothing. While the land was about to become a crossroads of political and commercial communication in the interests of a few alien officials and local *ricos*, nothing had changed in this regard among the people at large.

For the ordinary shepherd folk the land was still the primitive pastoral Canaan of old, and whatever new developments were taking place, or were about to take place, had to do much more with the Calvaries and

Bethlehems of their familiar Palestinian landscape than with any changes of governments in *tierra afuera,* or any exchanges of Chihuahua silver at their capital closer to home.

*   *   *

For exactly two hundred years, ever since the Oñate colonization of 1598, the Franciscan friars had been the sole ministers of the faith, much as they had been the only representatives of Rome in the Holy Land since the days of St. Francis. Suddenly the bishop of Durango, more than six hundred miles of perilous travel across the southern wilderness, secularized the parishes of Santa Fe and Santa Cruz in 1798. This meant the introduction of "secular" priests, who are the ordinary and most numerous clergymen of the Church. Unlike "religious" priests like the Franciscans, they take no vows in community. As independent individuals they are subject to their respective bishops in ministerial matters only.

From the beginning, the archbishops of Mexico and then those of Guadalajara had claimed jurisdiction over the New Mexican missions, picturing them as a fruitful source of tithes in a prosperous Kingdom that was said to resemble the two Castiles. The great distance and harsh circumstances of the times had kept those claims on a purely argumentative level. But by the year 1730 the bishop of a diocese established halfway in Durango made the claim more tangible by ordaining two natives of the land, and subsequently appointing them as his personal vicars. They were Don Santiago Roybal and Don José de Bustamante, the latter either a son or nephew of the current lord governor, and both are mentioned by name for being my maternal uncles seven generations removed. This helps confirm my mother's hunch about her family's traditional piety while furnishing historical threads other than carnal ones.

The presence of these supervisors had not changed the old Franciscan mission pattern, but now the arrival in 1798 of the first two secular priests as actual pastors of Santa Fe and Santa Cruz introduced a different kind of ecclesiastical regimen. For the past two centuries the Franciscans, deeming themselves missionaries to the Indians primarily, had regarded the Hispanic faithful in a more or less casual manner outside of the sacraments of baptism and marriage. Hence the people no longer knew what the dramatic liturgies of Holy Week were, as celebrated in the churches of Spain and New Spain. Through their own piety, most of the villages had built their own chapels, but they could expect mass in them only on rare occasions. All this was not solely due to lack of any zeal on the friars' part, but to distances of travel and because the friars had for long been dwindling down to a very few. In this respect, too, Mother Spain had lost track of her lost tribe.

The very first pair of secular priests arrived in Santa Fe and Santa Cruz in the spring of 1798, but they and their successors until 1821 kept returning to Durango after more or less brief stays. For this they blamed the ill will of some friars and public officials, but another reason was the poverty of the land. In between, the few remaining friars had to act as interim pastors.

After 1821 the bishop also began ordaining some native young men of New Mexico. As all these secular priests gradually increased in number, the historic old friars faded away from the scene, and it is during this period that two altogether new features make their appearance. One is the now famed chapel in Chimayó, commonly called El Santuario, with its Crucifix of Esquipulas and a pit of miraculous dust. The other is the first brotherhood of Penitentes which appeared full-blown in Santa Cruz with its distinctive organization and sanguinary practices having a long tradition elsewhere.

Incidentally, the arrival of these Durango clergymen also began popularizing the cult of the Mexican Virgin of Guadalupe. Creole friars in New Spain, who had accepted the legend of Lasso de la Vega, had first given this title to the one mission at Guadalupe del Paso, and after 1700 to the pueblo missions at Zuñi and Pojoaque. But now the first Hispanic chapel with this name was soon built in the western outskirts of Santa Fe, and it was followed by the very first parish church of Guadalupe in the newly founded Spanish town of Don Fernando de Taos. Subsequent chapels in other villages followed the example.

As for the Santuario of Chimayó and the Penitentes, the setting or background for these two new and strange phenomena, as regards both the land and its people, needs to be reviewed within the context of these times. A handy way of doing it is to imagine what passed through the minds of the different groups of secular priests as they made their way into what they had expected to be a prosperous vineyard of the Lord.

2. To High Upland Pastures

Two full centuries of travel had beaten a well-worn and readily visible trail from El Paso del Norte to Santa Fe, over the first path traced by the

Oñate colonists of 1598, and this a caravan of oxcarts and mounted travelers under armed escort was now following. Otherwise nothing had changed, save for the larger number of Apache bands which almost could be felt lurking behind some hill or around a willow-choked bend of the river. Seasoned guides pointed to a giant array of perpendicular crags to the east, whose now old name of Los Organos the newcomers easily guessed before being informed. Then they came upon the place of Doña Ana and the mount called Robledo, but no one remembered how these names had come about; likewise with regard to a spot called Rincón, where the caravan left the green valley and began the bleak traversing of La Jornada del Muerto in the desert.

But who was the dead man after whom this long stretch had been named? Many individuals had perished on it through the years, either from thirst or illness or an Apache arrow, yet it was not called the route of dead men in the plural. ¿Quién sabe? Then there were empty spots along the trail called El Perrillo, El Alemán, and La Cruz de Anaya, and away on their western flank rose the twisted shapes of barren mountains called Caballo and Fray Cristóbal. But whose horse, and what friar? Nobody knew. ¿Quién sabe?

Besides the goods-laden carts of a merchant named Pino, there were other such vehicles carrying the possessions of clergymen riding alongside with their black cassocks pulled over the saddle, and of members of their households who took turns riding less spirited mounts. For these secular priests from Durango were individuals of means as well as culture. Like all gentlemen from the lands far to the south in New Spain, they kept a houseful of familiares, whether relatives or personal servants. The men watched after the horses and cultivated the gardens, some of them doubling as valets and sextons; their wives and daughters were in charge of all household chores.

One of these "familiars" was a self-taught painter and sculptor whose surname was Molleno. His name turns out to be more important here than that of his clerical master, whoever he was, since no one knows which one of the priests from Durango Molleno accompanied all the way to Santa Cruz and Chimayó. And the trip with its impressions being detailed here could apply to any of the Durango priests who came between 1798 and 1821.

The grim Jornada safely behind them, the travelers descended into the river valley once more. Across the river well above its western bank, said the guides, once stood the Piro pueblo of San Antonio de Qualacú, and further upstream the one called Socorro, but no one knew how the latter had gotten its name. It was the same with regard to the place called Luis López, and the agricultural-minded newcomers wondered why such good land by the river lay fallow.

They were told that for the past century the Apaches had prevented the people of New Mexico from resettling the land; the Piro Indians had not returned to their pueblos, and their descendants still resided in the area of Guadalupe del Paso. The sole landmark left at Socorro was the walls of the old Piro mission of the Assumption, clearly visible in front of a great stone mountain to the west; also abandoned still further north, on the site of the much longer vacated Piro pueblo of Sevilleta, was a former Spanish estancia of the Robledos and Romeros, and now called La Joya de Sevilleta for lying in a hollow by the river.

Finally they came upon the first actual Spanish settlements at a place called Tomé; no one remembered that it had been the estancia of Tomé Domínguez de Mendoza. Just across the river was the new town called Belén, named after Bethlehem even if the flat site did not resemble the Lord's birthplace. Both here and at Tomé there were settlements of *genízaros*, who came in handy in parleying with their nomadic ancestors of the immediate plains and deserts.

If these gentlemen in black soutanes had expected to find prosperous towns with outlying ducal haciendas like those of New Spain, they were greatly disappointed. Nowhere in sight were there any white or pink houses of cut stone, or at least lime-plastered adobe, with red-tiled roofs in the already universal Spanish tradition. They saw no pillared arcades in the homesteads of landlords, no multistoried public edifices adorning cobblestone plazas, much less fine churches with tiled domes of blue and gold and tiered carven towers punctuating the wide azure sky.

What they saw on arriving at the southernmost settlements, and then along the river all the way to their final destination, were small drab clusters of mud houses with flat roofs covered with dirt. Meanwhile, the learned gentlemen kept criticizing their guides for many faults in grammar. For example, they chided them for saying *ciénega* instead of *ciénaga*, not knowing that with the second *e* it was a good Extremeño word. The same thing happened when the natives said *asina* for *así* ("thus"), and *muncho* for *mucho* ("much"). The priests also noticed that the people used *plaza* and *placita* for "town" instead of other Spanish terms like *aldea, pueblo,* or *población.* The word *pueblo* was here being used exclusively for the Indian villages.

Now, if any of these men had ever been in Palestine or Morocco, the sight would have evoked visions of towns in those faraway places. Round *torreones,* or bastions, and crenelated parapets along the tops of churches or taller buildings furthered the illusion. For these crenelations, or notched battlements, were peculiar to the Saracen fortresses of Palestine, Morocco, and Spain. Incidentally, here in New Mexico they later disappeared from the rooflines, as the wild Indian menace declined, and today we wrongly imagine that the mission churches and chapels of New Mexico always had smooth straight lines along their tops.

Here, the newcomers were told, these earthen towns were built around a square, with few openings to the outside, as protective forts against invasion from the Apaches to the south, the Comanches from the eastern plains across the mountains, and the Navajos from the western desert. Inside the square stood the local church or chapel, taller and with thicker walls but of the same undisguised mud, with front adobe belfries as unprepossessing as their unadorned façades. Their interiors were white-washed crooked walls with exposed pine trunks for ceilings, looking more like granaries back in New Spain. On the wavy walls hung oil paintings faded and cracked with age, or else crude drawings of saints on large thick *antas* or hides which, they were told, came from the *cíbolo,* as the bison was called locally, or from an unusually large deer of the region called *venado alazán* ("sorrel deer"), the local term for elk. The main altar itself lacked those ornate golden screens or retables so common in other Spanish lands.

Next to each settlement toward the riverbanks, the planted fields and orchards were miserably small, in the visitors' estimation, only what the thin veins of ditch water were able to moisten effectively. Some other outlying fields of corn or beans depended on the *temporal,* where crops were very liable to fail in drier seasons. There were thick groves, *alamedas,* of mountain or cottonwood poplars along the main stream, and some old specimens by the houses broke the monotony of bare outer walls with the cool patterns of their thick-leaved branches.

Actually, the Hispanic settlements looked hardly different in outward appearance from the nude Indian pueblos of Isleta, Sandía, San Felipe, and Santo Domingo, which they passed along the way toward the capital, except that they were smaller and more frequent—and shade trees grew closer to the walls.

These new priests could see that the inhabitants throughout the whole region, the rich as well as the poor, depended almost entirely on the grazing of livestock for their livelihood. They could readily see that the landscape was marvelously suited to it, for they had never seen such great sweeps of pastureland before. Large and small droves of cattle, horses, and sheep could be seen on higher terrain on either side of the river, like sprinkled grains of cinnamon, salt, and pepper in the distance. Closer by, bunches of goats or burros nibbled at the roadside weeds and native tawny grass.

In all this lay the people's prime source of food, woolens, and leather, but little else since there were no local markets to provide other staples or the barest of luxuries by way of trade. Only at long intervals were they able to barter them, and also the produce of their small fields and orchards in season, when a merchant train passed by on its way from Guadalupe del Paso to Santa Fe. And too often it was at an exorbitant rate of exchange. The few *ricos* and *patrones*, of course, could afford better raiment, tools, and household furnishings from faraway Chihuahua and Durango—and also an occasional wineskin from the vineyards of Guadalupe del Paso.

If all these factors began stirring misgivings in the breasts of these southern gentlemen of the cloth, what they saw in the inhabitants themselves made them wish that they were back home among the comforts and conversation of what they considered the civilized world.

*   *   *

The new priests' first encounter with what was supposed to be the cream of local society was with a very old man named Chávez, at the plaza of the same name just north of Belén, in whose large rambling house they stayed overnight. Here almost everyone seemed to be a Chávez, living in smaller houses around the big one like chicks gathered about the mother hen. One of the guides whispered with a guarded snort that there were more such anthills of them—*ricos* and *pobres* alike, but all cousins—all the way from Belén to Atrisco and Albuquerque. Here in this plaza their aged host was the patriarch of his clan.

That night, under the crude *vigas* of his long narrow salon, the old patriarch began boasting to his guests about his family, how it was the most prominent one among the descendants of famous *conquistadores*. At first the guests were interested and curious, for one seldom heard this kind of talk even among the most prominent people in cities like Guadalajara and Mexico. There their palaces and rich culture assumed their lineage for granted. As the eldest son of eldest sons, their host now droned on, he had inherited two precious objects brought by the very first Chávez, of whose entire lengthy name his scion was no longer sure. As he was saying this, one of his quiet sons brought out a gold signet ring which, upon close examination, revealed five very minute keys indented on a conventional shield. The second heirloom was a thin and very old printed volume, long shorn of its cover and now rolled clumsily in a swatch of tanned deerskin. The learned gentlemen gathered from perusing its torn title page and contents that it was a copy of a long poem entitled *Carlos Famoso*. Its author was a certain Don Luis Zapata de Chaves, and part of the date legible indicated the sixteenth century. Faded inked lines on the margin called attention to stanzas which told how the name "Chaves" had been acquired by two valiant brothers far back in the eleventh century.

At first the guests from Durango had shown themselves politely condescending, upon surveying the primitive character of the house and its few furnishings, the plain homespun clothing of most members of the household, the rustic simplicity of the old man's bearing and the archaic turns of his speech. The way he wore a fine pair of galooned pantaloons and an embroidered jacket, most likely tailored in Chihuahua, betrayed a use of them on the rarest of occasions. Now they were filled with pity, even though they suspected that his lineage and that of his several anthills of relatives could well be genuine. Their patriarchal host's recounting of begats, all illustrated with anecdotes like the one of his grandfather Don Fernando acting as royal standard-bearer under Don Diego de Vargas, kept them yawning far into the night. If this was a sample of the region's culture, what could be expected from the more common run of people?

These they had not failed to notice on the way, like the less endowed Hispanic folk—and especially the *genízaro* settlements. Their dwellings were much smaller, and empty of what one might call furniture. Still, they seemed happy and contented, having nothing else with which to compare their humble state of poverty, or even peonage in many cases.

The experience was repeated at the homestead of the merchant called Pino, the one who had accompanied them with his goods from Chihuahua; before going on ahead, he had insisted on their stopping overnight at El Rancho de San Clemente. His house was like the Chávez homestead, although better furnished; he proudly showed them a row of books which he said was the largest collection outside the Franciscan library in the mission of Santo Domingo. This very genial host made them promise to look up his elder brother, who was a prominent citizen in the Villa of Santa Fe.

And so it went on at other places where they stopped for the night. At El Rancho de la Peña Blanca, their host was a bellicose fellow named Baca, who insisted that his Baca ancestry was just as good and as famous as the one of the Chávez folk, and not only because the two clans had been closely interrelated from the very start. Besides, said he, his own family name came from that intrepid Álvar Núñez Cabeza de Vaca who had crossed a continent long before New Mexico was settled. He had no way of proving it with signet rings and old books, but one's father and grandfather ought to be taken at their own word.

At long last the party of extremely weary travelers reached Santa Fe. Ever since they entered the settled part of the country, the new clergymen had begun to appreciate the unique beauty of the landscape with its bracing air. Their first view of the Villa's panorama from a distance raised their spirits still more, even when they suspected that the town itself would be no different from what they had seen, only a bit larger. It was less of a fortress, they soon discovered, since its elevated position and its great sierra shielded it from enemy invasion.

The large treeless plaza, paved with the same earth that ran up the walls of the surrounding houses, was livelier with people of every age, and with uniformed soldiers crossing to and fro between the low-strung structure of mud, called the "palace" of the governor as if by a streak of irony, and the equally humble military chapel directly across from it, or the merchant houses lining the other sides of the square.

The Franciscan friar of Santa Fe, who was the military chaplain of the garrison as well as pastor of the large brown church of St. Francis up the street, promptly invited them to stay in the broken-down friary next to the church, but a merchant citizen by the name of Ortiz insisted that his house would be their home for the time being.

Ortiz and Father Hozio were close friends, and out of his commercial bounty Ortiz had just finished rebuilding the parish church as well as erecting a chapel, called El Rosario, at the spot outside of town where, he proudly claimed, his own grandparents had witnessed the peaceful reconquest of Santa Fe by Don Diego de Vargas. It would henceforth shelter the venerable statue of La Conquistadora between her processions, which had been going on ever since the city was reconquered. Their host's great house near the plaza, while still so primitive in its construction, was much better furnished than all the other residences they had seen, and the viands and wines were consistent with his position as a prosperous merchant.

Here also they met Don Pedro Bautista Pino, a very patriarchal fellow in his bearing, and they conveyed his brother's greetings to him. The governor and his staff also came from the palace to pay their respects. Some days later the new pastor took solemn charge of the capital's parish from the kindly friar, and the new pastor of Santa Cruz rode on northward to assume charge of his own parish.

And it was here in Santa Cruz de la Cañada, during his tenure and those of the other secular priests from Durango, along with the sojourn of their respective "familiars" from that southern land, that El Santuario and the Penitentes came into being.

3. The New Christ of Chimayó

The uniquely picturesque site of ancient Tsimayo at the headwaters of the little Santa Cruz river, and cuddled by the juniper-dappled foothills of the Sangre de Cristo, had been holy ground for the Tewa Indians from time immemorial. Their legends say that it had been a place where fire and hot water had belched forth in the days of the Ancient Ones, later subsiding into a sacred pool which they called *tsimayo-pokwi*. The water evaporated in time, leaving only a puddle of live mud, and this finally dried up into dust. But ever since those times the Tewa had been coming to eat of the mud and the dry dust, because they had the power of curing many illnesses.

After the founding of Santa Cruz de la Cañada, Spanish families began settling the narrow fertile valley of the village's stream as far as Tsimayo, which soon was pronounced "Chimayó" by the newcomers. The upper end where the Indian shrine was they called El Potrero, for serving as a grassy common where they penned their horses. But at the turn of the century it was the rancho of a certain Bernardo Abeyta, by whose time the curative *posito*, or little dust pit, was already being frequented by more and more of the settlers.

Father Domínguez in 1776 makes no mention of it, since there was no Santuario there as yet; nor had Bernardo Abeyta been born at El Guique across the Rio Grande on the opposite side of the Santa Clara valley. What we learn from him is that the Chimayó ravine was already very well populated. Most of the people, he said, passed for Spaniards, some having servants (genízaros), and all speaking the current Spanish of the region. He also noted that Chimayó itself had better farming lands and orchards than the Villa of Santa Cruz. It shows that these people as a whole had by now become more accustomed to an agricultural way of life, and this because the first settlers in 1696 were from among the new colonies from Mexico and Zacatecas.

Around the year 1813, either a pastor from Durango or those among his servant families told Abeyta a marvelous story, after learning about the sacred dust at El Potrero. Far to the south beyond the valley of Mexico, they said, in a country called Guatemala, there was a famous shrine at a place called Esquipulas very similar to this local pit of sacred earth. It was presided over by the great Crucifix of Nuestro Señor de Esquipulas in a magnificent church built there near a medicinal spring long known to the Guatemalan Indians. Abeyta was greatly impressed, more so since his Abeyta forebear had come from Durango, the native city of his informants. For soon he built a tiny shrine over the miraculous pit by his house in honor of the Christ of Esquipulas, and folks began making pilgrimages to it. Then he asked the friar who was acting as interim pastor to write the bishop for a permit to erect a public shrine, and by 1816 the present familiar structure known as El Santuario was completed.

While all this follows those much older instances in medieval Spain regarding the discovery of the many Cristos and Virgins which gave origin to the various patronal shrines all over the Iberian peninsula, in this particular case it is likewise redolent, not so much of still more ancient Bethels and Shiloams and Bethesdas in the Bible pages, as of the sacred groves of Baal in that same older world of a more or less agricultural folk. In this greener setting it is also reminiscent of the holy wells in medieval Britain and Wales, and the more modern waters of Lourdes in France.

In other words, the Santuario of Chimayó, for being agrarian and doubly Indianic in its earthy origins, was not strictly castizo. But for New Mexico as a whole, it was the first such phenomenon in two hundred years, ever since that incident in 1598 when a horse's hoof accidentally but providentially produced a waterspout from the desert ground. Perhaps also because of its picturesque setting, it grew with the years into a pilgrim Palestinian "Church of the Holy Sepulcher" and an Iberian "Shrine of Compostela" for the poor isolated New Mexicans, where the anima hispanica, for so long estranged from the typical miraculous shrines of Spain and Europe in general, and from those in the rest of Spanish America in particular, had been hungering for such things as it continued absorbing, days upon days of sun-drenched hours, a landscape reminiscent of age-old Palestinian theophanies and Castilian mystical experiences.

But it likewise filled a need in the Indianic blood memory of the *genízaro*, since arcane and occult shrines where the supernatural powers-that-be operated had always been a part of Amerindian belief on the Great Plains as well as among the Rio Grande Pueblos. For this same reason, the ever-conservative local Pueblo Indians, never too avid in accepting Spanish Christian worship in its totality, also took most naturally to the Santuario of Chimayó. It was as though their own venerable notion of Shipapu, the sacred earth-hole from which their ancestors had emerged, was being canonized at last by the European strangers who long ago had invaded their holy land.

No less novel than this Santuario were the Penitentes.

4. Brothers of Light and of Blood

Among the early pilgrims flocking to the Santuario of Chimayó were groups of pious singing men who called themselves *Hermanos de Nuestro Padre Jesús Nazareno.* Their headquarters were in the parish church of Santa Cruz. Within its sanctum, whips made of still-new leather thongs tied in bunches now hung in the century-old chapels of the Third Order of St. Francis and of the Associates of the Lady of Mount Carmel, each of which adjoined the big church's transepts on either side. Outside the church, lying lengthwise against the nave's flanks, were several large crosses of timber that had not yet aged to gray since the bark had been removed.

Some of those people from Durango who had informed Abeyta about Guatemala's Christ of Esquipulas had also proposed a novel idea to the Franciscan Tertiaries and Carmelite Associates of the parish. Far down in the backwoods settlements of Guatemala, they said, and also in scattered and isolated pockets in New Spain, there were certain brotherhoods which wondrously made the Fridays of Lent and the sad days of Holy Week come alive with a penitence worthy of the Crucified Redeemer.

The particular *Hermandad* which the informants knew about was that of the Slaves of Jesus as their "Father," and in his cross-bearing role of

Nazareno. This Brotherhood was divided into *Hermanos de Luz* or Brothers of Light, who took care of the necessary lighting and did all the singing, and *Hermanos de Sangre* or Brothers of Blood. These either scourged themselves in honor of Christ as the blood-striped Ecce Homo, or else carried *maderos,* heavy timber crosses, as Jesus himself did as the Nazarene.

As with every church confraternity, there was an elected *hermano mayor,* or head brother, along with other minor officials; one of the latter was the *muñidor,* or beadle, who also played the flute at the head of the processions, and hence came to be known as the *pitero,* or piper. Some of the informants also knew by heart many of the organization's *alabados,* or elegiac sacred hymns, which the brethren now added to the store of traditional sacred music.

The majority of Hispanic males who did not choose to join them might have entertained a private disdain for the new movement, but in their heart of hearts they regarded it with genuine awe. It was the deep respect of the Spanish soul for penitence in any form. Not only the nonmembers of the parish of Santa Cruz, but entire families from the settlements of the great valley of Santa Clara and the neighboring ravines of Nambé and Pojoaque—and from even as far as the Villa of Santa Fe—began coming to Santa Cruz for the ceremonies of Holy Week.

The current pastor of Santa Cruz carried out the customary liturgy of Holy Week, which included the evening service of *las tinieblas,* or Tenebrae, in their necessarily simplest form, and also the *Via Crucis* or Way of the Cross. But now, while the lone priestly celebrant was reciting each sorrowful biblical psalm and prophecy in Latin, prior to the extinguishing of each taper upon the multiple candlestick, the new slaves of the Nazarene sang the most sorrowful of hymns in Spanish. The words of repeated refrains relating the sorrows of the Passion could be so well understood, and the tune was that nasal wavering wail so dear to the *anima hispanica,* whether in times of happiness or woe.

When the thirteenth candle was snuffed out to signify Christ's death, plunging the church into total darkness, the slapping sound made by the Brothers of Blood was heard amid the rattling of chains and the clatter of wooden ratchets. Jesus was dead liturgically, but not quite enough to sate the popular hunger aroused by the sung *alabados.*

Now big *hachones,* or torches of pitch pine, were being lit by the Brothers of Light outside the door as their doleful hymns were resumed. The young *monecillos* in their surplices heralded a procession by starting out of the church bearing high the black-painted cross of the Via Crucis, and the *pitero* fell in with them piping his wooden flute. Outside, rows of bare-chested Brothers of Blood with black hoods over their heads joined in, whips ready in hand. Others of them began shouldering heavy crosses as *nazarenos*, to drag them between their flagellant counterparts as these began lashing their backs to the rhythm of the piper's tune.

Then the rest of the congregation, young and old, followed them in two files, the men on one side and the women on the other, out over the graveyard in front and then across the village plaza, towards a Calvary hill outside the town.

As the chanting Brothers of Light paced slowly across the earthen square, lighting up the path for the cross-bearers and the flagellants, the sharp tattoo of whips on bare flesh, first over one shoulder and then over the other, and all in grim unison which made the cracking all the louder, also made the women and children and even sturdier men shiver and cringe. The flames of the torches themselves with their long manes of black smoke fluttered sidewise back and forth as if to ward off the blows.

For it was the night wind now streaming down from the sierra, as the procession left the sheltering houses, which intensified the shivering of human limbs as well as of the flares. It also carried up into the yawning night the rending cry of the human heart pierced to its depths upon the kind of landscape that had witnessed the very first Holy Week, from the scourging in Pilate's Praetorium and the Via Dolorosa through the streets of Jerusalem to the hill outside the gates. For the basic melody of Spain, in plaintive minor key, goes far beyond the *cante jondo* of gypsy wailing, or the muezzin's lonely cry to his Allah—back, far back, to a primitive chant of times beyond recall from which the *Kol Nidre* also drew its soul.

Here under the typically immense clear firmament of this new Canaan, festooned with Yahweh's pattern of numberless Genesis lamps, and across the stark upland landscape of his shepherd people, went the simple *hesed* of Abraham once more, of Abraham and his son Isaac climbing up the mount of sacrifice. Here it was a score and more of just as simple Isaacs bent beneath the faggots of their holocaust, to pause at last upon the arid crest and find that here, after all, a victim-lamb had already been prepared. It was the Lamb of God represented by the big cross of the *Calvario*.

However, unlike the ancient patriarchs and their early progeny, these rapt creatures now had a more solid and visible sign. He was the very Jesús Nazareno whose long-familiar figure stood inside the church below, dressed in a long red gown bearing his cross, or else stripped like the Ecce Homo—the "Sangre de Cristo"—with all the red stripes of his flogging showing. And always he wore the long matted wig, as of a nazirite's unshorn mane, held in place by a crown of thorns:

> Seeing Jesus crimson-gowned
> is a thing so evident,
> going forth nettle-crowned
> as Nazarene and Penitent.

And here his nazirite disciples, who had never heard of the name or of its scriptural institution, nor yet about the long-haired Samson—here they stood upon the hill like so many Samsons, and as uncouth as he must have looked, their eyes now blinded by the sweat of their gory striving.

The heavy crosses having been laid down, the plash of the whipping grown silent, the *hermano mayor* began addressing the brethren and the throngs of onlookers gathered round. And what the man said with so much feeling, as though the One they mourned actually hung dead upon the Calvary cross before them, was uttered in words as simple as those recorded in those holy scrolls of long ago. It was like the sermon from another much more famous Mount. The speaker had never read the Prophets or even seen a Testament—in fact, he could barely read the simple stanzas of the scribbled *alabados* held in his hand. But as he spoke, there mingled with the thick smoke of the waning flares, like an incense wafting back from ages past the sad soul of Palestine, what long had been set down in Isaiah 53 referring to a suffering Israel. But the Church Fathers had long applied it to the Nazarene:

> A thing despised and rejected by men,
> a man to make people screen their faces . . .
> And yet ours were the sufferings he bore,
> ours the sorrows he carried . . .
> Yet he was pierced through for our faults,
> crushed for our sins.

Nor would that old *caballero* of Sevilla, Don Fadríque de Ribera, nor any of those penitents of former times as satirized in *Don Quijote* and *Fray Gerundio* have seen anything amiss. Even Cervantes and Padre Isla, stopped short for the moment, would have solemnly recalled that sonnet "To Jesus Crucified" which they wished they had written themselves:

You move me, Lord; what moves me is to see
you nailed upon a cross and laughed to scorn.
Your wounded body moves me while I mourn
those insults and your death that so move me.
It is your love that moves me: if there were
no heaven, I would love with love to spare;
were there no hell, my love would still be there.

5. The Return of Father Abraham

Don Pedro Baustista Pino was only about sixty years old in 1811 when he left New Mexico for Spain to represent his people at the first constitutional Spanish Cortes held in Cádiz the following year. In those days a lifetime's constant exposure to extremes of cold and hot weather used to hasten the outward marks of senescence in males well before its time, just as childbirth did with those of their women who managed to survive a string of yearly deliveries.

Not only did Don Pedro declare himself to be an old man, but he must have actually looked like a hoary bearded patriarch to his fellow deputies in Spain. For they actually referred to him, whether endearingly or with disguised sarcasm, as their "Father Abraham from New Mexico." But looks are deceiving, particularly with regard to patriarchs of an old pastoral tradition. By this time Don Pedro had sired at least thirteen children by two successive wives, and he was to beget five more in a young third mate after his return from Spain. Had his condescendingly amused peers in parliament known about such prowess, they might have compared him with Jacob instead, and with greater reason if they had also known how he had acquired a big fortune in sheep which enabled him to make the round trip to Europe at his own expense.

None of this is said to disparage the good gentleman; it is that he represented in his physical appearance, along with his ways of building up his resources, the other few *ricos* of his day.

A number of these contemporaries of his also wore out their own succession of Leahs and Rachels, subsequently consigning them amid the loudest of Semitic wailing to their landscape's silent bosom.

What is of main significance for New Mexico in this period is that

Mother Spain finally remembered her long-lost tribe after more than two hundred years, and that one tribal son sailed back across the ocean sea to plead in his people's behalf. He was also to be the last. As for what he said and proposed, it was summarized for him by a literate gentleman of Cádiz, where the Pino report on New Mexico was printed in that very same year.

Although his merchant father and grandfather, who were natives of the city of Mexico, had been newcomers to the land, Don Pedro's birth in the local landscape and his native mother's Sánchez milk had molded him in the upland pastoral pattern of her family. One can almost hear her voice when he proudly tells his royal Majesty and the Cortes that his ancestors had been made *hidalgos* two centuries before, by none other than King Philip II in a decree granted to Don Juan de Oñate. His august audience must have cocked its collective head quizzically to one side, the way Vivaldo must have also done when Don Quijote brought up the noble house of Dulcinea.

In his New Mexico, he said with a pride worthy of the man of La Mancha, there was no welter of mixed breeds as in New Spain, and particularly in the city of Mexico which he had seen with his own eyes on the way over. The inhabitants of New Mexico were either pure Spaniards or pureblooded Indians. Evidently, he considered the many local *genízaros* as pure Amerindian, and in this he was correct, but he was ignoring some intermingling which had been taking place. Nor could he have known that many generations ago, some Tlascaltec blood from New Spain had trickled into the bloodstream; yet, since it had already been absorbed within the preponderance of Hispanic genes, he was more or less right in this boast.

Curiously, what he strongly emphasized at the very start was the fact that there were "no castes of people of African origin." New Mexico, he said, was the only province in all Spanish America that enjoyed this distinction. By this time, of course, his people no longer remembered that the black-skinned son of a mulatto and his Tlascaltec wife had engineered the great Indian Revolt of 1680, and a black grandson the smaller one of 1696. Nor could they recall that the famed Don Diego de Vargas in 1692 had brought along a black drummer, a real jungle native of Luanda in Portuguese West Africa, whose grandchildren by his one son had been among the first settlers of Trampas.

But, then again, all this had happened so long ago that this minor African strain had become sufficiently diluted in the *genízaro* element to pass unnoticed. The numerous African-derived castes which Don Pedro had seen and marveled at in the port of Vera Cruz, where he embarked for Spain, were certainly not to be seen in his own most *castizo* homeland.

Much less, said he, was there any pauper misery in his beloved country, "no vagrants or beggars that swarm like ants in the viceroyalty of Mexico." Nor was there any unrest on this account, said he. In New Mexico every family had its own plot of land whereby its members could make a peaceful living from agriculture and other sorts of labor with their hands. All this was very true on the surface, since mendicancy is a distinctive blight of large urban centers, and his rustic New Mexico had none of these. One does not read about beggars among the early shepherd folk of the Bible, but there were plenty later on in Jerusalem.

Don Pedro claimed that even the poorest of Hispanic folks had their own homes, with some domestic animals and enough measures of victuals to tide them over the year. But, like most persons of means, he did not realize that these creatures who addressed him and his peers as *"patrón"* managed to survive many a long and cold winter, or a prolonged season of drought, with many a pang in their bellies.

He also told the European Spaniards that the homes of their New Mexican cousins were extraordinarily clean—"anyone who has seen the homes in Cádiz (with the exception of iron grillwork and balconies) has seen their equivalent." No doubt, he had been shocked by the filthy hovels of the different Indo-Negroid castes in Mexico and Vera Cruz, and he also might have had in mind the houses of the *genízaros* back home. But even among the lowliest of the Spanish folk of New Mexico, the interiors of their homes were spotless, although the floors might be of tamped earth and the ceilings of bare logs and unplaned timber. This particular observation of Don Pedro rings the truest, for utmost neatness is a distinctive character of even the humblest Spanish home in New Mexico to this day.

The hoary old fellow did not overlook the females of his country, as what upland sheikh or patriarch would. For he had to remark in passing: "The women (to whom nature has granted grace and beauty) wear dresses and small shawls, and they trim their hair, as has been the custom from remote antiquity, and as do our gypsies today." It seems as though the society ladies of Cádiz at the moment had adopted French fashions the way their men were practicing French politics, for Don Pedro to recognize the older tradition of Spanish female attire in the first gypsies he had ever seen.

To Señor Pino's greatest credit, for one coming directly from a primitive culture into the civilization of *tierra afuera*, he was not overawed by the architectural grandeur and the commercial bustle of urban centers in southern New Spain or in Spain herself across the sea. So clear did the native purity of his native landscape shine in his soul that, even amid the obvious advantages of cities built in much lusher surroundings, he could not help but be appalled by the material and moral squalor inherent in them.

Yet, because certain elements of this civilization were beginning to make steady inroads into his pastoral homeland over the commercial trail from Chihuahua and Durango, he was fully aware of measures that should be taken to prepare his isolated and long-neglected constituents for them.

                                    *   *   *

Everything that our Father Abraham proposed in the Spanish Cortes was quite practical, now that his pastoral Israel was about to become a crossroads of commerce. After outlining the natural resources of New Mexico, along with the produce from livestock and any improved farming, he suggested that the national government should establish small industries. Recently the viceroy had sent master weavers to teach the latest methods in the craft, and this was already doing very well. (One wonders if these instructors were among those other outsiders who had taught the folk of Santa Cruz and Chimayó about the Penitentes and the Christ of Esquipulas.)

Otherwise, said he, whatever little cash was paid in Santa Fe for raw products was promptly taken back to Durango as exchange for manufactured goods there. Precisely because of this the land's economy was of the poorest. Moreover, since there were no seaports at all, freighting costs were enormous—here he was speaking from his own family's experience—and each such enterprise could end in total loss at the hands of marauding wild Apaches all along the route.

All other departments, the civil along with the ecclesiastic, were in the worst need of royal assistance. The governor himself did not even have a secretarial aide, while the much-needed colonial militia was short of arms and largely unpaid. There was no education by and large; a college for laymen and seminarians had been authorized six years before, but nothing had come of it. Such an institute became every day more urgent. In this connection with religious matters, Don Pedro remarked that his countrymen had not seen a bishop for fifty years, and none had received holy confirmation—"I, an old man, did not know how bishops dressed until I came to Cádiz." As a result, first and second cousins, who had to marry one another because of the restricted population, were living in sin because it was so difficult to obtain matrimonial dispensations in faraway Durango. Therefore, Santa Fe should be made the seat of a bishopric.

Anyway, nothing came of Señor Pino's pleadings before parliament. For Spain's government was much too busy with civil upheavals both at home and abroad to pay any attention to the least of its subjects at the furthest edges of civilization. And so the sheep that had been found was lost again. Back in New Mexico the large Pino relationship, in tune with that brother of his at El Rancho de San Clemente, kept on boasting for years thereafter about their patriarch who had been a deputy at the Spanish Cortes. But the common folk looked upon the whole venture with the fatalism of the *ganadero* long inured to suffering and disappointment—yet at the same time sharply alive to anything savoring of the quixotic. Noting that Don Pedro had merely gone away and then returned, they immortalized the sterile trip in a *dicho* as concisely and witfully pregnant as any semitic *mashal* refrains in Proverbs:

> Don Pedro Pino fué,
> Don Pedro Pino vino.

It is also of the stuff which Don Quijote kept hearing from his squire Sancho Panza.

18

The Mexican Interlude

An amusing pastime, among publicists and private individuals in New Mexico today, is the collecting of historical and geographical blunders about New Mexico which are continually being made by people in her eastern sister-states. A private person or a business house in Santa Fe or Albuquerque will place an order with some commercial concern in New York, Boston, or Chicago, and a letter comes back stating that export duties have to be paid, or else that no transactions are being made outside the United States. And well before the tourist season begins, some naïve citizen from some other part of our nation will write to local chambers of commerce about necessary visas for visiting New Mexico, and also about such matters as the rates of monetary exchange.

One would expect that anyone who had any geography in school would readily recall that on our national map New Mexico, wedged between Arizona and the Texas Panhandle, is most graphically an integral part of the United States. Or that "New Mexico" with two words is totally distinct from the single-word "Mexico" designating the republic south of the border. Nor does it do any good to explain that New Mexico's name antedates the one of the Mexican republic by more than two centuries, and that to say "Old Mexico" is to express an anachronism.

A person can keep on citing in vain how New Mexico was under Spain for over two hundred years, and under Mexico for a mere twenty-five. Furthermore, she has since been a part of the United States for more than a century and a quarter. But it is like telling a certain type of mind that little George Washington did not chop down a cherry tree, or that a whale never swallowed Jonah. Perhaps it is this kind of hardshell mentality that explains it all.

Whatever the causes of misunderstanding, the fact is that New Mexico did belong briefly to the infant Mexican nation, from 1821 to 1846. Brief though this period was, it was an important one, for it marked her transition into the more prosaic modern scene from the halcyon days we have been following all this while with regard to the Hispanic notions of *hidalguía* and *conquista*. Old rustic fellows in every economic or social level might continue addressing each other as *caballeros* indefinitely, and a few will vaguely recall that their forebears were *conquistadores*. But the historical details are so blurred that these memories reach a point of pathetic myth if not ridiculous exaggeration.

The deep feeling of *catolicismo* remains as strong as ever, thanks to the language and the landscape, but with its sole remaining element of *penitencia* it is generally reduced to a pitiful reliance on such peripheral manifestations as can be found in the miraculous dust of Chimayó and the blood-letting rites of the Penitentes.

It is the external landscape that remains its own Palestinian-Castilian self, and for its complement within the people, the old language of Cervantes. While the general Castilian tradition which depends so much on literateness for its historical continuity fades away, the land and the spoken language will not let the last element of penitential awareness die. The Penitentes as such are only one minor tangible factor, and a recent one at that. From now on governments, whether civil or ecclesiastical, may come and go, but the land with its crystal sky by night and day, and the language in its unspoiled simplicity, keep on speaking of a *hesed* for so long as the distractions of an encroaching civilization do not start blurring its image and muffling its voice.

1. The Maccabees of Mexico

It might not be altogether apropos to compare the Mexican wars of independence with the struggles which the Palestinian Jews of a couple of centuries before Christ carried on against their Syrian and Greek oppressors. First of all, southern New Spain was not a Palestinian landscape, nor was the majority of its people a pastoral folk. They comprised a wide ethnic variety covering the whole gamut of occupations, and ranging from the greatest wealth to the most abject poverty, from highest culture to lowest misery.

As in ancient Babylon or Egypt, it was largely an agricultural activity supporting larger or lesser commercial centers. Furthermore, as purely children of the Cross in the Hispanic tradition, the inhabitants as a whole were less apt to make any biblical comparisons; yet, at least in one instance, some contemporary writer did make a reference to the insurgents' "Maccabean firmness." It is a handy allusion nevertheless.

Alarmed by the republican ideas which had been eroding the once absolute monarchy of Spain, the Spanish civil and church aristocracy in Mexico and other large cities of New Spain sought to preserve their old medieval privileges by seceding and setting up their own pure church-state monarchy in the New World. On the heavier side of the scale, the larger mass of common people yearned for the basic human privilege of being their own free selves under the libertarian principles of a new age. These aspirations had been squelched a decade before with the defeat of Padre Hidalgo and his banner of Guadalupe. Now, united in a common cause with the lesser but more powerful aristocracy, they succeeded in securing their independence in 1821.

The New Spain of the viceroys died, and their very own Mexico was born at last. Here the Maccabean comparison ends; for they were completely and permanently victorious, while there was no such thing as a Roman Empire to take over where Greek and Syrian despotism had left off in Palestine. True, the more powerful church-state aristocracy did set up a Mexican Empire, but it was short-lived.

Now animated by their newly gained freedom, the common people formulated their first democratic constitution, the famed Plan of Iguala of 1822, which made them one nation of Mexican citizens by obliterating all former references to racial origin. If they did not restore the Guadalupe symbol of Padre Hidalgo to their national flag, but chose the motif of eagle and serpent instead, it was because they had chosen the name "México" for their new nation.

*   *   *

In faraway and practically forgotten New Mexico—likewise named after the same ancient capital more than two centuries before, and for altogether different reasons as well as under very different circumstances —these revolutionary movements across the great wilderness in New Spain had caused only a ripple at best. While the few officials in Santa Fe or the few clergy were duly informed through their respective channels, their scattered subjects and flocks had no way of assessing what was taking place in *tierra afuera*. Still captives of their isolated landscape and its simple pastoral economy, all they thought about was how the uncertain vagaries of weather would affect their herds and flocks upon the open *mesta*, or their meager crops along the narrow stream bottoms. Or they might be wondering when the wild and fierce Edomites who surrounded them on every side would strike next—the Comanches from the eastern plains or the Utes from the northern mountains, the Apaches from the south or the Navajos from the western desert, to make away with their best horses and perhaps some of their children.

Beyond this there lay no other land worth considering, save for that heavenly place from where an inscrutable God watched over it all—"blessed be his Holy Name." All around them stood Calvary hills bearing their crosses long before the Penitentes began at Santa Cruz; and all the burdens imposed by weather or by the infidel Indians were as many crosses to be borne for the sake of the Nazarene who had carried his own as an example for everyone. What else could helpless man do in this vale of tears?

It was more than a case of simple ignorance when a child, in my own day, upon being coached by a nun to pray in English, "to thee do we cry, poor banished children of Eve," insisted on saying "poor Spanish children of Eve."

Séa por Dios, let it be God's will, was their last resort in the context of Judeo-Christian resignation, but it was also interwoven with threads of Moorish fatalism—*lo que será, será*. Yet through God's will and one's own penances nobly borne, things would turn for the better. *Ojalá que sí*, may Allah will it so.

All this should explain why the prescribed ceremonials in Santa Fe, which celebrated the Act of Mexican Independence on December 31, 1821, were tame and subdued. The town's cultural resources were not of the best, to start with, but it is interesting to note that for a pageant or tableau which was staged on the old plaza, no native citizens were among the chief characters. An officer called Abréu, who was from the provinces to the south, played the role of "Independence." The local pastor named Terrazas, a secular priest from Durango, represented "Religion." Old Padre Hozio, the Spain-born Franciscan who was still chaplain of the garrison, acted the part of "Union." Even the capital's current mayor, who was in charge of the activities, was an outsider from Chihuahua named Armendaris.

One native citizen named Vigil had been deputized to have an allegorical backdrop painted for the stage; that it was done to the satisfaction of the officials means that there happened to be another alien "Molleno" artist in town, possibly in the small squad of Mexican regulars at the garrison.

But what did make a lasting impression on everyone in the years immediately following, except among the Pueblo Indians, was that one law in the Mexican Plan of Iguala which stipulated that in the future no person was to be referred to by his racial origins, either in ecclesiastical or civil acts. The universal term to be used was a national one: *Ciudadano Mexicano.* The result was that in time everyone was proudly calling himself a Mexican Citizen. This means that the priests and magistrates, most of whom were from Mexico, rode the new edicts hard. One can almost hear a notary reading back the last will and testament to a dying patriarch as all his family and kin kneel around the bedside: "I, Manuel Castillo, *Mexican Citizen,* being of sound mind. . . ." Or an *alcalde* meting out justice to a poor fellow who had stolen a *rico's* cow: "You, Esquipulas Moya, *Mexican Citizen,* are hereby condemned. . . ." And much more solemn is the scene at the font when the padre says aloud for all to hear: "Francisco, *Mexican Citizen,* I baptize you. . . ." Or at the altar when he asks: "Will you, Antonio Salas, *Mexican Citizen,* take Juanita Trujillo, *Mexican Citizen,* for your lawful wife. . . . "

The Spanish people, especially those of the more affluent families, proudly adopted the new designation in its purely civic sense; otherwise, they continued esteeming themselves *españoles* and children of *conquistadores* in contradistinction to the *genízaros,* and even others of just as good Spanish stock who herded their livestock or swept their homes. Such things never die. These poorer and lowlier folk, no less Hispanic than their wealthier kin who sometimes kept them in peonage, took to the new term as though it were a sign of economic relief. But it was welcomed most of all by the *genízaros*—all bearing Spanish names and devout followers of the Spanish Cross, and speaking only the Spanish language, yet up until now being made to feel that they were an inferior class among God's children. It was as if the proselyte servants of Abraham or Jacob, while duly circumcized and instructed in the ways of Yahweh, had at last been told all of a sudden: "From now on you are full-fledged children of the Promise."

*   *   *

Already at this time, other events were beginning to prepare the way for a quick end to this Mexican interlude. Foremost was the Santa Fe Trail between Santa Fe and Missouri which started bringing in new ideas and a different kind of people. These new folk naturally regarded all of the region's Spanish-speaking inhabitants, except the Pueblo Indians, as "Mexicans." It was not only because New Mexico belonged to the new republic of Mexico at the time, but because her people were very proud of the name as citizens. But, when all is said and done, it is in a way unfortunate, if only because of the confusion current today regarding New Mexico's name, that the great new republic to the south chose the name "Mexico."

It could most appropriately have called itself "Azteca" or "Aztlan," in honor of that pre-Columbian native empire which represented the apex of Amerindian culture in that region. Its citizens would be known as "Aztecs" or "Aztlans" today. Or the new nation could very well have chosen "Guadalupe" from that miracle of roses that had created a people, and these would now be "Guadalupeans" or something like it.

Then our present New Mexico with her old historic name would stand free with her own clear identity in the eyes of the outsider. Her own distinctive landscape and heritage, however poor the latter may be, would not be aligned or confused with the Mexican. But this was not to be and, after all, Mexico had the fullest right to assume the name of her capital.

2. The Bishop

The portraits of Don Antonio de Zubiría show a Spaniard of most refined background and a man of very strong character. What we know of his life as bishop of Durango adds the qualities of highest dedication and deepest compassion. Hardly had he taken possession of his frontier diocese, which at that time was wild desert country outside his cathedral city, than he began a personal visitation in his immediate territory. This done, his eyes turned northeastward to that New Mexico he had been reading about in a journal written almost seventy-five years before by a predecessor of his named Tamarón. No bishop of Durango had gone there since.

Right away his resolve was made. In the early spring of 1833, after making his pastoral visitation of the young and thriving mining city of Chihuahua midway on his journey, then doing the same at the small mission town of Guadalupe del Paso with its adjoining farming villages along the Rio Grande, he entered what the oldest archival papers mentioned as a kingdom—and the rocky ford of El Paso del Norte as the gates of the kingdom. What he saw for the first hundred and more miles, including La Jornada del Muerto, was very much like the desert country he had traversed so far, except that distant mountains on the horizon were an extremely rich blue for being covered with forests, so it was explained to him, and because the glare of the sun was far less blinding than in the more torrid south.

When the trail sought the river valley once more, the eye could measure the ever-steeper incline of the land from the rushing downflow of the current. It had been aptly named the Fierce River from the North. Gradually and steadily, too, the drab Sonoran-type face of the landscape began showing a healthy flush in varied hues, like a person recovering from a long illness. The colorless mesquite which had become much dwindled in size with the land's rise was giving way to scattered stands of small evergreens on the hillsides which gave a fleeting impression of olive orchards. On the high mountains closing in on either side one could already discern small patches, and then bigger expanses, of cool pine and spruce. And the sky, because the sun was less and less a blazing furnace, shone a rich azure such as he had never seen except on a calm and cool ocean surface off Mazatlan.

His lordship began recalling a passage he had read with much interest, as part of his preparation for this trip, in a history of New Spain written by a friar of Jalisco. In it the author stated that, from what others had written, the northernmost Hispanic settlement called The New Mexico, "was most similar to the Spanish peninsula because of its fertility, climate, and products." "It is open and delightful, and embraces a part of the Sierra Madre which is considered a source of gold and silver. It would be a most prosperous country if the wild Indians were not so near."

The landscape did look Castilian, as he remembered it when he rode across its high plateau on his way to Rome and back. And the large number of mounted men escorting his party kept reminding him that somewhere among the hills and gullies on either side, groups of Apache scouts were assessing the armed strength of the escort. As for the gold and silver, however, the miners in Chihuahua had already told him that the people of New Mexico had never fully explored all the possibilities. The only placer gold mines there, at El Real de Dolores and San Francisco de Paula just south of Santa Fe, had recently been started by two European Spaniards who had operated in Chihuahua for a time.

The native New Mexicans had long been content to be cattlemen and sheepmen, they said, because it was their tradition and because their land was of the best for grazing. Occasionally they hunted the very large deer and elk of their mountains and the gigantic bison of their plains. All this was the New Mexican "gold" which the merchants brought down to exchange for goods and Chihuahua silver.

This alone could be a sign and promise of a very prosperous population. But once the newly settled town of Socorro had been reached, and then the more closely continuous villages and ranchos northward from Tomé and Belén on either bank of the large river, Bishop Zubiría began having second thoughts—as had the first priests from his diocese thirty-five years before. It was the same story previously related about those clergymen as they entered the land.

As for the people, how they gaped with childlike delight when he donned his tall silken miter and carried his golden crozier while administering confirmation in each major town. The answers the godparents and the adults being confirmed gave to his questions on matters of faith were just as simple—too simple, in fact, among a goodly number. At other times he overheard remarks having to do with witchcraft, such as the evil eye, but this was something he had experienced elsewhere, even among educated folk. And yet, he felt among these people an intensity of faith which he had seldom experienced before.

After having been received with the rudiments of pontifical pomp and circumstance which only the Villa of Santa Fe could afford, thanks to the governor's better resources and those of the town merchants, along with the salutes and color provided by the small garrison, the good shepherd proceeded on his visitation of the churches north of the capital. On the way over, certain thoughts which had lain dormant now began awakening in his mind. Among some mental notes made in Durango while perusing the reports of a previous inspector, he now recalled some disturbing ones dealing with a parish called Santa Cruz de la Cañada.

*   *   *

The pastor of Santa Cruz, a secular priest from Durango who had been in the region for several years, had no reason to hedge or dissemble when answering his new bishop's questions concerning the rows of cat-o-nine-tails hanging along the walls in the two lateral chapels of the Third Order and the Lady of Mount Carmel. Likewise, about the big timber crosses resting on their sides along the exterior walls of the church. The suspicious stains on all of them were relatively recent, since Lent had ended only a few weeks before.

All these paraphernalia and the bloodstains, the pastor said, belonged to a large confraternity in the parish which called itself the Brotherhood of Our Father Jesus the Nazarene. The people called them Penitentes, but the members liked to refer to themselves as brethren of the Third Order of St. Francis. The Third Order was no more, he said, since the last Franciscan pastor had left twenty-five years before, but they did use their old chapel for their meetings. There were over a hundred now in Santa Cruz alone, and new chapters had been started in most other villages of the Rio Arriba region.

His lordship, digging into his mental notes, remembered that only two years before his Vicar in Santa Fe had allowed these "Third Order" brethren, ninety of them, to hold their exercises in Taos—"provided there were no abuses." These abuses he could well imagine. His suspicions were confirmed when the pastor minutely described the scourging which took place within the church on every Friday of Lent, after the priest and people had prayed the customary stations of the Cross.

In the last three evenings of Holy Week, there was more of the same but with much greater fervor after the services of Tenebrae, followed by a general procession to a Calvary hill east of the town. He himself was greatly impressed, the pastor went on to say, both by the earnestness of the penitents themselves and by the great devotion displayed, not only by his own parishioners, but by other people who came from the surrounding countryside to watch the spectacle.

The next morning the church was filled to the bare walls with the pungent smell of the packed congregation, young and old, eagerly awaiting the ceremonial of confirmation. Standing in the less oppressive atmosphere of the high altar steps, the bishop was conscious of the impression he made upon them in his stately cope and miter; he also felt with humble compassion the heat waves of faith along with the glow of admiration as he counseled them in the ways of Christian living. Although not altogether pleased with some edicts of the new republic, he also reminded them of their duties as Mexican citizens of a new government which promised better things by way of education. In this connection he called for a native clergy, young men from their very own hearths who someday soon could instruct them more fully in the doctrines of Holy Church. He himself did not have enough priests to spare, and the Franciscan province in the Mexican capital was likewise short in personnel.

Without such instruction and guidance, he told his attentive flock, they could easily fall into many errors. Suddenly his fatherly visage changed to one of a stern schoolmaster when he began speaking about the blood-stained whips and crosses he had seen upon his arrival.

He left the gist of this discourse in a long pastoral letter and other instructions which he ordered to be read in all the parishes. After several pages of paternal exhortations, he then lashes out at the existence

> for a goodly number of years thus far, of a brotherhood of Penitentes without the authorization or even the knowledge of the Bishops, who certainly would never have given their consent for such a Brotherhood . . . because the excesses of most indiscreet corporal penances which they are accustomed to practice on some days of the year, and publicly at that, are so contrary to the Spirit of Religion and the decrees of Holy Church. We command, and lay it strictly upon the conscience of our parish priests in this Villa, the present one and those to come, that in future such assemblies of Penitentes shall not be allowed under any pretext whatsoever. . . .

In a separate instruction addressed directly to the pastor, regarding the sacrament of confession in particular, he returns to the same subject:

> In concluding this section, so as to forestall another great evil that can become still worse, I forbid for all time to come those brotherhoods of penitence—or, better still, of Butchery—which have been growing under the shelter of an inexcusable toleration. Each parish priest or friar-minister, in all the territory of his administration, will see to it that not a single one of these brotherhoods remains in existence, and that in no place will there be a collection or preservation of these big timber crosses and other instruments of torture whereby some half-kill their bodies, whereas one can see at the very same time that they pay no heed to their souls, letting them remain in sin for years on end. . . .
> Moderate penance is not forbidden, since it is so salutary for

the spirit, but let it be performed without assemblages wrongly called brotherhoods which have no legal authorization whatsoever. In conclusion, anyone who is moved by a good spirit may have the usual devices of penitence that he may choose for mortification, and not for destruction; but let him keep them private.

It was the second quarter of the ninteenth century, and yet throughout the Spanish world token flagellation (and sometimes the bloody kind) was still being practiced privately by some individuals in monasteries, while certain overpious laymen observed it in the secrecy of their chambers. But it always had to be under the discreet guidance of a spiritual director. This the bishop could not condemn, even if he wanted to, and now he guardedly approved of it. But public bloody flagellation, and worse still by societies formed for this one purpose, ran contrary to the norm of the times and current decrees of the Church.

He well knew that his fellow bishops in southern Mexico and Central America had long had this problem with similar penitential groups, and with worse manifestations such as actual crucifixions, among the lowest classes of *mestizos* and Indians in isolated pockets of their own dioceses. These had existed since the years following the Conquest of Mexico when public processions of blood had been suppressed under heavy penalties. Since then, church and civil attempts at suppressing them had proved futile.

Here, at the far edges of his own frontier bishopric, the problem was not so old and ingrained that it could not be nipped in the bud. His present firm condemnation should take care of it.

The pastor of Santa Cruz duly followed his orders, and the whips and big crosses disappeared from the parish church. But soon, well away from the town among the juniper-freckled eastern foothills of the Sangre de Cristo, there stood a lone adobe structure with no exterior windows. It consisted of a chapel with its small altar loaded with locally made *santos*, and the whips of the men who built it hung along the interior walls. There were other chambers for cooking and dining, or for periods of surcease from exhaustion and pain. Outside against the walls lay some large timber crosses, and a path led from there to the more prominent of the hills nearby, on whose top a big Calvary cross greeted the sky.

The lonely building was called a *morada*, from the verb *morar*—"to lodge for a while." For it was generally used only throughout the penitential season of Lent. But it did not remain the only one of its kind for long. Further up the Chimayó valley as far as El Santuario, each tiny community followed the example with its smaller *morada* somewhere nearby; and still further and higher up, there were others to be found near the villages of Quemado, Truchas, and Trampas, all nestling on the very lap of the great sierra now so appropriately being referred to as La Sierra de la Sangre de Cristo.

Good Bishop Zubiría made two more personal visitations, in 1845 and 1850, and each one more difficult for him as he grew older and the Apaches along the way more dangerous. In the meantime he had educated in Durango, and subsequently ordained, several young men from the region to administer the things of faith among their own people. One young priest in Taos by the name of Antonio José Martínez, whom his predecessor had ordained not long before his first visit, was most helpful in preparing candidates for the seminary. It was a most difficult if rewarding process, what with the great penury and lack of schools in the province, not to mention the perils and hardships of travel which he knew at first hand. When he came back on his third and last pastoral visitation, the country was already four years in the hands of the English-speaking Americans.

Yet, in spite of disturbances and changes, and the continuing illiteracy of the more common folk and the poor physical state of the churches, he still felt that quality of intense faith among the Hispanic people which had struck him during his first visit. Like their open and clear landscape, it was still the same. All that he could tell them now as a final farewell was for them to guard it all the more jealously among an ever-growing number of blond foreigners whom he naturally regarded as heretics.

3. The General

Two full centuries, and a good part of a third, had drifted over the Palestinian-Castilian landscape since the birthday of a people on that hope-filled April day at La Toma in 1598. To be sure, these were only a few grains of sand in the hourglass when compared with the duneful of dynasties in the ancient Near East, or the centuries of Spain since her own history began. But to this newer landscape's Hispanic folk, so woefully lacking in chronicles and scriptures of any sort, it could have been ages since the only two big names they could recall—Oñate and Vargas—had figured in the conquests of their beloved homeland. It was much like the universal case of simple Christians, or Jews and Muslims, shoving Abraham and Moses far back in time, into the misty era of the world's very Creation.

If those first colonists at La Toma, and then at the founding of Santa Fe and the Kingdom, could have been transported now in spirit, they would have recognized themselves in the faces and deportment of the greater part of the population. The language was the same, too, and most of all a staunch and simple faith bursting through the crust of so many familiar foibles.

The pastoral dukedoms for which they themselves had left their original homes were still there, albeit more replete with flocks and herds as there were many more widespread villages and ranchos, many of them with better farming pieces of land; but so were the fierce tribes harassing them on every side more numerous, and much better equipped with arms and horses. To their surprise, the mud look of the homes and churches had not developed into the old country's Mediterranean look of white arches and red tile, but this was of minor consequence; from their now detached point of view, it all went so well with the landscape. In fact, they rejoiced to see that their pastoral dukedoms seemed to have remained unspoiled.

But, on closer look, they found some things new and perplexing. Not only the manner of dress, but this matter of a Mexican republic which had erased all traces of their Kingdom. Then there was that part of the population, still occasionally referred to as *genízaros;* these were to be seen here and there, living at the edges of the Spanish towns, or else in their own villages strategically placed on the wild Indian frontier, like buffer settlements. In fact, these people did resemble the Indians of the plains and deserts in their faces and general bearing. Yet they were Christians and had Spanish names; and they spoke understandable Castilian even though they dropped more consonants (and letter "esses") than the Andalusians back in southern Spain.

And all, along with the Spanish people, now called themselves Mexicans, which was also most strange. For these transported onlookers, the term had denoted the Aztecs in their day, or, in a broader sense, any resident of the great valley of Mexico.

Still more amazing were other kinds of faces which had to be those of Englishmen, surely, although they were calling themselves Americans. But the onlookers' progeny called them *gringos;* this they readily understood, since the word was a corruption of "Griegos," which in Spain had been first applied to Greek foreigners, and eventually to all north European folks, the English in particular. Now these Englishmen who called themselves Americans were coming into the land in long wagon trains loaded with all kinds of interesting goods from a place called Missouri. These vehicles with great spoked wheels were just as great a marvel; if only they had existed in their own day when they crossed the great Sonoran wilderness to settle the land.

Not so amazing in themselves, but still a surprise because they were new in the land, were the scattered groups of organized Penitentes. Had Captain Villagrá been present also, he would have wondered how and when in the dickens—*¿como diantres?*—they had come. He remembered inserting that flagellation scene into his epic poem for dramatic effect, and as a pious boost for his leader; now the gallant soldier-poet considered himself not only a bard but a prophet as well.

Lastly, by way of ending this bit of fantasy, we can see the whole ancestral company showing considerable interest in a small civil war, when the people of the north murdered the Mexican governor; but they themselves had done the same to a royal Spanish governor when the Kingdom was new. How fondly they recalled those squabbles they had with many such sent by the viceroy. Hence they were not too much surprised at the political and military antics of a particular person who prided himself in being called "The General."

*   *   *

In 1837, the sixteenth year of the Mexican interlude, and only four years after Bishop Zubiría's first visit, there was a revolt in the Rio Arriba mountain country north of Santa Fe against the new republican government. It was mainly a question of taxes, a most distasteful thing which the New Mexicans had never known before. For this their ancestors had left feudal Spain and viceregal New Spain, preferring a primitive pastoral isolation to any civic and commercial developments which—as Samuel long ago had forewarned the Israelites—brought on the civilized burdens of systematic tribute.

This particular feature of Mexican citizenship nobody liked, and most of all the former *genízaros* who by now had developed their farmlands and herds whereby they lived comfortably if poorly. Perhaps also, something in their nomadic blood rebelled at the very thought of taxation. But, whereas the Spanish *ricos* as well as the *pobres* in Santa Fe and the Rio Abajo simply mumbled to themselves, the folk of the Rio Arriba were doing something about it.

That the rebellion caught fire in the northern mountain country, and was carried out with extraordinary violence, is nothing new in human annals; highland peoples have ever been the first to assert their independence in civil and religious crises, although often with a limited vision. As Jung once observed, mountains are not only geographical barriers but they also limit the horizons of the human spirit. It had happened at the miraculous hole in Chimayó along with the Penitente *moradas.*

Moreover, a goodly number of the protestors were *genízaro* descendants of the warlike Indians of the plains. The Mexican name and their equal status as Mexican citizens now gave them a pride and courage never dreamed of before. For several years now these same northerners had betrayed the same spirit, if only by silent protest, when they disregarded the bishop's strict orders and spread their Penitente *moradas* throughout the mountain villages. That these rebels were also Penitentes in great part is reflected in the language of their declaration of war at the decisive *junta* held in Santa Cruz—to be on the side of Jesus Christ, and to fight for Jesus Christ, until the last drop of blood was spilled in the struggle.

Their leader was José Angel Gonzales, nicknamed "El Angelito" from his middle name in diminutive form. Whether a tough little fellow or a powerful giant of a man, he was known as an intrepid hunter of bison all over the land. His father, who was descended from several sturdy plains tribes, and his mother, who was a Taos Pueblo woman, had lived the Spanish way of life in which Gonzales was reared as a *genízaro.* As such, and because so many of his followers were of the same background, he had no trouble enlisting the aid of the Indians of Taos and other pueblos.

To compress the story at this point, Gonzales and his wild army massacred Mexican Governor Pérez along with some of his staff from Mexico, and a couple of high native officials of Santa Fe. They took the capital without trouble and, like good Christians emulating the former receptions of the royal Spanish governors, they proceeded to the parish church to render thanks for the victory. Then José Gonzales was installed as governor at the venerable *casas reales* which for over a century now had been referred to as a "palace." By pure coincidence, yet as though history does enjoy being poetic, it all happened on the tenth day of August, the very day of the Pueblo Indian Revolt of 1680.

In sharp contrast, however, there was no further bloodshed. The native population of Santa Fe was left unharmed and also, to their great relief, the American merchants who happened to be in the capital. Gonzales then called a general assembly which was to draft a list of grievances for presentation to the supreme Mexican government. Some Hispanic leaders attended, and prominent among these was a certain one from the Rio Abajo named Manuel Armijo.

Armijo had been *jefe político* or departmental governor of New Mexico for a short term ten years before, and it was no secret that he sought the office again. Some believed that he had been an instigator of the revolt, using Gonzales as a cat's-paw in order to take hold of the government once more. But no one in the assembly spoke in his behalf, either before or after Gonzales declared himself the interim governor. The meeting over, Manuel Armijo returned to Albuquerque with new plans forming inside his head. For it was not only a personal disappointment that rankled inside of it. As a *rico* and an *español*, he felt that his homeland's government had been degraded by Gonzales and his motley mob. He also knew that his compatriots in Santa Fe and the Rio Abajo felt the same way.

Here we abbreviate events again. Armijo marched north in the following year at the head of his southern militiamen and a troop of regulars sent up by the Mexican president. He easily defeated Gonzales and his forces, which had fled to Santa Cruz, then promptly executed their leader with some of his officials. Before having Gonzales put away, Armijo told Padre Martínez of Taos, who happened to be present: "Hear the confession of this Genízaro so that they can give him five bullets." And so El Angelito fell before this casually ordered fusillade.

The Mexican government then rewarded Armijo by confirming him as governor and general military commander of New Mexico. What he liked best was the title of "General," the most high-sounding rank in modern republican armies. Now the General was on his way to his much-controverted tryst with destiny.

*   *   *

At this time New Mexico did not lack native sons of stout character and education, several of whom came to play very important civic and military roles during the Mexican interlude and well into American territorial times. The greater number belonged to the currently affluent families ranging alphabetically from the southern Baca, Armijo, and Chávez clans to the northern Martínez, Ortiz, and Vigil family groupings. Like

Manuel Armijo's, their lives spanned three periods of government: Spanish, Mexican, American.

By far more unfortunate is the fact that not a one of these excellent men can represent this important period of transition as fully, and as dramatically, as did Manuel Armijo. The mantle of an epoch's chief protagonist does not necessarily fall on the bravest or the most honorable individual. Nevertheless, Armijo happens to be a good composite of the native Spanish New Mexican in many ways, whether one likes it or not.

A rare portrait of him shows a genuine Spanish face, handsome but lacking the refined depths so evident, let us say, in the ones of Bishop Zubiría. The plumed admiralty hat that he wears even gives him a definite Napoleonic look, at least that air one associates with the militaristic and political opportunist. Although officially a Mexican *ciudadano* and *jefe político,* Manuel Armijo is a genuine sampling of the New Mexican pastoral *español* in whom the blood and instincts of the Oñate and Vargas colonists commingle. And, to flavor the native *olla podrida,* there is a dash of the landscape's own prehistoric salt.

His great-grandfather, Vicente Durán de Armijo, had come as a youth to Santa Fe in 1695, along with his parents and brothers who were in the colony from Zacatecas. It was a better than average family as regards material means and native talents, and also some education; his eldest brother was the first lay barber or surgeon to come to New Mexico. Sometime later, Vicente married María de Apodaca of Santa Fe, who happened to be half-Tewa, as the aftermath of one of those incidents in history which best lend it color and charm.

María's mother was a Spanish girl who had been taken captive along with some other women in the Pueblo Revolt of 1680. When rescued twelve years later at the pueblo of San Juan by Don Diego de Vargas and his troops, she had with her a small daughter (María) and a younger son—either one of them sired by one or the other of her Tewa captors. Little María must have been a most attractive child; when the soldiers offered to stand as godfathers in baptism for the children of the other captive women, Don Diego himself chose her for his own godchild. Later, Vicente Armijo must have found her beautiful also.

Vicente Armijo and María de Apodaca had three sons, one of whom, Salvador Manuel, married Aldonsa Lucero de Godoy in 1734; this pair had a dozen children, the eldest of whom was named Vicente after his grand-father. As a soldier assigned to the Villa of Albuquerque, Salvador Manuel

Armijo moved south to the Rio Abajo with his big family, and there four of the boys and three of the girls eventually married into the Chávez families which owned the Atrisco lands west of the river.

Young Vicente Armijo married Barbara Chávez in 1769, and these were the parents of Manuel Armijo, the governor-to-be. The progeny of this entire family became so numerous that their section of old Atrisco has been known as Armijo to this day. As for the young Manuel Armijo, the story goes that as a poor youth he had been obliged to herd sheep for others, but this is difficult to believe in view of the economic status of both his parents' families. That he helped herd the large flocks of the immediate clan is more likely, since the little Jacobs had to learn the tricks of pastoral living firsthand. Moreover, he must have received an adequate education for those times, if his firm and handsome script and other indications are any witness.

In 1819 Manuel Armijo married the daughter of a well-to-do livestock owner of Alameda or Bernalillo, the marriage being registered at the mission of Sandía. Eight years after the marriage he was serving his first term as governor or *jefe político* of New Mexico, and ten years after that the Gonzales revolution catapulted him to the heights of his power with the title of General.

The proud new General's ordinary chores during the next eight years should not have been too taxing for those times, except with regard to the continual defense of the peripheral settlements against the marauding wild Indians. But this was generally taken care of by the people of the areas concerned; whenever he dispatched his militiamen, he did not ride at their head. What interested him most were the duties paid by American and other merchants plying the Santa Fe and Chihuahua Trails, when he fixed the fees to his own advantage. It was in this same spirit that he made grants of enormous tracts of land to alien speculators with a largesse never seen before in colonial times.

But then there arose a crucial situation in which General Armijo had to act with dispatch. It was the first Texan invasion of 1841. Several years previously, colonies of American southerners had established themselves in southern Texas with the consent of the Mexican government. Some of their principal leaders, now the celebrated heroes of that area, even married local Mexican women. But the national politics of Mexico were in such a sorry state that they succeeded—and not without the aid of their local Mexican neighbors—in gaining their independence.

The southern curve of the long Rio Grande was designated by treaty as the Texan republic's southern boundary; but then, with the audacity of American enterprise, the Texans stretched their border *northward* along the river all the way to its very source. Washington officialdom backed their claim. In other words, the upstart republic now claimed the entire eastern half of the ancient Kingdom and Province of New Mexico, which included her venerable capital of Santa Fe and most of the larger settlements.

In the early fall of 1841, a motley troop of three to four hundred Texan men and boys left Austin with Santa Fe as their goal. Needless wandering all over the plains, many attacks by wild Indians, and some internal dissensions found them scattered in groups east of the New Mexican border villages and ranchos. Here they fell piecemeal into the hands of New Mexican militiamen whom General Armijo kept scouring the area for any such eventuality besides Indian raids. While these Texans were much better armed, their poor physical condition and low morale made them give in to the native squads which were armed only with oak lances, bows and arrows, and a few decrepit old muskets. These native soldiers, most of them *genízaros* in origin, and under an unsavory captain named Salazar, treated the captives with undue cruelty, particularly afterwards when conducting them down to Chihuahua.

General Armijo himself, whenever appearing on the scene in all his plumed and braided panoply, was no kinder in his conduct. Except for the savagery shown by Salazar and his men, this attitude can be excused, however. Military communications from Chihuahua had been telling of serious Texan forays into that region. But much more serious to the General and to the New Mexicans in general was the very fact that these captives of theirs, while protesting their intent of actually invading New Mexico, kept on insisting that New Mexico now belonged to Texas.

But one thing that has been overlooked, by both the accusers and the defendants regarding this incident, is what the surviving invaders had to say later on about the common people. Not only had the village leaders saved them from prompt execution, but these simple pastoral folks—reminiscent of Abraham's desert hospitality—treated them with utmost compassion in the face of their persecutors. The women, especially, went out of their way to ease the suffering of these *pobrecitos,* these "poor little ones," as they repeatedly referred to the prisoners. It is a term connoting endearment as well as pity, which is in most common use to this day. One of the prisoners remembered it so well as to dwell on it with grateful admiration.

The pity is that these kind women and girls of New Mexico were never rewarded by learning about the compliments that these Tejanos wrote afterwards concerning their feminine attractiveness as well as their Christian charity.

The General was still savoring this vicarious victory five years later when a really professional invasion was in the offing. The American Army of the West was already at the gates. With all his characteristic bluster, he assured the citizens of Santa Fe, and his mixed army of a few orderly dragoons from Mexico and his hundreds of poorly armed native militiamen, that the land of their brave forefathers would never fall to the Americans. His audience took all this with more than a grain of salt; besides being tired of his bluster, they were well resigned, and many of them eager to let the invader come in peacefully. It was the passivity of the early Celtiberians of the high Castilian plateau wondering what good things the Roman legionnaires might bring along with them.

When the moment of truth arrived, Armijo fled far south to Chihuahua with the dragoons, leaving the helpless native militia to straggle back to the capital. Saul had fled before Goliath because there was no shepherd David from the hills to come and save the day. Anyway, the slingshots of a mythical age were no match for the philistine weapons of a modern technology.

                        *   *   *

This is the last instance in which I can refer to any notable personage in New Mexico's long history by way of a personal genealogical aside. Since that time, the three or four generations of my direct forebears have come from among the minor children of large families, and hence are not numbered among the land-inheriting *ricos*. But there is a connection with the General which is worthwhile noting here for being illustrative of what has been treated all along in generalities. Manuel Armijo and his wife had no children of their own, but I am doubly related to him through both of his parents. When his father Vicente Armijo married his mother Barbara Chávez, Vicente's brother Antonio José Armijo married Barbara's sister, María Guadalupe Chávez. Hence the latter couple's daughter, Isabel Armijo (my paternal grandfather's great-grandmother), and Governor Armijo were double first cousins.

Consequently, the General and I not only share the same Armijo blood of the Vargas reconquest period, along with the much older Chávez and Lucero strains of the Oñate conquest period, but we also have as our common ancestress that lovely semi-Pocahontas figure of María de Apodaca whom Don Diego de Vargas picked out for his godchild. Somehow, I like this simple Aldonsa or Dulcinea better than those earlier Debborah grandmothers who were the wives of the first *conquistadores,* or those of a couple of royal governors and captains-general thereafter—or even that much more remote consort of King Fernando the Saint, were the wide assumptions of the Duchess of Noblejas in any way true.

19

Stars and Stripes

On August 18, 1846, General Stephen Watts Kearny and his Army of the West unfurled the seventy-year-old flag of the United States atop the flat earthen roof of the venerable Palace of the Governors in Santa Fe. It was the second flag to fly over it, replacing the twenty-five-year-old tricolor of Mexico. To say that New Mexico had been under the Spanish "flag" for more than two centuries before that is not quite correct, since horizontal flags are a later republican innovation.

Previous to that, the European monarchies had employed vertical stiff pendants or standards bearing the royal insignia, and these were not always used nationally. Each dukedom or province had its own. New Mexico's one and only pendant of this sort during her long Spanish colonial period was the royal *pendón* of the Virgin of Remedies with the quartered arms of Castile and León brought by Oñate in 1598. It was the very same banner which led the Vargas reconquest forces in 1692 and 1693. It was still at the Palace shortly before 1800, but, to our sad misfortune, it disappeared sometime after that. No doubt, its embroidered designs had been shredded away by so many hard years and by so many major and minor Indian campaigns, and with no appreciative soul around to save the precious remnants for us. It was like the disappearance of the Ark of the Covenant ages before.

One is tempted along this same vein to say that Sennecharib and his Assyrian army came down like a wolf on the fold, and his cohorts were gleaming, not with purple and gold, but with the blues and yellows of the U.S. Cavalry. The comparison fails, however, mainly because the invaded New Mexican people were neither maltreated nor transported *en masse* to the distant green lowlands of a Missouri-Euphrates or a Mississippi-Tigris valley. On the contrary, the invader had come to stay and was soon bringing in his own civilian countrymen in droves, whether in fringed buckskin or in fustian frockcoats, to lord it over the land.

A closer parallel could be drawn with the invasion of Mediterranean Europe by the Teutons and the Huns, yet here no destruction and pillaging took place to usher in a Dark Age. Still, the smell of a latter-day *Anschluss* is inescapable, since the invader had no right beyond his sense of Manifest Destiny to annex what was then the entire Mexican Southwest. But had not my own ancestors done the same with regard to the aborigines?

The Visigothic takeover of early Spain is a better comparison, in that an altogether different kind of people, as vigorous and as orderly in peace as they showed themselves in war, would usher in new and better forms and ideas in government and the comforts of daily living. But here they would go further, by diminishing the native culture and in some ways starting to transform the landscape itself.

Returning by long force of habit to biblical allusions, here we find a most apt one in the invasion of Canaan by Goliath and the Philistines, a Hittite nation which was wholly unrelated to the "sons of Shem and Ham" in the Near East. A taller and more robust people, they likewise came from the European or Aryan "sons of Japheth." But here in this New World Canaan there was no David with his slingshot to stem the tide. The American Goliath conquered handily and, just as it happened that the Philistines left their name in "Palestine," so the new Hittites brought the name "American" to cover and saturate New Mexico in more ways than one.

A still further inescapable temptation, this one prompted by this section's title, is to indulge in a bit of dour whimsy by saying that the common people of my penitential land saw a burst of stars when they were hit on the head by the hard facts of a strange industrial age pouncing down upon them; and their poor backs were covered with red stripes—like those of the Penitentes—by the lashes of an entirely new language and new codes of competition which so many could not understand nor cope with.

None of this in any way demeans our beloved Star-spangled Banner, which happens to be the most beautifully designed flag in the world. From the very start, as it fluttered over the Palace of the Governors that late first August afternoon, it fitted in gloriously with the background of deep azure sky and billowing white clouds, of carnelian foothills and the cobalt slopes of the Sangre de Cristo itself, just as it has done ever since in peace and war within the breasts of the native inhabitants.

1. Goliath and the Philistines

While leisurely strolling through the deserted streets of Llerena in Extremadura, during that trip of mine to Spain many years ago, I stopped to rest and muse a while at a table under the arcaded portal of a quiet tavern. The incident remains so clear in my mind because of an effortless chain of associations which took place at the time. Having ordered a small bottle of wine, I invited a modestly attired man standing nearby to share it with me.

"Caballero," he said, raising his glass, and I answered, "Caballero." Then there was silence. The amber liquid was the specialty of Jerez, the world-renowned wine center just a few hours' drive to the southwest from where we sat, and I recalled to myself how the French pronunciation of Jerez had given us the English word "sherry.'

My laconic companion then told me that his name was Durán, and I gave him mine. More silence, and now he began reminding me very much of a fellow back in Albuquerque whose name was also Durán. This made me think of the Spanish town bearing the original name of Alburquerque, which lay just a short drive west of Llerena. Even Spanish scholars have long disputed the origin and meaning of the town's unusual name. I remembered having seen the name of a village called *Al-bqerq* on a map of Arabia, and was sure there lay the answer, if only I knew what the term meant.

It was my turn to break the silence, so I began discoursing on the history of the man's own home city, how Llerena had been an important commercial center in Roman and Medieval times, and the original headquarters of the Order of Santiago after her reconquest from the Moors. She was also the birthplace of Don Luis Zapata de Chaves, Extremadura's most famous author and a contemporary of Cervantes. But now, having been cut off for so long from the main highways, sleepy Llerena seemed less than a shadow of her former self.

My table companion had begun showing a curious interest, as if what I had been saying was not altogether new to him. Then he leaned over and confided: "And things keep on getting worse. Do you see that mart over there, and the bakery, and the electric plant, and over yonder the *cine?* They are all owned by *forasteros!*"

This word means "outsiders," and I asked if they were Frenchmen or Germans.

"No," he answered, *"gallegos y vascos!"* They were Spaniards after all, but the more commercially and industrially minded Galicians, and the unique Basques, from the northernmost provinces. These were the "aliens" who were taking advantage of the more leisurely *ganadero* countrymen of Cortes and Pizarro, and of most of my ancestors, I began thinking to myself. For I recalled many a session with my own countrymen back home in New Mexico who, while implicitly regarding each other as proper "caballeros," mourned the fact that "foreigners"—the Anglo-Americans and the Texans —had made themselves masters of our own beloved homeland.

*   *   *

Following General Kearny's proclamations of genuine civil and religious liberty, and most especially of greater economic opportunities for all, the Hispanic New Mexicans wanted to become Americans more avidly than when they had accepted the name and status of Mexican citizens twenty-five years before. True, a handful of minor leaders in Santa Fe plotted a revolt the following year, but it ended quickly like a comic opera played by amateurs.

Much more serious was its continuation in Taos and other northern villages which was carried out by the same type of mountain people, along with the Taos Indians, who had followed José Gonzales in the rebellion against Mexican taxation exactly ten years before. These insurgents massacred the American territorial governor and other individuals, but they were summarily put down by superior American arms, which incidentally destroyed the historic pueblo mission of Taos in the process.

But these were not the sentiments of the main body of Hispanic leaders and of the people at large. Since the opening of regular trade routes with *tierra afuera,* first the Chihuahua trail and then the one between Santa Fe and Missouri, they no longer fully shared their proud forefathers' preference for complete pastoral isolation with all its primitive lack of comforts. They were also tired of wild Indian depredations, and welcomed the new well-armed dragoons of the United States as a much-needed shield—as had the Pueblo Indians appreciated Spanish arms when these first came. Most of all, the lost Rechabites of the entire countryside now coveted a fuller share in certain material advantages which only the few *ricos* of their Israel had been enjoying ever since the alien pagans began crossing their land with caravans of merchandise.

Maybe it was the fleshpots of Egypt in disguise, along with a bow to a golden calf which they themselves could neither afford or knew how to make, but it all looked so enticing in the midst of their loneliness and hunger. Now this self-assured tall General in plain dark blues, representing what was most evidently a stable and most properous nation, was promising them much more than had the turmoil-torn Mexican republic been able to fulfill through such representatives as General Armijo.

It was not only the superior household goods and better rural implements from the eastern states which had prepared the way. For the past quarter-century, American individuals with good English and Scotch-Irish names had settled in different parts and married native women; in the bargain they had readily submitted to the Catholic rituals of baptism and matrimony. Kit Carson is the best known example. Even before that there had been French trappers from Canada and the Mississippi valley who settled in Taos, and as strangers were considered on a par with the Americans. To Taos also came adventurers from Dixie, some of whom set up mountain stills, to the surprised admiration of the natives who for so long had utilized Indian maize for different corporal needs without ever suspecting that it harbored such a fiery spirit. With this burning water, or *aguardiente* as they called it, later nicknamed "Taos lightning" in English, the Nazirite sobriety of colonial New Mexico began losing ground rapidly.

Then there were those traders and land speculators on a more grandiose scale who, through the favor of Mexican *jefes* like Manuel Armijo, had opened leagues of wild Indian infested areas of mountain valleys and plains for more extensive grazing and farming. As a lot, the Americanos were pretty good fellows, they had come to think.

Many native sons of the landowning and commercial families, several of them first to third cousins of my own poorer forebears but lacking the notoriety of General Armijo, readily fell in line with the new order of politics, commerce, and the military, as well as the more modern methods of husbandry. What helped them primarily was an adequate education they had received, either from tutors who had come up from Mexico during the Mexican interlude or from their having attended academies in Durango or even Mexico City. Others simply had been taught the basics of learning within certain families which had nurtured such a tradition.

In Santa Fe there were such individuals as the Vigil, Ortiz, Alarid, and Pino men in the contemporary records who began blending the old New Mexican life with the new fashion. In the north were Padre Martínez of Taos and others of the same historic Martín Serrano clans, as also a José María Chávez of Abiquiú who became a brevet general in the U. S. Army and was awarded Santa Ana's sword by General Winfield Scott himself. In the south were the older Baca, Montoya, and other groups and, of course, the ubiquitous Chávez with their close blood-relatives of the Armijo, Luna, and Otero families. There were also the Pereas and Velardes with paternal memories from Guadalupe del Paso.

Special mention must be made of Colonel Manuel Antonio Chávez, romanticized by Lummis and then briefly by Cather, who was a key figure in the defeat of the Confederate forces at Glorieta Pass during the War between the States. There were many other single individuals representing different old New Mexican surnames who have been lost in the dusty scuffle of so many galloping events.

Had the shades of their ancestors of La Toma, from whatever Sheol they might now inhabit, been able to see what was happening to their progeny in their own pastoral Promised Land, they would have paled still further with deepest dismay. For the European feudalism which they themselves had escaped from was now taking hold of the landscape and their children under the guise of alien barons of industry and commerce. Yet they would have gloated a bit on seeing how so many of their sons were already mixing so well in politics, or attaining positions of military rank.

2. The Wild West Begins

The representative Hispanic leaders of New Mexico, sad to say, were far too few to compete fully with the ever-increasing number of eastern Americans of every description and profession, all wise in the tricks of the modern world of finance especially, which kept on coming every year. Many of them were now bringing their families. As for the rest of the Spanish population, while so sadly lacking in learning—and by age-old inclination wholly unattuned to the northern work ethic—it was also a very restricted one in comparison with the great reserves of people in the states now looking westward. While the new tide of immigrants kept repeating itself year after year, the native pool was not replenished from outside Hispanic sources.

Then there was that burden, referred to as such far back, which consisted of the people once called *genízaros*. They now made up a good part of the total native population still being designated as "Mexican" by the newcomers, long after it had accepted the name "American" with the promises made by General Kearny. Historically, these humble folk were a truly white man's burden to the Spanish people from the start, although most certainly not because of their Indian derivation. As the offspring of vigorous and highly intelligent mixed tribes of the prairies, they could well have contributed mightily to Spanish colonial times, and now to the new order as well.

But, as was stated long before when treating about their origin during the eighteenth century, the almost overall pastoral economy could not offer them either educational or any other material opportunities for advancement, much less a sense of pride in their origin; rather, it stamped into them a tradition of poverty and subservience which could not help but make them the prime victims of the new order as the lowest of the "Mexicans." More fortunate were many of them who had blended into Pueblo Indian life through intermarriage. Those whose spirit did manage to rise above so many serious drawbacks, like the brave José Gonzales, sorrily wasted their energies and their hopes in the futile revolutions of 1837 and 1847.

For them, as well as for so many of the poorer Spanish people, the new flag of hope could for long offer no more than stars of astonishment along with stripes of disappointment.

*   *   *

For the English-speaking American it was then easy in the extreme to begin and continue making New Mexico more and more his own, and in his philistine image. Whatever was "mexican," as he termed the entire regional tradition as if speaking in lower case type, had no place in the new scheme of things.

Especially after the railroad came, physical changes openly flaunted this attitude. The plaza of Santa Fe began turning into a replica of the midwestern town of brick and boards with false fronts trimmed with scrolled tin. New towns of the type sprang up by the railway depots, as at Las Vegas and Albuquerque, consigning the "old towns" to the less privileged natives. Other such new settlements appeared in outlying grazing and mining areas where no Spanish people had lived before because of the fierce nomadic Indians; this was made possible by the Army's continuing suppression of these "varmints" of the surrounding plains and deserts.

All in all, it was a hectic period of cattle barons, mining operators, dry-farm homesteaders, and assorted landgrabbers. It was also salted thoroughly by the wild antics of outlaw adventurers, whether singly or in gangs. It is the stuff that produced diaries and journals, many of which were published back East at the time; they are also the font from which old-timers have been drawing for their published memoirs down to this day.

In practically all such publications, the average native New Mexican fares badly, as he did when many of those things actually happened. He comes out as an inferior creature, whether depicted as a faithful honest hand or as a sneaky villain; and once in a while there has to be a lurid and most often imaginative reference to the Penitentes, as if these represented all of the New Mexican people and their faith.

In this respect, the New Mexican leaders themselves were of little or no help to their humbler and poorer countrymen. In what we now call "vanity biographies" appended to regional histories of the times, they falsely claimed that their immediate grandparents had come directly from Spain. It was a handy way of disassociating themselves from their less fortunate cousins bearing the same surnames, and with no Vivaldo around to question their quixotic pedigrees. This, of course, helped them in competing successfully with the newcomers, and they did draw the sincere respect of their Anglo-American business and political colleagues included in the same biographical pages. Intermarriage often took place among their families.

Despite all this, the common people were not altogether passive, particularly in politics. They loved election campaigns with a passion, no matter how humble their status; it satisfied deep *castizo* and *ganadero* instincts while letting them feel themselves a part of the American democratic system in which everyone is theoretically a king. In such involvements they often came to lose their shirts—and lands—not so much from failure within the new work ethic, as for lack of a working knowledge of a free enterprise system which holds that anything dishonest goes if done legally.

Thus, from the beginnings of American territorial times onward, the highlights of the history of New Mexico become increasingly Anglo-American. The once long-isolated pastoral life of the patriarchs, already fragmented during the Mexican interlude, falls wider apart. This is why this long pensive narrative about my people and our landscape—our Penitente Land in so many ways—now hurries to its close.

Not that these folk lost their identity altogether, or certain precious values which were the very essence of their lives. Fortunately, they were still on their very own landscape. Like a mute but tenderly loving mother,

she continued sheltering and nurturing them in a bosom which had little
else to give them now than a continuing if imperfect sense of that *hesed*
spoken of from the beginning. But this, too, came to be much misunderstood.

3. Kingdom of St. Francis

When Fray Marcos de Niza first saw the Zuñi pueblos of New Mexico
far back in 1539, he called the entire land "The New Kingdom of St.
Francis." It proved to be a prophecy. For it was three little Franciscan
martyrs some forty years later, in 1581, who gave New Mexico her civic
name, and their brethren who followed them from 1598 on were her only
godly fathers for two hundred years. The Franciscan image became part of
the very landscape as it had done centuries before in the similar ones of
Palestine and Spain.

Hence the many churches and chapels in New Mexico dedicated in
honor of San Francisco de Asís and his best known disciple, San Antonio de
Padua, and the prolific output by the *santeros* of their quaint little figures
dressed in blue. In Spanish, the friars' dwellings were called *conventos,* and
here, even a century and a half since their disappearance, the people still
call any priest's rectory a *convento*. A strong instinctive feeling also persists,
mistaken though it be, that all clergymen of whatsoever sort and rank ought
to observe strict Franciscan poverty; folks will readily overlook any moral
lapses, but any sign of luxury that reflects on their own poverty, or too
much emphasis on money, brings on silent estrangement. And the few
Penitentes that are left like to believe that they are genuine members of The
Third Order of St. Francis.

It is told that Bishop Zubiría's first gesture on entering the parish
church of Santa Fe was to kneel down and weep prayerfully before a small
stone sarcophagus near the high altar. It contained bone fragments of a pair
of saintly friars of New Mexico's first years, and may still be seen in the
chapel of La Conquistadora. The relics reminded the good man of the
simple and candid faith that had remained among the poor people. A year
or so after Zubiría's last visit, Jean Baptiste Lamy, as the first bishop and
archbishop of Santa Fe, was moved by the same instinct to dedicate the new
diocese and its cathedral in honor of St. Francis.

As for the simple faith of the people, a deep admiration was also evident, but at the same time it was just as deeply misunderstood. For this new church order was also philistine, along with its *romantic* admiration for St. Francis and his missionary sons of yore.

*   *   *

Sometime before the turn of the century, there was a somewhat deranged French priest who used to insult the plain New Mexican countryfolk with clever satire. Once during a sermon before a large congregation gathered for a patronal village fiesta, he told the story of Jacob and Laban, how Jacob had placed striped or mottled wands in front of Laban's ewes and nanny-goats while they were being impregnated; by this ruse Jacob got to keep the resulting pied lambs and spotted kids according to a pact the two men had made.

Then, glaring down at the many pregnant and nursing mothers before him, the preacher accused them of dropping such homely children as theirs were, in his estimation, simply because they prayed so much before the ugly homemade *santos* in their homes and in their chapels. These people took it all in good grace, however, because they knew that he was *poco loco* and because he was one padre who did not press them for money.

This incident, and many other stories about his clerical countrymen, were told to me years ago by one of the very last French pastors, who fancied himself a good raconteur. But the old fellow was unaware that he was illustrating for me what I had been gathering from written and other sources; while most of those Gallican clergymen were sincere dedicated men of God, they and some other ones of different northern European stock who dominated the ecclesiastical scene down to the period of World War I had considered my people an inferior breed of *pinto* sheep in the Lord's fold. What I myself came to learn among my own clerical contemporaries during thirty-five recent ministerial years was no different; such an attitude has a way of making itself known at unguarded moments, or through indiscreet conversations with outsiders who unwarily pass them on to someone like myself.

It seems as though the average missionary among peoples which are less materially advanced than his own, while in all holy zeal having dedicated his entire life even to the point of laying it down for his sheep, still has done it for "sheep" in his subconscious feeling of racial superiority. The pity of it is that he is the last to admit it to himself; nor does he have to be slightly deranged like that one priest and his story about Jacob's flocks. And to be fair all around, I suppose some of the old Spanish mission padres felt the same way with regard to the Indians. Still, the Nordic notion of superman is more compelling in this regard.

This state of affairs also pertains to the annexation of the entire Southwest by the United States. The Anglo-Irish American hierarchy, at the very start, got together to find a bishop for the vast new territory, and Jean Baptiste Lamy, a French-born missionary in Kentucky, got the papal appointment as first prelate with Santa Fe as his episcopal seat. The ancient little villa of adobe was the only choice possible, for being a historically famous capital as well as the only center of a large population which was entirely Catholic—but at the same time "Mexican."

Lamy was chosen on the philistine assumption that French priests, for speaking a language derived from the Latin, were ideally suited for a people who spoke a Latin-derived language of their own. This illogic has prevailed ever since, that a smattering of the language will supply for the grasp of a culture upon its native landscape. Sadder still, in subsequent times the most influential prelates of the nation, through a procedure which is suspiciously mattachine as well as philistine, have regarded the dioceses of the Spanish-speaking Southwest as their preserve for installing their favorites as bishops.

In *Death Comes for the Archbishop*, Willa Cather beautifully delineates the person of Lamy against this very landscape, particularly the backdrop provided by the Sangre de Cristo. It is a fine romantic picture of a great and good man upon the strange beauty of a land that she appreciates. But, as a foil to her hero, and to highlight his virtues and those of the French culture which he and his helpers brought along, the author makes a lecherous ogre of native Padre Martínez of Taos, while also demeaning his people in connection with the Penitentes. It is indeed a masterful painting of my Penitente land, but with penitential strokes that hurt.

For Cather's attitude as well as her information had its source, not only in what the civil newcomer had been writing for the past hundred years, but in the letters which the new clergy had written back home along with their pious publications which were replacing the story of the land's *hesed* with their own "Aryan" history. As with civil affairs, the highlights of faith no longer touched the landscape and its people, except for the fact that they furnished both pasture and sheep for the philistine apportionment of shepherds. Hence, in this regard also, this narrative must hurry to its close.

*   *   *

The clash which had occurred between the new and the native clergy was due to radical differences in training but more so to a centuries-long basic difference in outlook. The Frenchmen were, moreover, a recent product of strictest clerical reforms which followed a period of extreme laxity in their own country. Ashamed of Richelieu and Talleyrand, they looked down long Gallican noses upon what they considered "unclerical" deportment.

The few native priests were a part of their pastoral life and landscape, proud and easygoing like desert partriarchs. Besides, they had been educated in Durango when the spirit of Mexican independence was at its highest and, while some resented the American occupation as Mexican patriots, all balked at having an American prelate so close to home. The resentment grew stronger when they felt themselves regarded and treated as dust by the new broom. Chief among them was the famed Padre Martínez of Taos who, unlike his brethren who either left the ministry or exiled themselves to Mexico, stuck to his post and continued the good fight for his people against all abuses, whether civil or ecclesiastical. Unfortunately, his headstrong character caused him to be gravely maligned, even by a few of his own—and finally by the Cather novel—when he should long ago have had a heroic monument as Hispanic New Mexico's greatest son.

All this put an end to a native leadership in faith which Zubiría had so laboriously initiated, even when some native young men ordained by Lamy (again to his credit) labored faithfully to the end. It was his successors, and the continuing flow of priests from France and elsewhere, who now regarded the "mexicans" as neither morally nor intellectually fit for the priesthood. Years ago, when an old *monsigneur* publicly made such a remark, I hastened to remind him, by counting the names on my fingers, the larger number of his own countrymen and other aliens who had fallen by the wayside.

This is not to say that the majority were not sincere men of God willing to expend themselves for their sheep. Nor can one ungratefully pass by such benefits brought to the land as that of education under the generally kind tutelage of dedicated teaching brothers and sisters, or the first hospitals the land ever saw. But that same insidious feeling of superiority which revealed itself on the civic scene, in such banal things as eastern brick and tin, likewise showed its head when the old adobe churches were replaced by pseudo-gothic ones, and when the native *santos* had to give their place to cast plaster statues in romantically pretty poses and tints.

In Santa Fe the ultra-sweet Notre Dame de Lourdes banished the sterner Conquistadora to a dark corner, although her annual processions were too deeply imbedded in the people's hearts to suffer interruption. At San Juan, near the site of the first Spanish settlement in 1598, a gothic stone shrine was erected to counter the adobe one at Chimayó across the same valley, as if French water were more potent than native earth in either element's strange consortium with the expression of faith.

Or was it faith itself, through the subtle variances created by blood and landscape, which made all the difference? Even in my day, secular priests and my former Franciscan brethren—all of North European heritage—could never understand why my people could love Christ so deeply and passionately, and yet be so callous about current church ordinances like the "Easter duty" and the Sunday envelope.

Aryan faith versus *hesed.* As for the Penitentes it is a separate story.

4. Bones of Contention

There is the temptation to look back on the Penitentes of New Mexico, as Jeremiah and Amos had ages before recalled the primitive Nazirites of their pastoral past, through visions of radiant snow and coral and sapphire. Landscape and the more primitive times, it must be admitted, caused one to give fancy a free rein in describing the men of Santa Cruz when they first shouldered their timber crosses and felt the first sting of whips in their night of strange desires.

But the time comes when one must accept the more pressing realities, as Jeremiah also saw them, of "faces darker than blackness itself," of figures moving "unrecognizable through the streets," and their skin "shrunken against the bones." By the time the first eastern Americans were beginning to publish their comments on the Penitentes, unmistakable signs of decadence show through the biased or exaggerated accounts.

*   *   *

It was only the second generation of the penitential fraternity, but chapters of it had spread from the mountains and ravines of the Rio Arriba down to some in the Rio Abajo, as they did sometime later over the Sangre de Cristo to newer settlements on its eastern flank. By no means did they represent the majority of the Hispanic population; but the few from among the humbler Hispanic folk who were usually the leaders, and those of *genízaro* or mixed descent who formed the ever-growing majority of these brothers of light and of blood, all presented a grim spectacle which, from their being so much bandied about by the newcomers, were proving to be a source of embarrassment to the native population as a whole.

It is true that, for lack of a sufficiency of priests in the region, the flagellant brethren had furnished the only Lenten and Holy Week services in remote towns and villages far away from parish headquarters. Imitating the Latin liturgy of Tenebrae, their doleful *alabados* signaling the extinguishing of the thirteen candles, and then the rattling of chains and the whirr of ratchet *matracas* in the ensuing darkness, drew the faithful in moth-droves of sincerest devotion to the village chapel or else the *morada*. The pious spectators with stronger stomachs followed the procession of blood to the Calvary on a hill where on occasion some youth, robed in white cotton and with a black bag over his head, had himself "crucified" by being bound to a cross.

But much more appreciated were the services provided when death came to an isolated community. In those times, since the corpse could not await the arrival of a distant padre, the Pentitentes were ready at hand to solace the bereaved with their candles and prayers and hymns, from the start of the night's wake to the consignment next day back to the earth's maternal bosom. And some of their women provided the screechful wailing in a time-honored tradition going back through Castile's upland landscape to those much more ancient ones of Koran, Gospel, and Torah.

There is no reason to doubt the Spanish soul's genuine *hesed* within those Penitentes in whom there still flowed the *castizo* blood and instincts of Don Fadríque de Ribera, and of those rustic folk who were mistakenly assaulted by the mad Don Quijote de la Mancha one night, or preached to by the silly Fray Gerundio de Campazas. But among the increasing majority with *genízaro* antecedents, it necessarily had to be different. Not that these earnest men did not love the Suffering Christ any less than they; what made the difference, as it did in other things, is the single fact that they were not *castizo*.

This can be seen most plainly in the bizarre features which had developed since the original foundation at Santa Cruz some fifty years before. Cutting whips woven out of native yucca fiber had replaced the straps of leather; individuals sought new means of cruelest torture by tying slabs or branches of *nopal* and *entraña* cactus to their backs and chests; some now flogged each other in what one could suspect elements of sadism and masochism; initiates were now sliced down their backs with chips of obsidian, producing welts like the raised tattoos of primitive savages in various parts of the world.

And once in a while, not every year, a brother was so carried away that he insisted on being tied to the Calvary cross, where he soon fainted from his previous scourgings and the impeded circulation in his bound limbs. Whether he considered himself another Christ in his frenzy, or else the "good thief" atoning for a stolen cow, there is no way of telling. As to his simple sincerity, and that of all his brethren, there should be no question; but in all these extreme excesses the *anima hispanica* was no longer there.

Then somehow, and from what source we know not, there was introduced that ghoulish spectacle of a skeletal figure of Death on its cart, historically a spawn of medieval northern Europe's morality plays—yet not out of place in the Mexican Indians' preoccupation with skulls and bones. It was neither *castizo* in nature nor the gentle "Sister Death" of the good St. Francis. I myself once overheard some Penitente wives speaking of the horrible figure as "La Santa Muerte," as if putting it on a par with the *santos* which represented actual saintly personages who had once been living personalities. Here was an un-Spanish romanticism gone rampant.

As for real crucifixions, no records or traditions exist of anyone having been nailed to a cross, as in cases reported from southern Mexico since times past. But it could have come to pass someday, had the American occupation not occurred. It would have been the natural climax to the other bizarre practices being introduced, practices that had strayed far away from Hispanic *castizo* idealism and realism into the dark stoic romanticism of the Mexican Indian and the Plains Indian. Writers who have assumed that actual nailings did take place follow the same faulty logic which presumes that, just because so many Indians of Mexico and other parts were enslaved by the Spaniards, the Pueblo Indians had therefore been made slaves by New Mexico's Spanish people.

These Pueblo Indians, by the way, in spite of the Penitentes' new underlying Indianic elements, whether Mexican or *genízaro,* kept themselves aloof from the movement. Traditionally they had kept themselves culturally apart from the Spanish-speaking population; then, the same dearth of clerical guidance which had now encouraged the spread of the Penitentes

with all their subsequent aberrations also gave them completely free rein to
return more and more to their own ancient ways of worship. In this they
were largely left undisturbed thereafter, due to the separate and self-
sustaining communal life of the pueblos.

But in the new American religious and civic order, the Penitentes, for
being spread throughout the general community, could not escape the pen
of the curiosity seeker or in time the opportunism of the politician on the
one hand, and on the other the reform efforts of the churchmen.

*   *   *

It might have been on that same Easter Sunday long ago, during the
festive mass when the cobbler of my boyhood memories had returned from
his *morada* to inject his bass notes into the *kyries* in the choir loft, that our
pudgy French pastor berated the Penitentes for having missed their "Easter
duty" during Lent. His sermon could well have sparked my senseless act,
some days later, of insulting our friend with that verse about a stolen cow. I
know that I myself was to blame, since my partner in crime was a Protestant
lad who certainly had not heard the sermon. That he knew the insulting
verse was as much my fault as that of the older youths in town.

This boy's family and mine lived on the most neighborly terms, with
never a mention of religious differences, as we did with our own and all
other peoples. As for men like the cobbler, who disappeared from the
community during Holy Week each year, never a thought was given to the
fact that they were Penitentes otherwise. This is why my crime affected my
mother so much when he made his complaint on that unforgettable spring
day. Nor would that incident have taken place, I believe now, had not our
French pastor laid it on the Penitentes that Easter Sunday.

His attitude toward them was the one shared by all outsiders, lay or
clerical, Catholic as well as Protestant, as derived from a century of
sensational accounts by early travelers and preachers, and from condemna-
tions by priests and archbishops. The northern gothic attraction for blood
and darkness was now inspiring what was called "Penitente hunting," while
the worshippers of every word in a partly mythical Book, whether by way of
ritualistic dogma or pure verbal scanning, scorned what their ancestors had
practiced with an unredeeming fanaticism in the Middle Ages.

Today all that, along with further discovered material of the same sort,
is being published *ad nauseam* in endless publications which, as remarked
long ago in the Prologue, bristle with all such stuff but miss the very essence

of the subject. The same gothic fixation is still most evident, even if the modern writer does strive after sympathetic understanding as he sorrily misarranges his trove of literary potsherds. Nor has it been my intent to include all those arrays of facts here, but to search out their inner core within the larger and most necessary context of a Penitente Land with its Palestinian-Castilian background, as I have tried to do. Perhaps this will help to sift out the chaff of so much misunderstanding produced by racial and religious prejudice as well as by faulty interpretations of history during earlier American times.

Incidentally, it was in that period that Charles F. Lummis set himself up as the discoverer and historian of the Penitentes of New Mexico, and I return to him once more because, among other bits of information which he received from the family of Colonel Chávez of Civil War fame, he quoted that very same verse about a stolen cow which almost got me a whipping half a century later. In connection with Lummis another writer comes to mind, one who, perhaps for his being less self-assured as a humble "sinner," left something for us to ponder. In a magazine which he founded, Lummis assailed the character of a certain writer named George Wharton James, berating him as a dishonest ethnologist and as an ex-minister who had been defrocked by his church for some serious lapse. Later this same Mr. James wrote a book on the Indian and Hispanic people of New Mexico in which he repeats Lummis's faulty interpretations about the Penitentes, yet with such a deep feeling for what blood and landscape can effect in human beings that one cannot help but admire his own humanity. How much unlike the views of the smug priest or preacher, or pen-wielding traveler, is this passage concerning their flagellation:

> As to its being degrading to the Christian faith, that is purely a matter of personal opinion. I am inclined to have more faith in the simple, stern earnestness of a people who will whip themselves for their wrong-doings than I have in the professions of some people who never forsake their luxurious and sensuous lives even though they make weekly protest that they are followers of the meek and lowly Jesus who had not where to lay His head. It is easy to sing with unction the hymn: Nearer, my God, to Thee . . . but it is far from easy to embrace and kiss the Cross and actually suffer some, even [all?] of its agony.

20

The Spanish New Mexican

El que nace desgraciado
desde la cuna comienza,
desde la cuna comienza,
a vivir martirizado.

Anyone born disadvantaged
starts out from the cradle,
starts out from the cradle,
to be stepped-on and unwanted.

There is an infinitude of Mexican songs, basically Hispanic in their melody and in the thoughts expressed, yet *típicamente* Mexican in their dark soul and in the Indianic rhythm of most of them. In other words, the same tune with its words can evoke sentiments which are identical on the surface, yet inwardly diverse from the viewpoint of racial or national feeling. In some of the more distinctive *corridos* or popular ballads, there are echoes of the mournful *cante jondo*, and hence also of the *alabados* of the Penitentes—as if it were "a thing most evident" that Jesus had to be a red-robed, thorn-crowned Nazirite from the very manger.

In the example given here, the sentiment is likewise expressive of a classic Spanish poet's famous dictum that "man's greatest crime is to have been born." And both the music and the lyric echo the wistful "life is dream" in the *Canción de Cuna* of a later Spanish dramatist. Or go away back to Semitic Job in a similar drama complaining to God why he had been drawn forth from the womb, and then down to Shylock in another one declaring that "suffering is the badge of all our tribe."

The sentiment here is truly Mexican for its being a Mexican song expressing the heavy sadness that is a part of a land and its people. It is the dark lament of Moctezuma. But here the comment on life, for being so casually fatalistic, is also entirely *castizo* through the Hispanic lilt of both the words and the music.

1. Nuevo Mexico Castizo

The Spanish New Mexican has long forgotten the songs brought from Spain by his pioneer forebears. The archaic language brought by them, too, is fast on its way out, sad to say, although replaced in all too rare instances by its modern equivalent through individual effort. Having produced little or no genuine music or poetry of his own, he has for long come to depend on the rich musical lode of Mexico to express his loves and his sorrows. My New Mexican countryman, however, has become so confused as to call it "Spanish music," just as he misnames tacos and enchiladas "Spanish food"—or sees no incongruity when a youth with Amerindian features represents the person of a famous Castilian *conquistador*.

For this is the bane of a people who have lost sight of their factual "origins and history," even while these were being preserved underneath the surface by "landscape and language." And yet they do not wish to be identified as Mexicans, but correctly as long-time Americans by birth and nationality. Their not being accepted as such in the national picture of the United States has been part of their continuing penance. While being classified as Mexicans, which should bear no stigma at all, they do know, if more with the heart than with the head, that their own ancestry, language, and traditions are distinct from the Mexican, or perhaps that a difference exists like the one between a horse and a jackass without their knowing which is which—sometimes afraid that they might be the latter.

The Mexican Nationals and Mexican-Americans, as they are referred to in this part of the country, are just that: children of a large and populous nation called Mexico with a very rich culture and history of her own. As a result, most of them have inherited all kinds of useful knowledges and skills which the Spanish New Mexican is quick to notice. Contrary to a greatly undeserved reputation, the Mexican loves to work, but he does not let the labor of his hands become the master of his heart, and its killer as well. Whether they be considerably Hispanic in descent, or practically pure Indian as most of the poorer agricultural immigrants are, the Mexicans belong to one Mexican nation. For "Mexican" is a national term, not a racial one, except for the original Aztecs.

What is most admirable, these Mexican people are justly proud of their vitally intermixed descent and single national identity, while their love for their flag and their observance of patriotic dates are often more intense than those of most of us Americans regarding our own banner and the Fourth of July. Ever considered as aliens in this country, generations of their children born and reared in the big urban centers or agricultural syndicates in other parts of the great Southwest naturally fall back on their parents' and grandparents' national fealties by way of solace or mutual self-defense. The proximity to Mexico and a constant inflow of new immigrants do not help to relieve the problem.

In this regard precisely, the Spanish New Mexicans know that they are not aliens, but natives of their very own landscape for almost four hundred years. Except for the local Indians, all others are but recent immigrants. Unlike the Mexicans, however, they have not known what their original colonial banner was, or what it looked like, save for the nebulous fact that it was a "flag" borne by the only two historical figures they can remember, Don Juan de Oñate and Don Diego de Vargas. From here they skip to the Stars and Stripes which they deeply love and for which so many have died in several wars with as much devotion as any other Americans.

But all the while they are most conscious of their own Spanish individuality, and yet—like my mother long ago—frustrated by their not being able to explain it. This is not only due to their long isolation from Spain and a developing New Spain more than two centuries long, or because their status as Mexican citizens was so brief, or even because their only education as well as their national allegiance have been exclusively American for almost a century and a half. These are mere externals. The real causes run much deeper in what one calls the native soul.

*   *   *

Fully aware that he is no longer a "Spaniard" properly so called—*un gachupín*—the Spanish New Mexican still feels that he is somehow a true *español,* somehow a long-lost scion of Don Quijote's Dulcinea del Toboso even when a Vivaldo from Spain might raise an eyebrow. Likewise convinced that he is not a Mexican—*un serumato*—he will nevertheless refer to himself in Spanish as a *mexicano,* in the sense of "New Mexican," as though the Mexican nationals were interlopers. All these, too, are externals.

But what really makes him an *español* he cannot express in words because, like myself long ago, he never heard of the word *castizo* nor the wealth of meaning it contains, nor how much his very own landscape has to do with it as much as do his blood and his archaic language after so many generations of isolation.

He is the product of a centuries-long selection by roughest winters and summers from a series of periods of want resulting from the sky's inclemency and a history of poverty. As an individual he will greet you without big courtesies, halting and grave in his movements, and with a self-possession that makes him look like a king dethroned. But this only when he is not being wryly humorous as in the characters found in Don Quijote. Ordinarily he is taciturn, until his tongue turns loose.

His soul is the living soul of his forebears, gone to sleep perhaps, but nonetheless alive. Among those who have acquired a measure of latter-day culture, the marks of lineage might have changed but they are still there. As a rule, he resigns himself to the law or he ignores it, he tolerates it or he fights it. If he is beaten, he is a fatalist; but he is a firm believer in free will if he is on top. Doctrine is just a theory for conduct, not its guide. Hence such vigorous phrases on his lips like *"No me dá la real gana"* and *"qué importa!"*

His simplistic faith is the faith of the conquistadores, a faith in fate (or *kismet*): "Wish your son well and drop him in the sea." (Cortés burned his ships behind him, and Abraham not only left the safety of his tribe but calmly loaded his son with the wood of his sacrifice.) There is no middle ground, as when Pizarro drew a line on the ground with his sword, saying to his men: "From here one goes to Peru to get rich; and from here one goes to Panama to stay poor; let him *who is a good Castilian* choose what suits him best!"

And thus he can wait for *mañana,* which never comes, to see if *manna* falls from heaven. And if he has to die with his boots on, let it be like Samson pulling down the Philistines' temple upon himself. Even God is brought in by way of an excuse, as when El Cid asked: "What does God owe me more than you?" And in daily talk, when a little favor is asked "for the love of God," the answer for any help given is "May God repay you."

Our *castizo* horror for work is proverbial, as are our sly humor and our hoary idea that nothing debases a man so much as gaining his livelihood by means of a mechanical job. Such is the *castizo* Spanish soul, belligerent and indolent, passing from the violence of passion to complete apathy without bothering to blend the two in order to attain the sustained effort of labor. The poor Indians of El Dorado asked the Spaniards why they neither sowed nor reaped, and in vain did prudent minds in Spain argue that farmers be sent to America.

Now, while recognizing themselves in what has just been said, some of my *paisanos* will not approve of my saying it. *But the fact is that I have made up these last five paragraphs (except for what is put in parentheses) from phrases in Miguel de Unamuno's own assessment of his Castilian countrymen in Spain some decades ago!*

2. The Hesed of Landscape and Language

It is landscape which nurtures and preserves a basic culture, and language which assures its continuation even when historical tradition breaks down for lack of the written page. There is also that third factor, blood, which is somewhat less essential than the other two for its being more subject to periodic change through admixture. But so long as the basic strain also remains predominant, it plays its own extremely important part. We have seen this in the long story of the Palestinian and Castilian landscapes.

In the newer and decidedly much shorter story of the New Mexican landscape, the sixteenth-century language of Cervantes, specifically because it remained static and unaffected for lack of schools and reading matter, continued the same rustic spirit and tradition of the pastoral Castilian plateau of that very same period. The latter one in Spain herself had to be affected and modified as time progressed by the other surrounding Iberian provinces, and by the general history of Europe. But here in New Mexico it was affected only by the flora and fauna particular to the New World landscape, or by some minor customs of the aborigines.

But what about the goodly number of *genízaros* since the eighteenth century? It is as much an interesting phenomenon as it is vital to the story. They, too, fell into the general old Extremeño-Manchego pastoral life-pattern of New Mexico along with the language—but here up to a point. Since the Indianic tongues of their nomadic forebears employed more vowels than consonants, they tended to speak Spanish accordingly, especially by frequently dropping the so Castilian *s* sound. Hence certain current sociologists, who cannot tell the difference between folks of Spanish or *genízaro* descent, have wrongly supposed that the Spanish speech of New Mexico is Andalusian.

All this aside, it corroborates Unamuno's point about language, because the people of full or major *genízaro* descent and upbringing are definitely more Indianic in their outlook than they are *castizo* by their Hispanic contact. Significantly, in current revolutionary social movements, they are the ones who join the agrarian and urban Mexicans or Mexican-Americans in their social protests, and consequently like to be called "Chicanos" along with them.

The true Spanish New Mexican *castizo* does not, not even when he finds himself in need or when he feels himself "stepped-on and unwanted." If he is to be recognized, or employed, it is as a *castizo individual* on his own home landscape, and not for ethnic considerations in the mass. Finding himself ignored or shunted aside because of his racial background, he proudly withdraws from the offending circle to seek better pastures in another, and not necessarily his own people. Sometimes he does it with a flourish that might seem ridiculous to others, but that is what made Don Quijote and Sancho Panza possible in literature.

Especially in the pasturelands of politics, which he loves so much, he has been so individualistic for over a hundred years as to defeat any formation of a solid "Spanish-American block," or a solid "Catholic block." New Mexico has not had a governor, for this reason, of Hispanic New Mexican descent for over sixty years. The handful who have found their way to Congress have done it, for lack of a solid native backing, through such maneuverings as only the most seasoned politicians know.

Going back to those occasional non-Castilian admixtures in the properly Spanish New Mexican milieu, that is, throughout the Mexican interlude and the American occupation, we find them growing apace into our times. They are the Mexican and so-called Anglo-American infusions. At long intervals, some bachelor and largely Hispanic natives of Mexico, or fewer with their families, came to make New Mexico their home. But, as it has also happened in similar cases within my lifetime, their children lost all the national traits of their parent or set of parents by attuning themselves to the local language and ways of the land. In short, they became Spanish New Mexicans through landscape and language. This has also happened with regard to Spaniards from Spain.

More interesting, in a way, are the admixtures which took place when English-speaking Americans of British, Gaelic, Teutonic, and even Slavic descent took the Hispanic daughters of the landscape to wife. In cases where the English language prevailed in the home, the wife and children were lost to the Spanish native population and, sad to say, many were later ashamed of their "Mexican" grandparents and kin; today the tide has turned, with most of them harking back with pride to their Hispanic New Mexican forebears.

However, when the local Spanish language prevailed at home over the English, this produced genuine Spanish New Mexicans even though the surnames passed down were Conklin and McGrath, or Mueller and Koslowski.

Finally, simply because of our more remote and more general theme, of the utmost interest were some few alliances with modern Jews, and later also with some Syrians and Lebanese. But even when there was no intermarriage at all, there has always been a more brotherly rapport with these people, as if blood were calling to blood from loin and landscape beyond memory's recalling. As remarked many pages ago in passing, in our Palestinian landscape some Hebraic folks found the opportunity to own open grazing land on which to enjoy raising sheep and cattle after centuries of ghetto-living elsewhere in the world. And in New Mexico, ever since that brief episode when a Gómez grandfather was accused of being a backsliding *marrano* three centuries ago, anti-Semitism has been unknown among my people.

*   *   *

In the long run, landscape and language were the final arbiters in every phase of mores and customs. But when these two begin to change fast, as they are doing today, even to the dangerous point of losing their original identity, what can be expected of the people whom they have for so long nourished and preserved—and especially when they no longer own the land?

The Israeli are transforming the face of Palestine, but their vigorous vast numbers gathering in from all over the world, along with their peculiar genius as well as their preserved and now increased use of the Hebrew language, will insure the survival of a people as a people, just as a long cohesion of language with a badge of suffering held them together in the past. The landscape might no longer be the exact one of Abraham, nor perhaps their *hesed* quite the same either, but there will be survival.

Spain is becoming more European or cosmopolitan day by day, and the blight of concrete with the pollutions of industry can someday soon spoil the Castilian landscape that El Cid and Cervantes once knew. But, again, the many people speaking the language which made them what they are will still survive as Spaniards, even if not quite as *castizo* as were their forebears of the Moorish Crusade and the Conquest of America.

But when the landscape of New Mexico, already alienated for the most part, has been largely churned up by the bulldozer, and the air filled with English sounds in the accents heard from New England down to Texas, that is, when the old language of Cervantes is no more, it can only mean the end as an entity for an extremely small population. Their long experience of suffering has nothing to hang on to. On the one hand, the true Spanish New Mexican is steadily blending into the general English-speaking American milieu, despite all the pride of surname he may keep or any desperate efforts at preserving local bits of folklore, social and religious customs, or native architecture. On the other, the one with *genízaro* antecedents tends to identify himself with what he considers his brown brethren from south of the border.

Many years ago, when I was in my late teens, a local newspaper quoted a novelist in Taos as having declared that the Spanish people of New Mexico were "a washed-out race." I believe it was in connection with a book written around the Penitentes. In my youthful anger I wrote a letter to the editor suggesting the trite American idea of having the offending writer tarred and feathered, and then ridden out of the region on a log. But the thoughts of youth are long, long thoughts. Whatever the author meant in his own mind, the words he used were not so wrong after all. So be it.

This tree that I have painted down to its furthest roots, one which grew through a lifetime out of a boy's lively curiosity, was not meant to be a commentary on current ethnic and social problems, but simply a nostalgic story as promised from the very beginning—the soul story of my Hispanic people of New Mexico wrestling for centuries with her God upon a Bethel landscape made to order up to the day that stronger alien forces brought on significant as well as irreversible changes. It was painted to show them, and all our other fellow Americans, that we can look back with tender pride, and without having to live in it, to a most colorful past bred by brave stockmen ancestors from Castile as a most distinctive contribution to this great nation of ours.